THE FOREIGN LEGION

The Foreign Legion

Breaking the
barriers of
European
cycling

Rupert Guinness

SPRINGFIELD BOOKS LIMITED

TO PHILLIP AND GRAHAM

© Rupert Guinness 1993

This edition first published by Springfield Books Limited, Norman Road, Denby Dale, Huddersfield HD8 8TH, West Yorkshire, England

First edition 1993

Photo credits

The author and publishers wish to thank the following photographers:

John Pierce for the photos on the title and contents page, and p93 lower. Presse Sports for the frontispiece and photos on pages 8, 21, 35, 54 lower, 71, 72 upper, 79, 81, 89 lower, 88, 93 upper, 135 lower, 146. Graham Watson for the photos on pages 24, 26, 28, 29, 31, 36, 54 upper, 57 lower, 77, 90 upper, 89 lower, 107, 108, 125 top left, 147, 148, 162. Phil O'Connor for the photos on pages 35, 59 right, 70 left, 84, 86, 63 upper, 120, 122, 125 top right and lower, 126, 130, 135 upper, 143, 144, 159, 161.

The rest of the photography has been supplied from the archives of *Cycling Weekly* and *L'Equipe.* Our special thanks go to their staff for their cooperation.

Acknowledgements

The author and publishers would like to thank the following people for their generous help and support:

Members of the Foreign Legion: Paul Sherwen, Graham Jones, Robert Millar, Phil Anderson, Stephen Roche, Sean Yates, Allan Peiper. The management and staff of *Cycling Weekly,* Philippe Bouvet and the cycling department of *L'Equipe,* John Wilcockson of *VeloNews,* USA Claude Droussent and Jean-Michel Guerinel of *Velo* France, Phil Liggett, Mike Price, Samuel Abt, Graham Watson, Luke Evans, Kenny Pryde and Jean-Marie LeBlanc Director Sociètè du Tour de France.

British Library Cataloguing in Publication Data
Guinness, Rupert
Foreign Legion
I. Title
796.6

ISBN 1 85688 035 4

Design: Chris Hand, Design for Print
and Gerrard Lindley

Typesetting: Paragon Typesetters, Queensferry, Clwyd

Printed and bound in Hongkong by Colorcraft Ltd

Contents

Tom Simpson on the 1960 Tour de France

FOREWORD

Images of a certain white jersey with the Union Jack on the shoulders are still very clear to me: there was the jersey of Brian Robinson, the first British rider to win a stage of the Tour de France and whom I admired since my young days in shorts. Another was that of Tom Simpson, I had the honour to ride with him in the peloton when I became a young professional. As an amateur I also rode with Barry Hoban, Vin Denson and several others. There was Alan Ramsbottom, John Clarey, who finished the 1968 Tour de France alongside me – that's to say way at the back!

My first contact with English-speaking riders was in competition on the road. I can honestly say that even in the 1960s there were many riders of true class who crossed the Channel to take their chance on the continent.

The late 1970s and early 1980s was a truly impressive era which saw the English-speaking rider assert himself in the world of professional cycling. By this time I was working as a journalist and year after year – often by the canal of the ACCB club in Paris – I met names like Paul Sherwen, Graham Jones, Phil Anderson, Robert Millar, Stephen Roche, Sean Yates and Allan Peiper. Then there was Sean Kelly, Greg LeMond and several others. They represented the development of cycle racing in their own countries from Ireland to Australia, where we, the French, hardly knew if the sport even existed there

I gradually learned what difficulties these adventurers experienced at the start of their careers. They uprooted themselves from their homelands, without money or family in Europe; they were forced to speak a new language, and adopt a new lifestyle. All for the dream of success as a professional cyclist. Whatever recompense came along, it was nothing but justice. I really felt sympathy and admiration for all of these sporting 'exiles', for they were ambassadors of the new cycling nations, who asked only to learn by experience and were granted no special favours.

During my era as Chief Editor of the cycling desk on *L'Equipe* I remember a lunch in Paris with Graham Jones – a great champion. He had all the excellent qualities needed as a *rouleur* and climber, but he lacked that little bit of physical endurance. Today whenever I meet him, I still call him *mon favorit*.

Equally I recall the amazing debut of Anderson who attacked and attacked incessantly. His first *maillot jaune* – yellow jersey – in 1981 was by no means a present found in the chimney from Father Christmas! Rather he fought for it like a tiger, and won it with his legs, even though the task was as difficult as climbing a greasy pole.

There were those who became big stars like Kelly and Roche, who were far from spoiled in their early years. What an example they both make for our young hopefuls who so often get so much – money, equipment, hotel expenses – without having touched the age of 20 or proved anything. I am certain that the careers of Kelly and Roche have inspired so many young Irish cyclists.

Their story reflects the universal magic that exists in top level sport, especially cycling. What an adventure life really is, if one wants to take hold of it like a set of handlebars – with two hands and a clear head.

Thank you Rupert for bringing back the memories in this history of cycling Anglophiles in Europe. I hope your readers enjoy it.

Jean Marie LeBlanc, Directeur Société du Tour de France.
Former journalist for *L'Equipe* and professional cyclist.

Anderson's historic first day in yellow — Tour de
France 1981, stage 7 time trial

INTRODUCTION

The news room of the *Sydney Daily Telegraph* was extraordinarily quiet on the afternoon of July 3 1981. The chief of staff was festering over a lack of incoming newsworthy stories, so much so that in desperation he even poached one from 'Sports' and inserted into his news list for afternoon conference.

It seemed reasonable enough, although nobody **really** understood the magnitude of it. It was an item about the Tour de France and Phil Anderson, who, 24 hours earlier had taken something called *le maillot jaune*.

Looking back, wire reports labelled Anderson's accomplishment as historic and incredible, but even stranger was the lack of understanding of what he had done even after it led the sports page, the features page and even got a mention on the front page. A memory that will never leave my mind is the sight of our leading feature writer scrambling through a sparse clippings file on Anderson trying to rummage up enough material for a one-page profile on this unknown Australian who the French called *Le Skippy*.

It was also the day that I fell in love with European professional cycling. I was like millions of Australians who hadn't even heard of Anderson. As we huddled around our feature writer's desk we all joined in with a chorus of 'Aagh ... yeaghs' especially when one cutting fell out and reminded us of Anderson's 1978 Commonwealth Games gold medal victory. Sadly, national interest in Anderson petered out when he lost the jersey a day later. But, his 24 hours in the *maillot jaune* – yellow jersey – converted me to the cause of cycling and an almost ritualistic following of his career. We received European magazines three to four months after they were published featuring events curiously called 'classics' or tours. And time and time again in the following years Anderson's name came up in the results, as did others like Stephen Roche, Robert Millar, Sean Kelly and Greg LeMond.

It was exciting to write about these names, and my first big opportunity was at the 1986 Coors Classic in the US where I first met Anderson in person. By March 1987 I was standing on the finishing line of the Tour of Flanders and watching him and every other rider, I had only seen in glossy colour photos, go rushing past at 60kmh. Since then I have been swept up in their pursuit to be champions in one of the toughest sports in the world.

It struck me straight away how many English-speaking riders were top rated in a sport so reputed for its nepotism, and chauvinism against any non-European. Not only did these riders have physical resilience and aggression, but they were also instilled with a psychological mettle which seemingly grew stronger with every hardship. As a result every single major race in the world has an English-speaking name on its honour roll.

At that time cycling was not a mainstream sport in Great Britain, Ireland, the United States, Australia, New Zealand or South Africa. It still isn't. But the influence on European cycling of those riders who came from afar was nothing but major – and not just in the mid-1980s but ever since the sport began. English-speaking riders were a novelty to begin with, yes. Today they are just as respected as any Belgian, French, Italian, Spanish or Dutch rider, and in many cases they are more highly paid!

'The Foreign Legion' was the title given to those riders who passed through the French amateur Athletic Club de Boulogne–Billancourt (ACBB) and then into the professional circuit by way of team Peugeot in the 1980s. And while their story is the crux of this book, *The Foreign Legion* is also a testimony to the achievements, efforts, anguish, and triumphs of every English-speaking rider who has tried to enter the closed doors of European cycling.

As the main people featured in this book face retirement in 1993, in fact Paul Sherwen, Graham Jones, and Allan Peiper have all retired, for the others their racing careers can only expect one or two more seasons – one can only hope that the legendary Foreign Legion continues. If not, this book may one day sadly go down as its epitaph as well.

It is first necessary to look at the events before then, beginning with the pioneering European exiles like Australia's Sir Hubert Opperman, Ireland's Shay Elliot, England's Barry Hoban and those others who came first. Not every anecdote, race result or personality can be written about. It would take several volumes to do that. And the book is not intended as a patronising gesture of praise for the past. For the riders concerned it certainly wasn't all rosy. But I hope if anything, that the following pages stand as a respectful, historical and interesting account of the impact of English-speaking riders in European cycle racing.

1 THE PIONEERS

In a sport which took on competitive status in 1869 with the inaugural edition of the amateur Paris – Rouen classic in France, English-speaking riders broke new ground for others to follow; Paris – Rouen was after all won by Englishman James Moore. Despite Moore's victory it took a long, long time before English-speaking riders were regarded seriously abroad. No doubt for those who first came, taking on Europe's best at their own game was probably just part of a big adventure. As pioneers they could not have known what lay in store.

By the late 1970s however, English-speaking cyclists had made their mark. Looking back at the evolution of such achievements and at the personalities who initiated it, history is clearly divided into four transitionary phases defined by each passing generation of cyclists, and beginning with the single-minded ambitions of these key riders: Sir Hubert Opperman, Brian Robinson, Shay Elliott, Tom Simpson and Barry Hoban.

1914 – 1939 Sir Hubert Opperman

Records go back to 1914 of the first participation by an English-speaking rider in the Tour de France – Australians Don Kirkham who was 17th at 11:53.39 to Belgian winner Philippe Thijs, and Munro who was 20th at 12:34.57. Kirkham was the Phil Anderson equivalent of Australian cycling at the time. It was his success which inspired others to follow. One was a small 15-year old named Hubert Opperman. Opperman, 63kg when dripping wet, was not a name to be reckoned with. In fact it took him three years before he won a race – in 1922. This success came after Kirkham had taken the young Opperman under his wing. 'He was the pinnacle for me,' Opperman said in *Pedal* magazine. 'I learned what to do, when and what speed and gears. I took it all in. Above all, he taught me to look for shelter in a bunch – behind the biggest rider.'

Passing on that knowledge was like planting a seed for the cultivation of a crop of English-speaking riders in the European peloton. Several other riders made the voyage from Australasia and the United States before Opperman first rode the Tour in 1928 and finished 18th. Australians Percy Osborn, Ernest Bainbridge, Frankie Thomas and New Zealand's Harry Watson went for the 1928 Tour with 'Oppy' as he was called. And in 1929, Canadian Adolphe Cockx tried, but failed to finish.

At the age of 27 Opperman lined up with 161 others for his first Tour. His talents as a Tour racer were totally unknown, but he was without doubt a world class record-breaker. He twice set world bests for the 24-hour record and was Australian record holder for 100 miles when the idea came up for him to race the Tour with the other Australasians – Osbourne, Bainbridge, Thomas and Watson.

It was a project thought up by his mentor and manager Bruce Small and sponsored by the Melbourne *Herald* newspaper (now *Herald-Sun*). The idea was for them to ride in a composite team with several French riders. Yet before the race began, it seemed the project was doomed when the French didn't ride. 'They gave us no chance. ''Experts'' reckoned we'd last three days since the formula for the 1928 Tour was 15 team time trial stages, plus six road mountain stages. We were riding with the whole of Australia on our backs. We couldn't back down,' Opperman said.

They didn't back down. In fact Opperman finished 18th and took third place in one stage as well. 'It was the hardest thing I ever did,' says 'Oppy' today. And while Bainbridge and Thomas failed to finish, Watson was 28th, and Osbourne 38th. English-speaking cycling history was first made by Moore in Paris – Rouen and then with Kirkham and Munro in the 1914 Tour. Nevertheless, these fleeting visits by Australian riders were regarded as a novelty by the locals.

Oppy quickly earned cudos as a legitimate star by wining the Bol d'Or 24-hour race later that year. So impressive was Oppy in winning that he was ahead of schedule to break the 1,000km record if he continued. And he did, after much pleading from his confidante, Small.

Opperman recalled the moment in the Australian magazine, *Cycling World*: 'Bruce ran alongside me and said to go on to the 1,000km. I said to hell with that. I stopped and he grabbed me and said: "you'll never be forgotten in France if you do this." The manager came across with tears were running down his face. "I cry for you Oppy" The crowd was chanting "Oppy! Oppy!" It was easier to give in than argue the point. So I pushed away and the track was cleared. That hour and 19 minutes were just a joy. It was easier than at any time in a race.'

Opperman returned to Australia and dominated the racing scene before returning to Europe in 1931 for the Paris six-day race and another assault on the Tour with three other Australians, Richard Lamb, Ossie Nicholson and Thomas. Only Opperman and Lamb finished the 1931 Tour (at 5:29.05 the last finisher from 81 starters) and Opperman's 12th place at 1:36.43 to Frenchman Antonin Magne, would stand as the best overall result by any English-speaking rider for 31 years, until 1962 when Simpson was sixth.

Meanwhile as the Tour became the season's objective for riders, teams, and later, for the sponsors, Opperman saw it as just a preparatory phase for something more important to him – the 1931 marathon 1,200km Paris – Brest – Paris classic, which was then a professional event and not the open *cyclo-touriste randoneé* it is today. 'I found the Tour was an excellent training ground for form,' he once said.

The field for the 1931 marathon included two Tour winners – the 1927 and 1928 champion Nicholas Frantz of Luxembourg and 1929 winner Maurice Dewaele of Belgium. But Opperman also ranked amongst the favourites too. 'The first leg was ridden in darkness and then into a howling gale and driving rain. It took us more than 25 hours to get to Brest. On the way back, riders were all over the road with fatigue.' Except for Oppy, who not only had to battle against the elements but also the teams as he was an independent entry. Yet he overcame all this and found himself in the winning five-man break which contested the first ever sprint finale. And the winner was convincingly Opperman.

Opperman's two seasons in Europe are the most noted, however, he went on to set world records for the motor paced 1,000 miles (1932); the Lands End to John O'Groats in Britain (1934), and a collection of bests in end-to-end distances in Australia before setting the world unpaced 24-hour record in 1939. Then came World War II and for Oppy the start of a distinguished political career in the Australian Government which saw him become the Minister for Immigration and later, after being knighted, the Australian High Commissioner in Malta.

Opperman redrew the boundaries for non-European cyclists. While the Second World War delayed the flood that would come, others were starting to follow his initiative and pioneering spirit before the outbreak of hostilities. In 1937 Bill Burl and Charlie Holland signed their names on the start sheet of the 1937 Tour de France.

They were the only Englishmen to race in the Tour before the war. It was not an experience that dealt kindly with them. Burl crashed on stage one and was eliminated on stage two when injuries sustained from the fall left him to finish outside the time limit. Then Holland, while riding strong until the mountains, owed his eventual retirement to a series of punctures which literally saw him left behind by the entire race. At the stage finish in Luchon he was so far back that every race official was gone when he arrived. It was as if he had been forgotten.

Holland unceremoniously took off his number and retired, not only ending his Tour aspirations, but apparently any hope that – apart from Oppy – English-speaking cyclists could be a serious force in European racing. There was certainly no indication that by the mid-50s interest in European cycle racing would be revived, and that new blood would soon be ready to take over from those pre-war pioneers.

1952 – 1959 Brian Robinson

The new era began in 1952 with Australian pioneer, John Beasley. After Burl and Holland he was the next to turn to Europe and the Tour. But he was unable to finish that year, or in 1955, and never succeeded in emulating the feats of his predecessor, Opperman. The only Australian who had shown any sign of doing that was Russell Mockeridge who excelled on both track and road. Others would succeed in Europe, even to race the Tour, like Reg Arnold in 1956 when he was 86th, and six-day track star Don Allan in 1974 and 1975 when he was 103rd and 85th respectively. But neither was a sensation like Mockeridge. His initial fame came on the road, years before his 64th place in the 1955 Tour. He had taken up cycling at the age of 18. He excelled, winning 'handicap' races everywhere. Then came his victory in the 1947 National Road Championship, which earned him selection for the 1948 Olympic Games road race in London finishing 29th. By 1952, he was an established track star as well. Confirmation came when he won a gold medal in the 1952 Olympic tandem with Lionel Cox; and the prestigious Grand Prix de Paris sprint title against Britain's triple winner, Reg Harris and reigning Dutch professional world champion Jan Derksen.

One of the saddest chapters of Australian cycling history, occurred when the bespectacled Melbournian was killed just three years after contesting the 1955 Tour, when he hit a bus during the Tour of Gippsland in Victoria, Australia. Monday September 15, 1958 is a date that sticks in every Australian cycling fan's memory.

From the hilly heartland of British cycling, Yorkshireman Brian Robinson took up the trail. Like so many of his countrymen, Robinson came from a time trialling back ground, but unlike so many, he would become one of Britain's greatest roadmen in Europe. He was the first to win a Tour stage, and from his seven starts he would finish five Tours, two of which saw him take 14th and 19th places overall. His successes in the Tour and other European races began a record of British success that spanned the 1950s and 1960s.

As Europe recovered from the economic, political, and social rigours of the war, Robinson's achievements came at a time when cycle racing in Europe was at its peak. Increased public interest in the sport was a healthy reflection of social change, and it helped encourage national pride. This made the challenge all the more daunting for an Englishman to try to break through a system led and ruled by Belgians, Italians and French. It took true determination and adaptability: Robinson clearly had it.

Robinson's place in the European peloton was aptly summed up by Dennis Donovan of *Cycling Weekly*. He wrote: 'He was the complete *coureur* in a hard school where the tutors were Fausto Coppi, Jacques Anquetil, Louison Bobet, Ferdi Kubler, and Rik Van Looy.' For one generation such names are the greatest ever in cycling. Whether for respect, adoration or fear each was revered in Robinson's day just as Roman Emperors were thousands of years ago.

It helped Robinson that he had experienced racing in Europe before turning professional. Before the 1952 Olympic road race in Helsinki he had ridden the 1952 Route de France amateur stage race in a composite British team of Army and National Cycling Union riders. Others in the team had been Peter Procter, Bernard Pusey and Les Willmott of the Army, and Brian Haskell, Des Robinson, Dick Henley and Alan Ashmore from the NCU. The outcome was heart rending: Procter was best finisher in 15th place, and Robinson finished 40th after being in fifth until the Pyrenees with three days to go. 'We were raw amateurs with no experience and no equipment. We were thrown in at the deep end. We went over the Pyrenees. I had never seen mountains like that before. It was a big learning session.'

Still, the experience didn't stop Robinson from pursuing his racing career. He finished 27th at the Helsinki Games road race in which Anquetil was 12th. In the world titles in Itay that September, he was equal eighth with Anquetil. Another Tour winner of the future, Charly Gaul of Luxembourg was also in the same group. Then in 1953 he became an 'independent' for the Ellis-Briggs team in England and rode for them in the home calendar before turning professional in 1955 with the Hercules team. Hercules, a British bicycle manufacturer, was an integral part of British cycling history. It came into the sport with one big ambition, to race the Tour de France. And in 1955 – when the Tour was raced by national teams – it backed Britain's first ever professional team. The full Tour team selection was: Robinson, Pusey, Dennis Talbot, Freddy Krebs, Clive Parker, Ken Joy (who was replaced by Bob Maitland), Arthur Ilsley, Derek Buttle and Dave Bedwell.

Hercules knew that continental experience was a must if dreams of competing in the Tour were to be realised when the team headed for Europe. Optimism for their success quickly took hold. No one could have declared disappointment: Robinson was third and Krebs sixth in the Tour of Calvados in France. Then Tony Hoar won a stage in the Tour of Holland and was second in another. In the Belgian Ardennes classics, Krebs again shone with tenth place in Liège – Bastogne – Liège, while Robinson was fourth in Flèche Wallonne. Nearer the Tour date, Robinson was fifth in the Grand Prix de Moulin and tenth in the Grand Prix du Havre. Suddenly, the British were becoming established names to reckon with.

As always the Tour yielded startling results. The 1955 edition proved that the Continentals were champions of their own game. Only two Brits finished the race which was historically won for the third time in succession by Frenchman Louison Bobet. Robinson was the first ever British finisher with his 29th place and Hoar, with his 69th and last position, claimed the distinguished title of *lanterne rouge*.

Bobet's dominance at the time had a bearing on the Yorkshireman's instinct for survival. Like Anquetil, Belgian Eddy Merckx and Frenchman Bernard Hinault in years to come, Bobet's authority as *patron* was never questioned. That Robinson learned in a post-Tour criterium in 1955 when the often moody Frenchman threatened to end his contract if he didn't let him win.

Team members came and went, Robinson lived on a day-to-day basis never knowing if his place on the team was secure. Eventually he joined a combined British–Swiss team named Cilo, led by Switzerland's Hugo Koblet. Several heads turned in the Tours of Spain and Switzerland where he was overall eighth and ninth respectively. Robinson was a natural selection for Gaul's Tour de France squad of 1956.

As Robinson took the step up towards elitism, the year introduced a new English-speaking professional, Irishman Shay Elliott. Elliot had raced for ACBB in 1955 and earned his professional contract by winning five amateur classics in the season. As fate would have it, by July and the Tour de France, both would ride together in the international team led by Luxembourg's Charly Gaul.

The Tour results saw Robinson in 14th overall and his best stage placing was third on stage one. Gaul was 13th. It was clear that Robinson had potential to do better. Elliott failed to finish the Tour, but this was his debut season in the paid ranks and the Dubliner's best was yet to come.

The 1957 season saw both riders get off to an aggressive start. Robinson claimed his first professional victory in the Grand Prix de la Ville Nice beating of all people, Bobet, by 0:50. Then Robinson and Elliott took the headlines in the Belgian classic Het Volk, where they were in a day long break, being caught just before the finish. Finally, Robinson confirmed he was definitely on an early season roll when he took third in the first major international classic for the year, Milan–San Remo in Italy.

Ironically, that major classic result also signified his biggest regret. As any rider knows, being so close to winning a big race is often worse than finishing last. And on this occasion Robinson felt he might have won were it not for team orders to help Spaniard Miguel Poblet. His team had business connections in the cycle trade with the Spaniard. When Robinson attacked on a climb, he was quickly reminded of his orders, and as the results showed, he bit his lip and followed them to the letter: Poblet first, Belgium's Fred De Bruyne second, and Robinson third. 'Had I won, I would have been made for life,' he says today.

The same season also saw a second disappointment. He was the sole English-speaking entry in the Tour which saw the first of Anquetil's five career wins. Yet for Robinson a crash on the fourth stage to Roubaix broke his left wrist, and he was forced to abandon.

Robinson was forced to abandon again in the 1958 Tour which saw his old team leader, Gaul claim his only win. That year 69th placed Stan Brittain – another new name to earn plenty of attention later – was the only English finisher.

The race was still an important bench mark in English cycling history. Everything was geared to the next Tour in 1959. The careers of Robinson, and Elliott who was now settling down, revolved around the Tour. Elliott took second place on the sixth stage to St Brieuc – for a day the highest place ever earned by an English-speaking rider – and then went on to finish 48th overall and claim his first Tour finisher's medal. And Robinson claimed the first stage win by any English-speaking rider on stage seven from St Brieuc–Brest.

The only hitch to Robinson's celebration was that the stage win came by default. He was actually second to Italy's Arrigo Padovan but was given the win when Padovan was disqualified for dangerous riding in the finale. But any frustration for Robinson not having finished first on the stage was swept away in the 1959 Tour, eventually won by Spaniard Federico Bahamontes, the 'Eagle of Toledo'.

As another Englishman named Tom Simpson began his professional career, Robinson grabbed the headlines with his 19th place in that year's Tour. He was one of four Englishmen in the race. Vic Sutton was 37th overall while John Andrews and Tony Hewson did not finish. Elliott was again in the starting line-up but abandoned as well. Meanwhile Robinson chased away any mid-race blues with a marathon 140km attack on stage 20 from Annecy to Chalon-sur-Saone. He won, fair and square, by an incredible 20 minutes and six seconds.

Robinson was a sporting hero who deserved whatever recognition he got. In future years the opportunities would not be so great; Simpson was closing in as the next English star after his fourth place in the 1959 world championship road race, at Zandvoort in the Netherlands.

1960–1967 Tom Simpson/Shay Elliott

Two stark parallels would be drawn between these riders. Both would wear the yellow jersey for the first time ever, for their respective countries – Ireland and England. And both would meet premature and tragic deaths.

They did not compete alone, for there was a handsome crop of strong English riders racing on from the late 1950s such as Robinson, Brittain, Coe, Sutton, Hewson and Andrews amongst others. However, the years from 1960 to 1967 would be most remembered for Elliott and Simpson's achievements.

Simpson was the first to make the historic claim to the *maillot jaune*. His first chance came in the 1960 Tour de France which was contested by national teams. He and Robinson were in an eight-man British team and while outnumbered by rival teams of up to 14 riders, Simpson was never frightened to attack. After stage one he was sixth overall thanks to his presence in a winning 14-man break. Then two stages later he was in an eight-man break which gained enough time for him to become leader on the road. By the end of the day, however, he was third, and the collation of time bonuses did not tally in his favour.

An exhausted Simpson finally finished his first Tour placed 29th overall, three places behind Robinson. Yet so drained of energy was Simpson that he swore he would never do it again. So many have said the same and yet come back year after year. Simpson proved no different.

Signs that Simpson's cycling career would carry historic proportions were clear in 1961 when in April he became the first British winner of the Tour of Flanders in Belgium – one of the top five one-day 'monuments' in the sport today. He started the Tour with an injured knee, and before stage three was finished, he was forced to retire. That year only three of a nine-man 'British' team made it to Paris: Robinson who was 53rd; Elliott, 47th; and Scot Ken Laidlaw, 65th. Anquetil, Elliott's leader on the St Raphael team, won the second of his five Tour victories.

Next year 1962, brought Simpson even greater success. Then riding on the French Gitane team he didn't win the Tour of Flanders as he did in 1961, but his fifth place confirmed him as an ever-present contender for the classics. A month before, in Paris–Nice he finished second behind Belgian Joseph Planckaert. But the best was saved for July and the Tour, where on stage 14 from Pau to St Gaudens in the Pyrenees he finished in the winning break and took the yellow jersey. 'Major Tommy' as he was known because of his ever-present joviality was the first Briton to don it. Unfortunately, Simpson wore his trophy for only a day. Arriving in Paris, still placed an incredible sixth overall, Simpson was on a high.

Meanwhile, Elliott was establishing himself too. Major victories had eluded him, none more so than the 1962 world road race title at Salo in Italy where he went for gold and won the silver medal. He was in the winning move, but with his French team-mate Jean Stablinski who attacked in the final kilometres won the gold medal. As soon as 'Stab' attacked, Elliott had no choice but to stop the other attackers from chasing him down. 'I couldn't chase after my friend attacked,' he reportedly said in frustration after finishing 1:22 behind Stablinski and 0:22 clear of the rest of the chasing group.

For Elliott the 1963 Tour was an occasion for Stablinski to repay his world title debt. And that moment came on stage three to Roubaix when the pair were in a stage winning break which gained a nine-minute lead on the peloton, which included their St Raphael leader Anquetil. Elliott and Stablinski did their duty and held back from working in the break. But both were ready to make the best of the opportunity. Stablinski's help came when Elliott punctured. The Frenchman slowed the break down long enough for Elliott to rejoin quickly after changing wheels. Then with six kilometres to go Stablinski winked at Elliott before leading the break off the cobbles and onto the adjoining bike path. This was Elliott's moment to attack and he took it to win the stage and the coveted yellow jersey. It was the pinnacle of the Irishman's career. He savoured it for just three more days before Anquetil took the jersey back with victory in a time trial. Three days were long enough for Elliott to etch his name in English-speaking cycling history as one of the pioneering greats.

As quickly as Elliott became a household name, however, the Irishman took the road to retirement in 1964. He had few results that year and even failed to finish the Tour. He returned to Ireland where he tried setting up a metal working firm with his father. But he was never able to adapt to a quieter life off the circuit, especially after his French wife left him in 1966 and returned to France. The next year Elliott attempted a comeback in the London–Holyhead race, but his 21st place was proof that his best days were gone. Elliott carried on riding and coaching juniors. Adjusting can't have been easy, and the cycling world was devastated in May 1971, one month after his father died, to hear the news that Elliott was also dead. It was at his Irish home that his body was found. He died of shotgun wounds which were rumoured to be self-inflicted.

By contrast it was a glorious year for English-speaking cycling enthusiasts. Simpson did not tackle the Tour of 1963, which saw Anquetil win for the third successive year and fourth time in his career. Instead, he continued to impress with victories in Bordeaux–Paris, the Grand Prix Parisian, and the Roue d'Or. Simpson was one of the year's most consistent performers in the classics: in Paris–Brussels and Ghent–Wevelgem he was second, then in the Tour of Flanders he finished third, by the year's end he was second in the Super Prestige Pernod Trophy series based on overall results.

The next year would be remembered more for consolidation than celebration for other older European-based English riders. Simpson was 14th in the Tour which also saw Denson claim his first finish with 72nd place, and another Englishman, Michael Wright finished 56th. Wright, who rode seven more Tours and even won a stage in 1965 and 1967, always made interesting copy for Tour journalists. He was unique in two ways, one for his bike racing prowess, and also because he was an Englishman who didn't speak English. His family moved to Belgium when he was six and he only spoke French. But he always kept his English passport, and was still registered as an English rider!

Simpson's performance on the circuit was to prove that he not only had winning potential for the Tour and one-day classics, but the world professional road title as well, placing fourth at 0:06 to Dutch winner Jan Janssen in the title race at Sallanches in France that September. His next most noted performance was to finish third in the two-man Italian time trial, the Baracchi Trophy with Germany's 1966 world champion Rudi Altig.

They were good results. And the momentum was to grow with the arrival of a new English name on the top of the result sheets – Barry Hoban. Hoban had been offered a professional contract in 1962 with Pelforth which was then directed by Frenchman Maurice de Muer, who would take on Peugeot in the mid to late 1970s. But Hoban wanted more amateur experience first and gave himself another two years before joining the Mercier-BP team directed by former French Tour winner Antonin Magne.

The cycling world had shared euphoria and heartache with Simpson. Euphoria came in the form of his victories and top results in 1965 when he rode for Peugeot, highlighted by his gold medal win in the world title at San Sebastian in Spain. His other wins that year were in the Italian Tour of Lombardy and London – Holyhead. He was also British Sportsman of the Year and second again in the Super Prestige Pernod series after adding third places in Bordeaux – Paris, Flèche Wallonne and the Grand Prix du Midi Libre to his season credits.

Heartache came two years later on July 13 during the 1967 Tour de France when Simpson collapsed on the sun-baked, barren scree-slopes of Mont Ventoux in Provence, where he died.

Simpson came into this Tour with victory in mind. He had won Paris – Nice earlier that year and used the Tour of Spain, in which he was 33rd overall, as preparation. And when Tour organisers reinstated the system of fielding national teams, Simpson carefully selected a ten-man team that was tailor made for his interests. The line-up was: Simpson, Hoban, Wright and Denson who shared a vast knowledge of European racing; and Colin Lewis, Arthur Metcalfe, Pete Chisman, Peter Hill, Albert Hitchen and Bill Lawrie. It was a team bolstered with one ambition – to bring home the first British Tour champion. No one was prepared for the tragedy which followed.

It all happened on stage 13. Under a burning summer sun Simpson was struggling up the long, twisting road towards the 6,250 foot summit of the extinct volcano, Mont Ventoux. He was suffering like hell, but giving up and letting go was never a trait of Simpson's character. He was a rider who would always go to the limit. But this time he went too far.

Suddenly with two kilometres to go on the 35km climb Simpson stopped and collapsed. His team mechanic Harry Hall rushed to his side and tried reviving him before Tour doctor Pierre Dumas arrived and rushed him to hospital. But it was too late. Dehydration, lack of oxygen and an overload of physical effort that day was ruled as the cause of death, despite the discovery of amphetemines and alcohol in his body in an autopsy. Such elements were never labelled as the cause of Simpson's passing away, although their trace did lead to the start of widespread drug testing not only in cycling, but all sports.

Simpson's fate left an eternal impression on the sport. Today a granite memorial stands at the very 33km mark where he collapsed on Mont Ventoux. Racers passing it nearly always take time out to pay special hommage to a man who was not only an English sporting hero, but a Continental one as well.

The day after his death, a mourning peloton granted the demoralised British team – of which only Hoban, Lewis and Metcalfe finished the Tour – the stage win as a token of respect to Simpson. That 'honour' came for Hoban who merely slipped off the front of peloton and soloed to the first of eight career Tour stage wins. 'I don't count that stage win. It was symbolic – a gesture to Tom. It just happened,' reflects Hoban who, like his team-mates, had become a dear friend of Simpson's.

1968 – 1978 Barry Hoban

As well as a friend, Hoban also became an apt successor to Simpson as the guiding light of English cycling on the Continent. He assumed the role superbly well until 1978.

He fully adapted to European life, spoke fluent Flemish and French and was a daily pick for journalists at every race he entered. It was clear to everyone that Hoban would never be a Tour contender like Simpson, instead Hoban had great stage and classic winning potential which the entire peloton recognised.

He actually only won one classic, but came close to his first victory in the 1967 Paris – Tours, when he was outsprinted by Belgian Rik Van Looy by half a wheel. Victory was finally his in 1974 when riding for Raymond Poulidor's Gan team he won Ghent – Wevelgem in a glorious sprint from none other than Belgium's Eddy Merckx and Roger De Vlaeminck.

He may have tallied numerous top placings in other classics, but his Tour record was a victory in itself. He rode it 12 times and finished 11 of those; 1970 being the only year he didn't make it to Paris. And he won eight stages – in 1967, 1968, 1969 (two), 1973 (two), 1974 and 1975.

Hoban won two stages of the 1964 Tour of Spain, which was won by Frenchman Raymond Poulidor. Two months later Poulidor, the perennial French runner-up in the Tour de France, pushed Anquetil to a meagre 0:55 victory in the French Tour for his hardest fought fifth win. It was in that French Tour that Hoban made his debut, after impressing his director for selection earlier in the Midi Libre with a stage win and victory in the climbers' category from Spain's 1959 Tour champion, Federico Bahamontes.

Like any rider, Hoban was impressed by his first Tour experience, he came 65th overall. He has clear memories of riding with the big stars like Anquetil, Poulidor and Bahamontes: 'They aqua-planed above the ground and we were mere mortals who grovelled along,' said Hoban once in *Cycling Weekly*. Hoban quickly saw that he had to adapt to the system. And like Simpson and Elliott it was several more years before he would produce his fabulous best.

The passage of generations between him, Kelly, Sherwen, and the lesser-known riders like Italian-based American Mike Neel, began soon after. He rode the 1977 Tour where Bill Nickson made his debut and failed to finish. 1978 saw his last Tour, which was Kelly and Sherwen's first. After that Hoban raced mainly in England, although his last victory before retiring in 1980 was Germigny l'Eveque in France.

In 1981 as Hinault would win the third of his five Tours, Boyer and Mount were American cycling stars, although that was a label they would soon find themselves sharing with a certain Greg LeMond. By the time Mount retired after 1983 and Boyer after 1988, LeMond was more than an historic 'finisher'. He was an outright winner.

However the Americans were not alone, in the competition for hometown attention, Kelly was already a big star, Sherwen was an established professional. And with the 1980s came a flood of talent into Europe which the pioneering efforts of those before them had created.

Barry Hoban, Tom Simpson, Shay Elliott, Brian Robinson, Sir Hubert Opperman and others all won and lost in their years of sufferance on the uncleared and rocky path to European cycling fortune. But were it not for them Kelly, Sherwen, Nickson, Mount, Neel and Boyer – and all those who followed – may never have picked up the trail to a professional cycling career in Europe.

2 THE CONSCRIPTS

The men who joined the French amateur club Athletic Club de Boulogne – Billancourt, known as ACBB, established and improved conditions for English-speaking riders in Europe. Eventually they formed the new guard, being the conscripts who became the foreign legion.

Paul Sherwen

Date of birth: 7 June, 1956

Place of birth: Frodsham, England

Teams: ACBB (Fra), FIAT (Fra),
      La Redoute (Fra), Raleigh (Eng)

Turned Professional 1978

Retired 1987

The bitingly cold wind was blowing fiercely off Blackpool beach. It was not a nice day for cycle racing, but then as most professionals quickly learn, few are. You wouldn't have guessed it by watching Paul Sherwen who whizzed past our press car before a stage start in the 1987 Tour of Lancashire. Crouched only on his left pedal and precariously poised like a trapeze artist yet in total control, he was making his way to the start line.

Sherwen shouted something at his apprehensive, shivering and much younger rivals. Their reaction was of apparent annoyance. After all, this was a national classed pro-am race, and they were trying to prepare themselves for a race that bore great influence on upcoming Milk Race selections, but it held virtually no personal importance for Sherwen at all. How could it? Here was a man who had ridden seven Tours de France and numerous one-day classics. His words were smothered by the roaring gale. However his cheeky smile – his trademark – made you think that he was mocking the locals. After all, compared to the hundreds of days spent racing in his ten years on the Continent, conditions here were not that bad. Well, the home boys didn't think so.

Sherwen was always different. Having lived in Kenya until the age of 13 and still making regular winter visits, his was not a regular background; he accepted the individualist's tag and had no trouble living with it.

In his heyday he was always regarded as an outsider by British and Continentals alike. When he returned to English shores to ride out his career with the

British Raleigh team in 1987 he saw no reason to expect that those who did resent him would feel differently. His detractors must have felt a chill down their spines when he won the British road championship of 1987.

Sherwen has always said that people got the wrong impression of him. They still do. He still laughs at the occasions when I would angrily take the defensive on anti-Australian jokes. And looking back on how I took the bait, it's reassuring to know that dozens of others have been caught the same way. Many still are!

He reeks of a psychological resilience which critics unfairly label as aloofness, arrogance and superiority. But without these qualities he wouldn't have survived his decade on the Continent. Indeed, the lack of such characteristics often broke the Continental ambitions of other riders with far greater raw ability.

That's not to say Sherwen was without ability. He left England rated a star. And when he rode for ACBB he confirmed that with several big wins. Such results eventually led to professional contracts with FIAT and La Redoute before his move to Raleigh in England. Adaptability and an inner determination to get the job done were Sherwen's greatest traits, being adaptable helped him to become 'one of them' – one of the French – and be accepted; his determination was for success, as one of the few English-speaking riders on the Continent, he wanted to make his mark and not return home a failure. Barry Hoban was at the end of his career when Sherwen arrived. While Sherwen was not destined to be a champion like Hoban, as a boyish 20-year old he wanted to do justice to his time there. He quickly learned when to help others and when to stick his neck out and do something for himself whether by words or action.

It was a strange coincidence that his first win in France was the Grand des Ouefs Dure or 'Hard Eggs'. He is one – a much shared sentiment by the peloton and race organisers. Never was it so perfectly illustrated as in the 1985 Tour de France; it was his last and he battled to finish.

Since his retirement from professional racing he became a respected television commentator and his annual insights on the Tour are screened by Channel 4 in England, CBS and ABC in the United States and SBS in Australia. He also spent two years as *directeur-sportif* of the Raleigh team. More recently he has become one of the few respected media-liason officers on the European circuit, having worked with the American Motorola team since 1991.

Sherwen is just as much a professional now as when he was racing bikes. He does admit to feeling nervous sometimes – no doubt when he turned professional – perhaps it was mixed with expectation and wonder on his first day with Motorola, again on stage one of the 1991 Ruta Del Sol in February, again when he took on the job as *directeur-sportif* of the British Raleigh team in 1988, did his first stand-up in front of a television camera and no doubt when he first lined up for the start as a racer for ACBB. He was probably just as nervous when he got married in late 1992! All impressive landmarks in a varied career that directly stems from his dedication to cycling.

Graham Jones

Date of birth: October 24, 1955

Place of birth: Manchester, England

Teams: ACBB (Fra), Peugeot (Fra),
　　　　Wolber (Fra), Systeme U (Fra),
　　　　Ever-Ready (Eng), ANC-Halfords (Eng)

Turned professional 1979

Retired 1987

The melting bitumen and simmering heat were relentless. After 70km of the sixth stage to the 1987 Tour de France, the peloton was approaching its first climb of the race, the Col du Champ de Feu in the Vosges. The real battle was about to begin for the leader's yellow jersey, between Carrera's Erich Maechler, the Swiss winner of Milan – San Remo four months earlier, and eventual winner and team-mate, Stephen Roche.

　　Not many people were paying attention to what was happening at the back of the peloton where Graham Jones, a member of the ill-fated British ANC-Halfords team, was about to confront a physical and mental battle just to finish. But with nine years of professional racing behind him, he must have sensed his imminent fate.

　　In the Tour, riders always forecast their performance by how their legs feel at the start of a race. As Jones pedalled towards the seven kilometre first category climb, his legs were already turning to jelly. To onlookers his previous day's award of the Prix de l'Amabilite and the £100 that went with it must have seemed a cheap alternative to a gold watch for his retirement. For here was one of the classiest bike racers Great Britain has ever produced being sent to the executioner. The axe fell as soon as the peloton began ascending. Within minutes the airwaves of Radio Tour crackled and the hoarse voice of Albert Bouvet confirmed Jones' doom. *"Jones est laché"* (Jones is dropped) said Bouvet with an almost sympathetic and sorrowful hesitancy.

　　Unlike his ANC team-mates, Jones was well known by everyone in the Tour – riders, team managers, the press and organisers. More importantly, he was highly respected for his dedication, ambition and ability. He had **earned** his right to be there. And in a better team with better support and consequent better form and morale, Jones would normally be up near the front of the peloton. It pained Tour purists like Bouvet to see riders like Jones bow out of the limelight this way.

　　Jones was not the only rider to be dropped so early. Nor was he the only ANC rider – an apparently 'fresh' Paul Watson was there right alongside him until ANC *directeur-sportif*, Phil Griffiths, ordered Watson to ride on and leave Jones unless he wanted to risk being eliminated as well. Meanwhile Jones, his shoulders hunched and face contorted in pain, took one pedal at a time. But each could have been his last. He made it over the 1,100m summit, and over the next second-category climb, the Col du Donon at 92km. But he was resigned to the fact that he would not finish. As Jeff Connor described in his book *Wide Eyed and Legless* which documented the ANC team's 1987 Tour assault, Jones' last words to Griffiths before he drove off to help other ailing team-mates were: 'It's no good.' And when Jones stopped after 100km and climbed into the 'broom wagon', so too did a professional career that **should** have ended on a far more glorious note.

On that day, Monday July 6, 1987, his nine years as a professional meant nothing. He had quit the Tour for the second time in five attempts. He might have been the Merlin Plage series winner in his French amateur days at ACBB in 1978; he might have ridden as a professional with Peugeot for four years and been one week short of finishing in the top five of the 1982 Tour where illness saw him fade to 20th place – itself a career best; and he might have ridden with distinction at the French Wolber and System U teams before returning to England where he rode with Ever-Ready before joining ANC in 1987. But nothing hurts a rider's pride more than pulling out from the Tour, especially his last. And Jones was hurting bad.

Unsurprisingly Jones made an unceremonious exit from the Tour later that day. Having to surrender his number and spend the rest of that stage in the broom wagon behind the race was punishment enough. Back at his hotel he quickly showered, packed his bags and then bought a beer before bidding farewell. As the Tour unfolded, his story became just one of the many tragedies behind the ANC-Halfords story.

In later years I got to know Jones better and realised that although the general consensus was that he was a very quiet person – a loner but not selfishly so – it's also true that he was perhaps too giving to the needs of his teams and their bludgeoning tendency to over-race him, and waste his undoubted climbing qualities.

Today, having returned to 'civilian life' as a travelling salesman, Jones has not cut his ties with cycling. Far from it in fact. Like many of his peers – including his close friend and one time team leader, Jean-René Bernaudeau – Jones has returned to the Tour de France each year in the capacity of driver for the British press. Many other ex-professionals do the same – even Bernaudeau. It's their way of maintaining old friendships in the peloton that would otherwise be lost. The scene of many a stage start is akin to a school reunion. For three weeks every July, Jones and those he raced with and against know they can relive cherished and unique memories.

Phil Anderson

Date of birth: March 20, 1958

Place of birth: London, England

Teams: ACBB (Fra), Peugeot (Fra),
       Panasonic (Neth), TVM (Neth),
       Motorola (US)

Turned professional 1980

Not yet retired

The morning after Anderson lost the 1988 Tour of Flanders I was due to interview him. Knocking at the front door, I wondered if he regretted agreeing to it. Only the day before, his breakaway companion Eddy Planckaert dusted him in the finale. When he opened the door, the mask of disappointment was stuck to his face like wet mud.

For hard, tough, one-day classic riders like Anderson, the Tour of Flanders is not 'just another race'. Winning it is as good as a world championship and better than a Tour de France stage. And equally, letting slip a winning opportunity is a painful legacy to bear – even more so for a rider like Anderson who had already suffered humiliation. In 1985 his Belgian Panasonic team-mate Eric Vanderaerden rode off from the decisive break which included Anderson, leaving the Australian with the duty of blocking while the Belgian took the spoils.

Anderson is a rider who doesn't like losing. He feels the Tour of Flanders is a race he 'should' win. Although he has had plenty of success in his career to sooth the frustration: a run of 11 days in the yellow jersey; a number one ranking in the world cup; numerous victories in races like the Amstel Gold, Championship of Zurich, Creteil – Chaville; and stage wins in the Tour, the Nissan Classic, Kellogg's Tour of Britain, the Tour of Romandy and Tour of Switzerland.

His gritty determination, brute strength and aggressive racing instincts have always been the hallmarks of his career. On the morning after losing the Tour of Flanders, there was no reason to expect him to explain why he lost at Flanders. It hurt him to talk about it. He knew what winning would have meant. He was in a new and small Dutch team, TVM, which was little rated by the critics who also labelled Anderson as 'washed-up' after a sad departure from Panasonic the year before. But after several minutes he did come round. He must have known, deep down, that he wasn't finished and that opportunities to prove it were just waiting for him.

Who could have predicted with any confidence, back in 1986, when he recovered from an hereditary back condition, which not only caused him to lose the 1985 Super Prestige title, but almost forced a premature retirement, that he would ever return to the podium? But he pulled through, winning Creteil – Chaville and the New York City Tour, and finishing third behind Bernard Hinault and Greg LeMond in the Coors Classic later that year.

Sadly in 1987, his last with Panasonic and Peter Post, there was little to smile about – especially after his devastating time trial at Futuroscope in the Tour which once more saw Anderson's attackers bring the knives out. One was Peter Post who, according to one Belgian journalist, reportedly said Anderson rode like a 'retarded human being'. Hence he found himself riding for TVM in 1988 in that fateful Tour of Flanders, which could have seen an embarrassed Post had he won.

Next to Anderson's dogged racing spirit, it is his ability to bounce back that is so inspiring. He has had numerous victories since 1988, that his rivals never forget. He may be one of the oldest members of the peloton, but he is the type of racer who will always be marked until the day he decides to hang up his bike.

It's ironic that he has chosen to ride the remaining years of his career based in southern France, where much of his cycling career blossomed. Since moving into a two bedroom cabana overlooking the Mediteranean waters at Miramar, Anderson has rediscovered his past. The old training routes of ACBB and Peugeot are still firmly etched in his mind . . . like the memories of races and training camps past.

His training is still hard, bloody hard. But it is not the 'task' it used to be in Belgium where wind, rain and cobblestones create further hardship. The thinking that such elements made you 'tougher' may have some truth, but they also weaken riders and invariably bring on injury. After 14 years of professional racing, Anderson hardly needs further tempering. These days he is far more at ease with himself and his surroundings. His distinct crew-cut of the early 1980s, once replaced with long Samson-like locks, has now returned along with a deep hunger to win. In early 1993 he was put out of racing because of a terrifying tally of injuries which included a fractured knee-cap, dislocated shoulder, badly bruised ribs and index finger, torn chest muscles and bronchitis. He desperately wanted to race. He had to keep reminding himself of how he has always come through just as people have written him off. He did it in 1991 when he won 12 races and announced to his critics that he was back. After a poor start in 1992 he did it again in the Nissan Classic, Grand Prix of Isbergues, and a sixth in Paris–Tours.

Doing it again seems a wild hope, but hope goes a long way in cycling. And who knows, by returning to the roots of his early racing career he may rediscover the winning essence that once made him the name on every headline. That's not to mean Anderson aspires to win the Tour de France. Such dreams are long past. But there are still other races, Tour stages and major World Cup classics to be won – especially that 'darn' Tour of Flanders.

Robert Millar

Date of birth: 13 September, 1958

Place of birth: Glasgow, Scotland

Teams: ACBB (Fra), Peugeot (Fra),

Panasonic (Neth), Fagor (Fra), Z (Fra),

TVM (Neth)

Turned professional 1980

Not yet Retired

It was 11pm on July 10, 1989. That day's ninth stage of the Tour de France from Pau to Cauterets in the Pyrenees, and Spaniard Miguel Indurain's stage victory, was the subject of most people's conversation.

A rake-thin figure entered the hotel dining room from the darkness of the outside. It could have been any bike rider. After two weeks of the Tour they all bear the same ghastly emaciated look – except of course Miguel Indurain who won that day. But as this approaching person emerged into the light, I saw it was Robert Millar: Britain's best ever performer in the Tour de France – fourth in 1984 and King of the Mountains, and always a force to contend with once the gradient goes up.

Renowned for his acid tongue on and off the circuit, I was prepared to be swamped by a barrage of Scottish sarcasms about what journalists eat and drink. It was a relief to be greeted by that wiry Scottish grin. In fact our evening on the Tour passed pleasantly, he sat down and ordered a whopping great big ice cream. As we ate we barely talked about cycling. It made a change from the day's events and eventually he offered to drive me back to my hotel. When we parted ways, he had not passed one derogatory comment against me, I realised how clouded an impression one gets of somebody. The evening revealed no sign of pressure, or tension in this notoriously difficult rider. It seems incredible that the next day Millar went on to win the tenth stage from Cauterets to Luchon-Superbagnères.

My first meeting with Millar at the 1987 Tour de France made no startling impression on either of us. I tried to be polite and introduced myself. 'Gee Whiz...,' he replied barely looking up, he finished his speech with a rude expletive. I was wounded by his indifference, and decided to adopt the same policy, even if he went on to win the race. Luckily he didn't and my foolish conviction went unchallenged. Three months later, at the announcement of French teams for the 1988 season in Paris, I met Millar again – warily. He had just signed with Stephen Roche for the Fagor team and an ill-fated year. Someone noticed my frosty look. 'Robert have you said something to offend him?' they asked. Millar looked with that wiry smile – the same I'd seen at Cauterets on the Tour – 'Did I tell you to sod off or something?' he asked. My reply was direct: 'Yes, something like that, but I thought sod you too.' There was nothing else to do but laugh at the stalemate.

Knowing now the type of person Millar is, it was probably that confrontation which established a rapport. It was a type of 'cut-the-bullshit, lets get on with it' association he wanted. And he got it.

Millar still likes to make occasional jibes. He has his moods. But he has his lighter moments too, even so, his quick doubled-edged jabs can be laden with sarcasm. But for some reason it no longer offends. Maybe he has mellowed: fatherhood, age and his imminent retirement would certainly contribute to anyone's outlook and behaviour. In this respect why should Millar be any different? The pressures on him now must be substantially less. Perhaps, like Anderson, he enjoys life a little more and is more at ease with himself. Some people believe Millar today is just biding his time until his retirement arrives. But give him steep mountains and a race winning opportunity, and his climbing prowess is always polished. When wins become scarce, as they have been in recent years, it's easy to forget his achievements.

Besides the Tour in which he has won three stages, he has twice finished second in the Tour of Spain – in 1985 when the Spanish peloton combined to knock his leadership on the penultimate day and in 1986. He was second again to Stephen Roche in the 1987 Tour of Italy. And even in the one-day classic Liège – Bastogne – Liège he came close to winning in 1988. He was in the winning break, but was outsprinted by Dutchman Adrie Van der Poel and Belgian Michel Dernies.

Who can forget the image of Millar towing a tiring and yellow-jerseyed Frenchman Ronan Pensec up the L'Alpe D'Huez in the 1990 Tour when he – had he been allowed – might very well have won the stage himself?

Then there is his unexpected success on British soil in 1988 when he won the Kellogg's Tour of Britain and finished second the following year by four meagre seconds. So much for assuming – wrongly – that Millar's self-inflicted exile on the Continent means he can't win elsewhere.

On first meeting, Millar might not seem the friendliest rider in the peloton. But he is a man who grew up needing his instinct for survival. It's easy to forget that since he left Glasgow for Paris in 1979, he has had to fight, and fight hard. He has done so probably harder than most of us will ever have to. Today he knows what he wants. He is certainly one of the most astute riders around. When Millar does retire from the peloton one thing is sure, he will be missed, for watching him race at his best is nothing less than impressive.

Stephen Roche

Date of birth: 28 November, 1959

Place of birth: Dublin, Ireland

Teams: ACBB (Fra), Peugeot (Fra),

La Redoute (Fra), Carrera (It),

Fagor (Fra), Histor (Bel), Tonton

Tapis (Bel), Carrera (It)

Turned Professional 1981

Retired 1993

The heavy fog fell across Luz Ardiden, the rain continued, the temperature dropping at every minute. A lack of spectators at the Pyreneen summit finish of the 1992 Tour of Spain's ninth stage said it all – there were obviously better places to be.

As Stephen Roche reached the finish line 7:23 behind stage winner, Spaniard Laudelino Cubino, his face was frozen blue, his eyes bloodshot and his teeth chattered like an electric typewriter. He was pushed towards the Carrera team truck and an awaiting soigneur whose forlorn look, when he saw the Irishman, resembled a doctor's in a hospital emergency ward. Roche – suffering from an agonising back injury which would have stopped any lesser mortal long ago – had gone too far this time. Prised off his saddle, he spent a good three minutes trying to straighten his back as he leant against the truck. In between wipes and rub-downs from his soigneur, Roche coughed, spluttered and finally heaved a painful cry as he rediscovered an upright position he had not felt for seven hours. He slowly pulled himself into the truck, sat down and looked at me with a sunken expression which was so self-explanatory that it defied any sense in asking the inevitable: 'How are you Stephen?'

I didn't ask, I couldn't. There was absolutely no need. Suddenly, in the stark absence of the usual tension and excitement of a race finish and sensing the seriousness of Roche's condition I simply asked if he saw the risk of doing irreparable damage by continuing with a race he did not want to start. Roche sighed, tried in vain to crack the beaming smile that television screens see day in and day out of the Tour – but failed – and said: 'Perhaps, I don't know. I just have to finish this race. If I don't, I won't be ready for the French Tour.' His head fell back into his hands, and I walked away feeling total admiration for his courage.

There has probably been a no more charismatic member of the peloton in the last 20 years than him. He is a born winner and he proved it in 1987 when he did the remarkable and won the Tours of Italy and France and the world professional road championship – being only the second rider after Eddy Merckx in 1976 to do so. The signs were there well before then too: in 1981, his first year as a professional, he won the Tour of Corsica and Paris–Nice to everyone's surprise, including his.

Furthermore, his record of successes has come from a popular aggressive flair which has won the hearts of so many. Even off the saddle Roche has left the public and media swooning after him – no matter what country or language, be it France, Italy, Spain, Belgium, England or Ireland, he seemingly fits into any environment.

Adding to the impact of Roche's versatility and manner are also his looks. His chirpy smile, sad blue eyes, black curly hair and open face, ooze with sympathy. It sounds over the top, but its true. It sometimes seems that he just can't go wrong. Of course this is not so, for a rider blessed with so many advantages, there has been a hefty dose of trouble thrown into his life: knee and back injuries, sponsor troubles and, as a consequence from the pressure, personal strife. All this has put him on the brink of retirement at least twice since 1987. He won the 'Triple Crown' that year, so rare was the feat that everyone said it would be unfair to expect Roche to do it again. But nobody was prepared for the remorseless flow of misfortune which then beset his career.

He developed – however unintentionally – an awkward knack of giving two versions of the same story. Or, even worse, in attempting to lighten journalists' affinity with him, Roche has sometimes targeted one for a public ribbing without realising the ridicule being heaped on them. Yes! I have been the victim of both, but to his credit he has always apologised – an admirable act with which not many in the racing world would bother.

In many ways Roche's 1992 season – which ended with him saying he would retire at the end of 1993 – was his greatest victory of the lot. For while it was not laden with great wins (although many great rides) it marked the end to the wave of misery he rode on after 1987. It also secured his hope of a celebrated rather than commiserated end to his career.

The most celebrated of his 1992 performances was his ninth place in the Tour de France. He also won the 16th stage to La Bourbole after several nail-biting close calls in stages leading up to this cold, foggy, glorious day in the Massif Central. And his 15th place in the Vuelta was a triumph which deserved more recognition than it got – if just for his solitary and very unglorious struggle.

He is every bit the showman as much as he is a champion. But if ever a cyclist was to prove the value on not giving up in life, then Roche is that man.

Sean Yates

Date of birth: 18 May, 1958

Place of birth: Forest Row, England

Teams: ACBB (Fra), Peugeot (Fra), Fagor (Sp),

Fagor (Fra), 7-Eleven (US),

Motorola (US)

Turned Professional 1982

Not yet retired

Sean Yates was sitting quietly on a bench, looking out across from Grasse to the lowlands of the Alpe Maritimes and the blue Mediterreanean sea. It was late October, 1992 and he was taking time out from a light training ride.

With only the Grand Prix des Nations and Florence – Pistoia time trials to go Yates was happy: the racing season – his tenth as a professional – was at its ebb, just as it was on the tourist-free Cote D'Azur where he has lived since 1988. In a reflective mood, aware that his racing commitments were just about over, he had just endured three hours of questioning about life at ACBB, Peugeot, Fagor and Motorola. And he was two weeks away from getting married.

Yates was waiting for me to return from the travel agent's office. I was crossing the road to join him when he was suddenly confronted by a shuffling, rotund *Grassois* who bore a ruddied nose – the common trademark of a truely vintaged wine drinker. He was another of the many old retired French cyclists, who pop out of the woodwork when you least expect it. His attention was caught by the shine and sparkle of Yates' team issue Eddy Merckx bicycle, which encouraged him to make a comparative description of his velo. Yates politely nodded, 'aha-ed' and even offered jocular responses to the happy veteran's banter. Then came the big question: 'Have you ridden the Tour?' he asked Yates with a spark of anticipation that perhaps, just perhaps, he may have stumbled upon a star. Being caught on a good day, Yates was happy to oblige: 'Oui,' he replied calmly before halting for a fleeting second – as if to keep the suspense hanging. 'Neuf fois,' he added with a pinch of a grin creeping through. The bulging eyeballs and raised brows of Yates' inquisitor confirmed that he was impressed. And then the verbal confirmation came: 'Ah... bon.' And just as quickly, the *Ancien* hobbled away, no doubt ready to tell his friends of his encounter with a nine-Tour veteran.

A few minutes after, Yates looked at me, then laughed: 'Ha . . . I love saying it that way'. I wondered what he was talking about. 'Oui . . . nine times! That really gets 'em'. The media gets so easily swept up by the pomp and circumstance of the Tour, and it is easy to forget the personal triumph that riders like Yates feel for finishing it once, let alone nine times. And Yates, never one to be outwardly boastful of anything, is rightly proud of it.

He mightn't be a Tour de France winner – although his tally of top results is nothing to joke about. Amongst his credits are victories in the Tour de France time trial stage from Lievin to Wasquelhal in 1988, stage 12 to Jaca in the 1988 Tour of Spain, the Tour of Belgium in 1989 (including two stage wins), the 1989 Grand Prix of Eddy Merckx, and stages in other races like the Midi Libre (1988), the Dauphiné Libéré (1991), the Nissan Classic (1991) and Paris – Nice (1988) when he also wore the leader's white jersey.

In addition Yates' best attribute is to endure the pain, suffering and sweat that goes into racing the Tour, the world's hardest event. Very few riders can sit on his wheel, whether in a team time trial or in a chasing peloton on the flat at 60kmh, or on a descent at 100kmh. Whenever he pedals his 77kg and 187cm tall body to the front, the haggard looks of his rivals around him suddenly turn to fear.

Invariably his sacrifices have been for the sake of another's glory. Our meeting at Grasse was probably as close to a boast as Yates could get. While possessed with a demonic streak of toughness and a frightening ability and love to ride the legs off his counterparts, Yates is also very much the gentle giant whose loyalty and sincerity is without question. He is a man who doesn't bother about the frills. Everything is black and white, shades of grey are virtually non-existent. More often than not, as Yates sees it, the grey is where excuses are found.

'We weren't good enough,' is a common reply in defeat. Asked why he refused a feed bag in his first Milan – San Remo in 1983 where he later blew up with hunger, he said: 'Wasn't hungry, was I.' And when asked why he denied himself a drink at a legal drink zone in the 1988 Ghent – Wevelgem – when in the winning two man break all day long – he simply said: 'I wasn't thirsty.' Such is the man.

His need for honesty means he says what he thinks. During the 1988 Tour de France, he had blasted the best time triallists in the world, winning, ironically, the Race of Truth to Wasquelhal in record time. He was 0:14 from the yellow leader's jersey. And for the press, this was pretty exciting stuff to write about. There I was, desperately trying to get him to say he would go for the race leadership and become the first Englishman since Tom Simpson in 1962 to do so. But he wanted nothing of it. And to make it worse he closed the subject by picking up on a caption error I had made in *Winning* Magazine which I edited at the time. As he lambasted me for not getting facts right, my focus on Yates and the yellow jersey was totally obscured. Yates to this day, never lets me forget it.

Allan Peiper

Date of birth: 24 March, 1960

Place of birth: Melbourne, Australia

Teams: ACBB (Fra), Peugeot (Fra),

          Panasonic (Neth), Tulip (Bel)

Turned Professional 1983

Retired 1992

Australia, November, 1984 and summer was just around the corner. The cricket season was coming up, so too was the tennis, the golf and all the major leaguers. This followed a winter season of Australian Rules football and assorted stereotype mainstream sports, but no cycling.

Word was out that Allan Peiper was in town – like a breath of fresh air – I wanted an interview, and after a few enquiries it was all arranged. We would meet on the Melbourne to Frankston coast road and ride together on our bikes. He would be coming up from Frankston: 'You won't miss me, I'll be wearing black and white cycling gear with Peugeot on,' he said. He probably thought that I had no idea of who he rode for, or anything about European cycling for that matter.

Finding him was no problem. His Peugeot colours stood out proudly like a beacon. And as we rode together, Peiper's pride in what he was, his career, the tradition and his ambition stood out just as clearly. He carried a certain reverence for the sport and kept on talking about 'The Tour' and 'The Classics'. And he said it with so much passion that you had to simply nod and try to mirror his enthusiasm. I knew he really was committed when, on what was a 28C degree day, he explained why he was still wearing leg warmers: 'I haven't shaved my legs for a while. I wouldn't be seen dead with hairy legs,' he said sternly.

It was another three years before I saw Peiper again: just 30 minutes after Belgian Claude Criquielion had won the 1987 Tour of Flanders. Peiper was riding with Phil Anderson for Panasonic. Anderson, along with all the Panasonics, was furious for having lost, and suggested I go to Peiper's house which was only 300m away. Following the directions, I came to a house full of people walking in and out carrying bags and bikes. There was Peter Post himself, looking as stern faced and formidable as ever and still giving orders, perhaps even more than normal considering Panasonic's loss. This couldn't be Peiper's house.

I explained to someone that I was looking for Peiper. And I was invited inside and told the kitchen, where he was, was straight through. Showered and washed, Peiper looked so tired that it seemed on first glance his entire body had shrunk into the thick layer of clothes. Sitting at the kitchen table he was trying to revive himself with homemade health cookies and herbal tea to a background chorus of Flemish and Dutch chit-chat between various riders. They were everywhere. Eric Vanderaerden, Eddy Planckaert, Theo De Rooy, Guy Nulens and more . . . all the names I had only heard about. Peiper's household was always used by Panasonic for showers after the Tour of Flanders. It was a tradition. The kitchen door was flung open and Peiper's wife, Christine, entered in a flurry and quickly confirmed it was accepted under duress. 'That bloody Peter Post. He thinks he owns the place . . .' she said to her husband, unaware of a 'press' presence.

On that day, at that hour, things did look that way. Peiper kindly offered me a sandwich, a cup of tea and a thought provoking insight into the race. He didn't mind about Post. You could tell he was just happy to be a part of it all.

In years to come, years in which Peiper continued to play major roles in many significant victories in one-day classics and stages of the Tour of Italy and France, he passed on vast amounts of that passion to me. When I missed the notorious snow-ridden Gavia stage of the 1988 Tour of Italy which led to American Andy Hampsten taking the pink leader's jersey, Peiper said: 'You should have been there ...' His pride for having ridden it glowed from every syllable.

Like Sean Yates, Peiper is one of the best in helping others win. He was also one of the best paid for that service. He learned how to make a living out of that when he was a junior in Belgium and fine tuned his talents later on at ACBB and then Peugeot and Panasonic. Towing the peloton at 60kmh and with pain etched across his face was a common and glorious sight to see on television.

There have been moments of triumph too. His time trialling prowess was established in 1982 when he won the amateur Grand Prix des Nations. As a professional he followed that up with prologue wins in the 1984 Dauphiné Libéré and Tour de L'Oise which he also won overall, 1985 Paris–Nice and the time trial of the 1984 Tour of Sweden where he was again first overall. Also amongst his estimated 35 career wins were stage wins in the 1990 Tour of Italy, the 1990 Tour de France team time trial, the 1987 Kellogg's Tour of Britain where he also wore the yellow jersey for a day, and the 1988 Nissan Classic. And in the 1987 Tour of Switzerland, a second place on stage one saw him enjoy a four-day spell in the leader's yellow jersey.

The only real blemishes on his career have been his near-misses in two of the biggest one-day classics in cycling – Milan–San Remo in 1987 and the Tour of Flanders in 1989. In both, he was in winning breaks and let the opportunity to win slip past. And at Panasonic, a rider was not allowed to make the same mistake twice. Peiper did. And it was after his seventh place in the 1989 Tour of Flanders that his reverence for everything Post stood for turned to fear. His private turmoil was often the subject of many enlightening articles he wrote for cycling magazines around the world. But it was clear that self-confidence had its ups and downs in Peiper.

Two weeks after the 1989 Tour of Flanders, Post gave Peiper a rocketing outside the changing rooms, witnessed by 40 or so fans at the Schelde Prijs in Belgium.

Peiper always said Post had a knack of playing on personal weaknesses, and here they were clearly exposed. It was at this time when I thought of Peiper as a bike racing fan accidently swept up by the peloton, rather than as the hardened, tough and relentlessly intrepid pro he can be.

Peiper eventually escaped from Post's bullying in 1990 when he joined Tulip. It was a hard decision to make, but one that had to be faced in order to be his own person again. Like many, I wondered why he joined Tulip – a team blessed with ambition but no hunger to achieve it. And after two uneasy years there Peiper's own doubts about the team finally gave rise to a conviction to retire.

Fittingly, his adieu in the 1992 Paris–Tours was historic, if not for what he did at least for what he was a part of. After all, it was the fastest ever race with Belgian Hendrik Redant winning average speed over the marathon 286.5km clocking 46.745kmh. Peiper hung on to the front group until the last hill and finished alone, 2:22 after Redant.

His 63rd place may not have stirred the slightest interest amongst onlooking fans. But for Peiper it was as important as any race in his career. It meant he would leave the sport as he came in – using every ounce of physical and mental resource right to the end.

3 RECRUITMENT: THE ACBB AND WHERE IT ALL BEGAN

Competition between French amateur clubs has always been fierce. Naturally regional and personal pride fires the competitive instinct of each to be better than the other.

In the late 1970s one amateur club, the Athletic Club de Boulogne-Billancourt (ACBB) wanted to stand out above the rest. It had already battled against other clubs and tested the local talent, but it wanted something special, something different, something that would put its name on the lips of every cycling fan, sponsor and media outlet.

The ACCB's pioneering roots go back to the 1920s when Paris was gaining its second wind after the First World War. Industry was picking up, jobs were on offer and Parisians in their thousands were using bicycles to get to and from work.

One such Parisian was Firmin Terrigny: employed at a locksmith's workshop at Rue Pasteur in Boulogne, on the south-west outskirts of Paris, his passion for cycling led to the founding of the Velo Club de Billancourt in October 1924. In 1928 the club became part of the Association Cycliste Boulonnaise and hence was renamed Association Cycliste de Boulonnaise-Billancourt.

Albert Gal and Eugene Gribeauval directed the club, which aquired legendary status over a marathon spell of 40 years. The ACBB made its first global mark in 1930 on the track in Brussels when 18-year old Frenchman Louis Gerardin beat Britain's Sid Cozens for the world amateur sprint title.

The club changed its name to Athletic Club de Boulogne-Billancourt in 1943 when the local council amalgamated it with several other sports to have an overall membership of 600 people. In the late 1970s and 1980s members of the cycling club, at this time one of the most feared, still wore orange and grey jerseys. And any *Acebebiste* was termed a *petit gris* because of it.

After the Second World War, the ACBB wanted to make a new impact on the sport. So with this vision, in 1949 Gal recruited Paul Weigant to direct a professional ACBB team. Weigant, nicknamed 'Mickey' because he always wore a Mickey Mouse badge on his jersey during his amateur racing days, was to become one of French cycling history's most reputed personalities. Sponsored by Philippe Potin who worked in the cycle industry, and Helyett cycles, the Weigant-directed team entered a golden age. Between 1955 and 1963, those who rode for Weigant were heroes – Jacques Anquetil, André Darrigade, Jean Forestier, Jean Stablinski. Ireland's Shay Elliott also rode there as an amateur before turning professional in 1956.

Sadly the 1960s saw the ACBB pull out of the professional circuit. As French society became more *bourgeois*, cycle sales dropped and public attention turned to other sports. Basically, there was less money in cycling to fund a professional team. Weigant and the ACBB had no choice but to channel its main interests into the amateur team alone. Weigant never changed his philosophy and the club continued to run as any other professional outfit and hence became known as the premier stepping stone to a professional career in the 1980s.

It had to readapt to the ways of amateur racing, which was clearly no problem as its status as the top amateur club in 1971 was quickly established when French

Anderson now in the best young rider's white jersey, still up with the top riders of the 1981 Tour de France on the Col du Pra de Lyse

Millar in the 1985 Tour of Spain *amarillo* jersey. His smile and jersey were swept from him one day before the finish

ACBB member Regis Ovion won the world amateur road title, the Tour de L'Avenir, and the amateur Grand Prix des Nations in 1971. The ACBB was known in France and internationally as **the** French club to be in.

Elliott may have been the first English-speaking star at ACBB but his term there did not trigger the Anglophile invasion. That began in the late 70s when ACBB started looking around for foreign talent in the same deliberate and pioneering fashion that created a professional team of the 50s. This international recruitment programme not only tapped into a new source of talented riders, but also a cheaper and very expendable one. It began with Paul Sherwen, who walked out of his Cheshire home and 12 hours later arrived on the concrete steps of ACBB. Sherwen was not the first English-speaking rider after Elliott to don ACBB's colours. Jonathan Boyer spent several months there in 1974 before joining the rivalled US Creteil club. But from Sherwen's full season there came a constant flow of Anglophile brilliance that would kill any myth that cycle racing was a European's game.

In reality, the flood of English-speaking stars which followed Sherwen was not part of any grand plan. Nobody foresaw the sudden rise to fame that they and the club would attain. They didn't even know if Sherwen would survive his first year at ACBB let alone open the door for others to follow. If anything, taking on a simple 'roast beef' was a shot in the dark. Sherwen proved he did 'have it' and gave ACBB officials the confidence to take on more English-speaking riders. His departure in 1978 left a vacant spot to be filled. And thanks to his suggestion, the offer to fill it was given to Graham Jones.

By the time Jones left in 1979, both he and Sherwen had stepped up to the professional ranks without stumbling. The ACBB management may have foreseen a success story evolving. The 'Foreign Legion' label was still a long way from being coined, but Sherwen's proven grit and Jones' astounding ability was enough to keep ACBB heads looking across the French border.

To a French team, there was certainly a novelty in having English-speaking riders on board. And because ACBB was a Paris-based club and close to the centre of a cosmopolitan and international society, its image as an international hub of cycling gave it an upper-class and more professional standing. And inevitably that made ACBB more attractive to prospective sponsors, race organisers and the media.

The ability of English-speaking riders to adapt to an unflexible French system and lifestyle, combined with the fact that they raced and trained so hard after coming to France at very little cost, gave sporting justification to rider importation. And because of their success, French riders, angered by the allotment of team berths to foreign riders, had very little to argue against.

How then did ACBB strike it rich when other clubs didn't? Perhaps limiting the other clubs' desire to follow suit was the fact that they were distanced from the international ambiance of Paris. For example, a Breton club may have wanted Breton members and Breton winners. Whereas ACBB just wanted winners. It was well known that riders who didn't make the grade were quickly pointed to the English Channel or Charles de Gaulle airport and the first flight home.

The club may be on a sad decline today, but for Anglophile cycling fans then the name ACBB was just as well known as its professional counterpart, the Peugeot team. It was synonymous with European cycling and basically the stepping stone to greater success. The system of recruitment of English-speaking riders at ACBB was pretty simple. Each foreign arrival undertook to find a 'successor' at the club when he turned professional. Also, the club itself grew to be an attractive destination for aspiring professionals as word spread of each members' success.

ACBB focused on the big amateur classics which were centre stage for professional head hunters to take their pick of the best for the coming season. Riders had to fight for their place in the classics. Missing the big races meant less chance of capturing a professional manager's attention. And inevitably that meant little chance of a professional contract.

Joining ACBB was like going to a top preparatory school for professional racing. They were taught tricks of the trade like what to do before a wheel change when you puncture, how to go through a feed station in a big bunch and how to read a Continental race. There are still non-European based riders who have been professionals for years and still don't know some of the basics that ACBB amateurs learned in their first week.

An off-the-saddle education was also vital. At ACBB, foreign riders learned French, they had to if they wanted to communicate – French was and still is the official language of cycling. And because of their isolation from family and friends, they had to develop a strong sense of survival – in many ways stronger than the local riders. There were no warm baths run by their waiting mothers, as for other ACBB members after training or racing. Neither were there cooked meals, washed clothes and someone to drive them to and from races. They had to cook and wash for themselves, and make their own way to races. They did it. There was no alternative. They lived with it and it made them tougher. No doubt their constant run of success was greatly due to their resolve to win against the odds.

Inevitably by 1980 it was clear that ACBB was committed to its foreign recruitment policy. The string of successes by the foreigners stirred a fever of jealousy amongst home riders, until then those who rode for ACBB were never really confronted with the problem. But from 1980 – when the amateur Merlin Plage series was open only to French riders after Graham Jones and Robert Millar had won it in 1978 and 1979 respectively – it was clear to all that the French didn't like having 'their' races monopolised by outsiders. Not that it mattered, it was unlikely that ACBB was going to stem the tide of foreign success. A win was a win. And that's what ACBB wanted.

Furthermore, the rising power of English-speaking riders gave club officials a lever with which to pressure French riders. Seeing the foreigners become so strong and self-reliant quickly exposed the deficiencies of the French. And by saying to a French rider who was taking it easy: 'Look at these English, they are stronger than you without any help', the rider could hardly argue the point.

For the legionnaires, the mere chance of becoming professional was enough of an incentive to put up with the hardships. By the early 1990s foreign ACBB riders were receiving salaries of about 1,000 francs a month. That is not a lot, but in earlier days some French members received payouts of 3,500 francs, and all that was offered to English-speaking riders was free accommodation, a bike and supply of race clothes.

In any case, foreign recruits didn't ride at ACBB to make money. Prize-money was supposed to be given back to riders at the end of the year. Yet much of that was gone by October as riders would often ask for advances for food, clothes and other odds and ends.

A white haired, burly and broad shouldered man, Mickey Weigant was the most influential figure in the ACBB story. He left the club after 1985 to run the Toulon club in the south of France. He died in May 1991. Some people believe it was indicative of Weigant's influence that after he stood aside from his role as team manager, ACBB started its decline. Claude Escalon had risen from his position as team mechanic, to *directeur-sportif* and eventually to manager, but he never really filled the void left by Weigant.

Within a season of Escalon taking control, the club lost its traditional sponsor Peugeot when the French car/bicycle manufacturer pulled out of the sport altogether. In 1987 it rode under the label of Renault, which itself hit financial strife in the late 80s and then dropped ACBB, leaving the club short of finance to run as it should.

In many ways, when Weigant and Escalon ran the club together the two worked hand-in-hand – a bit like a 'bad cop, good cop' routine. It was clear to anyone that Weigant was the man in control, but there was always a quieter air about him. Although when one of his riders was in a winning situation and Weigant was following, nothing could stop him from bellowing threats and orders from the attendant team car like a captain in a cavalry charge. But when Weigant became ill, his presence at races was saved for events in the south of France where he lived in Les Issambres. It was then that Escalon took a firmer grip on club affairs. However every rider remembered Weigant as the 'Godfather' of the ACBB. Even Escalon didn't forget, even though he clearly wanted control of the team.

Escalon was the unfortunate bearer of the nickname 'Claude Balls' – no one really knows why. And while such a moniker may have led one to doubt his authority, it was never successfully buried. Perhaps it was because of the more discreet manner of Weigant that Escalon took a ruthless, tougher and more obvious hands-on approach to affairs. There was less of the diplomat in Escalon and the generation gap was narrower between him and the riders. But thanks to ACBB's reputation as a holding house for future stars, he knew he could use a blunter approach to business. And not surprisingly, he has made his share of enemies.

It was soon made known if you were 'in', and your future in the club was secure; but if you were not, then the future ended right there. With up to ten foreign riders anxious to fill the allotted six berths in the team, Escalon and Weigant always had the upper hand.

Weigant was pretty open in his adoration of big strong riders who could win a time trial. It may have seemed prejudicial, but it was the way Weigant worked. And often when a time trialling strength joined the club he would find himself invited to stay at Weigant's house while the others took rooms at a nearby hotel. Even after he left ACBB and directed VC Toulon, Weigant was known to 'adopt' time triallists as they prepared for races in the south of France. Year after year he would pride himself on offering his protégés the use of a prized set of wheels that Anquetil had used to win the Grand Prix des Nations on five ocasions.

There were many reports of discontent about Escalon's manner after Weigant's departure, from a more contemporary circle of ACBB riders. Despite their misgivings those from the late 70s and early 80s accepted both Escalon and Weigant for who they were. 'Claude was pretty shifty, but so was Mickey. But Mickey was just a little bit more subtle,' reflected Phil Anderson once.

After all, the foreign *Acebebistes* of the 1980s came from countries where cycling was less organised and they knew no better. Now when they hear complaints from newer members it's easy to understand how they regard it as a weakness.

By the mid-eighties when the rise of English-speaking talent was at its zenith, being one of Escalon's favourites meant you had to be a champion. He didn't care if you were a time triallist or not, as long as you were a winner. When Sherwen rode for one year at ACBB and was a founding member of the foreign legion, matters were very different: he still recalls Escalon as being his first close friend on the Continent. But then Sherwen was a winner, further advantaged by the fact that he was the first of a line and there was not the same high expectation of him which burdened those who followed.

Come the late 1980s, ACBB's fervor for drawing on international talent met with set backs. The club continued to contract foreigners thus Danes and Poles joined the English-speaking recruits in greater numbers. But the effects of the recession tolled heavily on the club: Peugeot's 1986 withdrawal from cycle sponsorship and then Renault's own financial troubles drained ACBB's kitty. Wins still came ACBB's way, but by the end of 1992 the Boulogne-Billancourt city council murmured about pulling out its backing as well. Also, other clubs were by then in on the act, often being more professionally run than ACBB. The ACBB cycling team was still on the road in 1993, but its sorry state was reflected in its inability to make the French Cycling Federation's inaugral top 21 *Division National* when the season began.

It would be wrong to say that ACBB missed English-speaking talent. Basically, there was none about, none prepared to make the jump like those in the late 1970s and early 1980s. Riders like Sherwen, Jones, Anderson, Millar, Roche, Yates, and Peiper may have been the source of the team's success. But after their spells at ACBB, not one other ACBB recruit from English-speaking shores managed to fill their shoes. Several riders in ACBB's colours got halfway: John Herety, David Akam, Paul Kimmage, Deno Davie, Laurence Roche and Clayton Stevenson all took the step to professionalism, but their careers were short lived.

Whatever the reason, one cannot help but wonder if the English-speaking rider is suddenly not up to it? Such a generalisation may be hard to justify. But that mere suggestion and the problem of finances are probably the main factors leading to ACBB's more recent look towards Eastern-European riders who come just as cheaply as Sherwen did in 1977.

1977

Sherwen's debut at ACBB followed his victory in the Pernod Grand Prix series in England in 1976. Winning meant travelling to Paris where he was presented with his prize at the end of the year at the Super Pernod Trophy awards. Here Sherwen met Weigant who knew of his reputation as Weigant's ACBB team always competed in the British race.

Without hesitation Weigant offered Sherwen a place on his team in 1977. And Sherwen didn't hesitate to accept. Because he was committed to university studies that year, he could not join the team full-time until the end of the year. So until he packed his bags for good Sherwen's aggressive racing talents had to be confined to home-based events like the Pernod Grand Prix which he won again, or events held over the holidays enabling him to do a three-week spell with ACBB on the Continent over Easter. It was just before Easter Sunday that Sherwen lined up for his first French amateur race for ACBB. 'I got knocked off in the first race and then won the second . . . by about five minutes,' reflects Sherwen.

During the 1977 season he won a number of races, including amateur classics like Paris–Barentin in a solo break, and Paris–Maubeuge, he also won the Tour de L'Essonne stage race. And by the end of the year which included 80 races, he was second in the Merlin Plage series thanks to a set of consistent placings which included

Sherwen's victory in the 1977 Pernod Grand Prix opened the floodgates to English-speaking recruits at ACBB

third in the amateur Paris – Roubaix.

Finishing second in the Merlin Plage series was one of Sherwen's greatest personal triumphs, and in addition it carried the reward of 3,000 francs prize-money. ACBB policy was that all prize-money goes to the club and is given to the rider at the end of the year, but only after various deductions for seasonal expenses. But because the series organsers signed the winner's cheque in Sherwen's name, it went directly to him. 'They (ACBB) couldn't get their hands on it then!' adds Sherwen, still shining with pride.

A major factor in his success was his adaptation to French life. He learned French at school and when he arrived he was aware that it was up to him to fit in. As the first of a wave of English-speaking riders at ACBB he was not perceived as a threat to anyone. 'It was different then, had there been four, five or six foreigners in the team, then there would be animosity. I was the only guy and had no problem.'

One of Sherwen's first and closest friends was Escalon. Sherwen was often invited for dinner at the Escalon household where, almost nightly, the two would 'do the French thing' – as Sherwen calls it – and rush from the table to watch television movies within seconds of their last mouthfuls. Next to his ten years in the peloton, those movies were the greatest influence on Sherwen's street knowledge of the French language.

Sherwen demonstrated a tremendous inner drive and commitment to his spell in France. He was not there for a holiday; he was there to compete. And in order to bring out the best of himself Sherwen lived like a virtual monk in Paris. He raced, trained, ate and slept. He never went to the cinema or cafés and bars, not even the popular tourist sites like the Champs Elysees, from where he lived only two and a half miles away. Every moment of every day in 1977 revolved around cycling. Sherwen lived by himself in a bedsit and had little if any contact with English-speaking people. It was a lonely existence, but one that Sherwen became accustomed to.

Despite his successes Sherwen also felt the need to help others to win. And one regular beneficiary was Frenchman Serge Beucherie who would later become a professional cyclist and finally assistant *directeur-sportif* to Greg LeMond's team. 'He was always wanting these local races because it was his uncle's birthday, or his mum's birthday or his dad wanted him to win because it was his birthday. He always had a reason to win. So I used to help him.' It might have cost Sherwen his own winning opportunities. But Sherwen didn't mind. He made a lot of friends that way – in Beucherie's case 'because he had a lot of uncles'.

As the end of the 1977 season drew near Sherwen developed strong ambitions for a professional career. His desire to move up was so strong that when ACBB suggested he stay amateur for the first months of 1978 to race the amateur classics and then join Peugeot in May, Sherwen declined. Instead he signed, with Weigant's support, a contract with the French FIAT team for 3,000 francs a month.

1978

Back at ACBB, the rider to take Sherwen's place was Englishman Graham Jones. But even before Sherwen departed and Jones took his place, it was obvious the club was aware of the advantages of having one or two more foreign novelties.

One of them was South African Alan Van Heerden who spent several years with ACBB, one with Sherwen in 1977. Sadly, political wrangling always got in the way of his amateur career because of the ban that was then on South Africa from participating in international sport. In attempts to cover up his nationality, Van Heerden rode for ACBB under the name of Van Harden. And before the truth caught up with him in 1978 when he won the Paris–Orleans and Paris–Varennes amateur classics, he had kept one jump ahead of controversy by riding under different nationalities. When his South African nationality was leaked to the press, he turned professional to avoid being sent home. Joining Peugeot for the 1979 season, he rode there during 1980 and part of 1981.

Sherwen has a lot of admiration for Van Heerden who still races in South Africa today. 'He rode one year as an American, one year as an Australian and then came back an Englishman. But then someone said: "this is funny, he comes back every year as a different nationality." Then it got out to the press that he was South African. So he turned professional and they couldn't stop him from racing. He was a damn good pro, but then the political thing got too big and he had to go home.'

Unlike Van Heerden, when Jones joined the ACBB fold in 1978 it seemed he was destined to enjoy his time there. He quickly asserted his star status, leaving in his wake not only Van Heerden and the other two English-speaking riders – Englishman

Nigel Hartle and Irishman Oliver McQuaid – but every Frenchman as well. The fact that he came to Weigant and Escalon with Continental experience must have helped. He spent much of 1976 racing in Holland, and committed himself to a full European assault in 1977 after winning the Grand Prix of Essex in England. That win saw him head to Belgium where he raced for five months before Sherwen directed ACBB's attention towards him.

Life was hard for Jones in Belgium. As a 19-year old, he went there the day after winning at Essex. 'I'm going for good. There'll be no more Pernod events for me,' he said at the time. Yet armed only with the dream of a professional career, Jones left having to cover virtually every expense himself – new tyres, bike repairs, food, clothing and accommodation.

Not long after setting up base in Ghent Jones saw some results: he was 20th in his first race on the outskirts of Brussels, then his first win came in his second race at Anvaing, where he finished alone and 0:40 clear of the peloton. But even though much success came under Jones' wheels that year he needed more to secure a professional contract. He suddenly realised that he would need another season as an amateur to achieve it. At the time his intentions were to move to Italy. But Sherwen was about to change all that. A long and trusted friend – as well as his former training partner in England – Sherwen had kept in touch with Jones during that season despite their separate paths. Aware of Jones' troubles and ACBB's willingness to try out another Anglophile, Sherwen didn't hesitate to put his name forward.

Jones was not unknown to Escalon and Weigant. That year he came third in the Etoile des Espoirs after the world championships in Venezuela. It gave the club some idea of his ability. 'It also showed I could race in France which was an important thing in those days,' he says.

Aboard a bus and bound for Paris, Jones left England with another invited rider, Hartle. But the latter would never match Jones' ability and after several months he was on his way home. But when Escalon first met the pair, there was little cause for their fuming new boss to discern any difference between them. As they would later discover, excuses never counted for much in Europe.

'I still remember that trip so clearly. I thought we were never going to get there. We took the bus and during the journey there was very bad snow which blocked the motorway. We got to the pickup point very late that night and Escalon was there, but he wasn't very happy,' says Jones. One can see why Escalon would fail to make the rendezvous with many arriving Anglophiles in years to come. It was so late that Escalon and his new charges spent the night in the nearest – and smallest – Bed and Breakfast they could find. There was not even time to eat dinner, let alone get back to Boulogne-Billancourt and ACBB 'HQ'. With no command of the language and fatigue from a 12-hour trip, they were completely disorientated the next morning. It was a dishevelled pair of bike riders who met Escalon: 'We couldn't speak French but we managed to figure out something about somebody coming to pick us up and take us to ACBB,' says Jones.

Jones was determined to prove that Sherwen had not erred in recommending him. And his first chance came a few days later at the team's camp, held each February in the south of France. In his first race, the Grand Prix de Sanary, Jones startled everyone by attacking from the gun and soloing with nothing more than a minute's lead for the next 80km. He was caught and Escalon labelled his fate as a just reward for 'foolish English racing.' But Jones still finished 13th. And more importantly he proved that though he lacked tactical skill, and in Escalon's eyes deserved another rocket for showing it, he still had plenty of spirit.

Escalon's fury for the premature attack didn't upset Jones too much. Rather the biggest disappointment was the absence of Weigant who he had still not met. He suspected that Weigant would have at least appreciated his courage if not his brains. But Weigant, normally preying on his new riders like a school teacher at a new term, was more than 100km away in hospital in Nice, having a pacemaker fitted. Jones' frustration eased, even if it didn't lead to the pat on the back he had hoped for. 'I got told off by Escalon, told that here in France you can't race like an Englishman. Then suddenly he took me to see Weigant in hospital. There he was lying in hospital, just after having his pacemaker put in and being told by Escalon what happened. Then somehow he managed to tell me that what I did was no good and that I need to attack at the right moment,' says Jones.

The blond Manchester star heeded the advice – it came from the top. And by now Jones was aware that 'second chances' are rare. He won his second race, the Grand Prix de Toulon in a two-man break with another ACBB Frenchman. But even with his first bouquet under his arms, Jones was still the open-eyed innocent. Because of his poor French, the other ACBB rider spent most of his attack blabbing away in French trying to pay Jones off in return for the win. 'The guy wanted to buy the race but I couldn't even understand what he was trying to do. But even if I'd known, there was no way I was going to sell it,' says Jones.

Diplomatically Jones could have pleaded ignorance for his unwillingness to keep a local rider happy. But in the Grand Prix de Saint Maxime the next day he found the best way to avoid a similar predicament: he won the race alone and with a seven-minute lead! Now Escalon was smiling!

Having proved his class and ability to learn, Jones was asked to take it easy at the Grand Prix de Grasse the following day. He did, as the first international race of the calendar, the amateur Tour du Haut Var was nearby, and he wanted to win that, then head for the Spring classics near Paris, and keep in the running for the season long Merlin Plage series, with every ounce of condition he could muster. The Tour du Haut Var, amateur and professional editions, has always been a tough race; the route is littered with twisting hills, some short but then others frighteningly long so early in the season. The winner is a rider worthy of notice, even if the race has reaped little media interest outside of France.

Jones didn't win, but the circumstance of his eventual second place to Daniel Willems of Belgium, was arguably more notable. Willems won alone, but he was part of a four-man break which included Jones before the attack. Willems' winning move came after the Englishman punctured and was floundering, having to wait for a team car and a wheel change. There was nothing until the peloton arrived. Yet undaunted the Englishman attacked in pursuit of the break and miraculously caught it. The only thing was that Willems had already gone off alone and was within sight of the finish line at Draguignan when Jones drew up level with the two others. 'I am sure Escalon still remembers that day,' says Jones with a smile and a shake of his head.

Once more Jones was able to look at the positive side of his near miss. Such a successful chase proved he was in top form for the coming March classics which began with Paris–Ezy. He was second there, beaten by a team-mate who sat on throughout their attack, winning thanks to Jones' help. 'That probably had a lot to do with why I never came across any resentment from the Frenchies as a foreigner,' he says.

Jones hadn't lost his taste for personal success. He took leadership in the Merlin Plage series with victory in the next Spring classic, Paris–Evreux and then

Paris – Troyes and Paris – Vierzon before an iron deficiency saw him succumb to poor form. He came out of it in June after missing the Milk Race in England. But then at the Sealink International he struggled. 'In the prologue I wasn't feeling good and never got better. I finished the race, about 15th or something but I just didn't feel as I should have,' recalls Jones.

Jones still feels his poor form in the home race was seen by critical British selectors as reflective of an apparent lack of regard for them. He was still called up for the Scottish Milk Race and told all his expenses would be paid. But the 'low cost' 24-hour journey on trains, buses and ferries from France to the start was hardly what he had in mind. 'Then when I checked into the hotel who was there checking in at the same time? The French team which had just flown in. I could have been on that plane. You can imagine how I felt!' says Jones.

If nobody knew how he felt then, the following day's prologue time trial made it clear. With his ill-health and the frustration of the previous day's trials, he simply stopped, got off his bike and quit the race.

The selectors were not impressed. And when Jones told BCF selector Jim Hendry that he wanted to miss the Commonwealth Games in Edmonton, Canada later that year to prepare for the coming world titles in Nurburgring Germany, they took matters further and omitted him from the British worlds team as well. 'They thought I just wanted to race in France and make money and couldn't care about racing for Britain. That wasn't the case. I wanted to do well in the worlds and couldn't see the reason for going to the Commonwealth Games for two weeks for one race, when I could be training properly for the worlds in Europe. Finally I was not in the team, although guys who were totally unsuited for the course were,' says Jones.

Shelving his world title ambitions, Jones settled back into France and ACBB's programme. And left the BCF selectors red-faced when he hit another winning streak. His Merlin Plage lead had never been challenged since his victory at Paris – Evreux. And his ensuing wins in the Grand Prix de France and Grand Prix des Nations left him with an amazing series victory by 100 points.

He may not have been the toast of the BCF's annual awards that year, but at the annual Pernod awards in Paris he surely was. Standing alongside Italian great, Francesco Moser, who won the Super Prestige Pernod professional award, Jones was heralded as a champion for the future. His dream of being a professional was now to become a reality. With Peugeot and FIAT both offering contracts, it was only a question of which path to take. And by joining Van Heerden and signing for Peugeot, Jones and the 'Peugeot Foreign Legion' took off.

1979

Weigant and Escalon were now rubbing their hands in sheer delight. Here was another ACBB discovery to put on the club's honour-roll. Would there be more? Certainly Weigant and Escalon were keen to try and find out. But not even they were prepared for the lucky find of two champions in the same year. They were Phil Anderson and Robert Millar. One came from the middle-class and pretty much well-to-do Melbourne suburb of Kew in Australia. The other from a depressed suburb of Glasgow in Scotland. Their personalities were different in every possible way. But to this day, both have distinct parallels between their careers. Both spoke English, both began cycling at the age of 16, both were to prove distinct winners at ACBB, and in years to come they

On the attack in the 1979 Tour du Haut Languedoc, Millar's climbing prowess was clear from his first days at ACBB

would ride for the same teams – Peugeot, Panasonic and TVM – although Anderson went on to join Motorola.

For Anderson the opportunity of a European career arrived at Noumea late in 1978. It was there where Weigant met Gerald Georges, an ex-patriat French restaurateur now living in Melbourne. Both were attending the Noumea six-day race and after striking up a conversation with Weigant, Georges dropped Anderson's name. A member of the Hawthorn Cycling Club where Allan Peiper was also registered, Anderson had won the Commonwealth Games road race gold medal and Dulux Tour of New Zealand that year. And such credentials made Anderson the ideal candidate for Weigant's 1979 plans. Weigant didn't waste time in telling Georges that a place was available in his 1979 line-up for this unknown Australian should he want it.

Georges, a portly man whose passion for cycling is second only to the French cuisine he serves at his West Melbourne restaurant, returned to Australia with the offer. And boosted by Georges' offer to pay his air fare, Anderson accepted just as quickly. There was nothing to lose and everything to gain.

At the time, the awaiting adventure was nothing more to Anderson than a

The 1979 Grand Prix de la Boucherie – another Millar victory

means of preparing for the 1980 Olympic Games in Moscow. He hadn't even considered turning professional. 'I thought joining the ACBB would be a good chance to get experience of racing in Europe,' he recalls. 'I realised that in the Commonwealth Games we were pretty sheltered because there were only the Commonwealth countries. We needed to race the Europeans more. And this was the chance.'

Meanwhile, on the other side of the world, Millar's burning ambition of becoming a professional was several years old. But then deliberation had never existed in Millar's racing career to date. Like many boys he started riding bicycles with his friends around the streets. Then his best friend joined a club, the Glenmarnock Wheelers, and coaxed Millar into doing the same. Within a year he won his first race and then soon after the 1976 Scottish Championship; this led to his move to the Glasgow Wheelers in 1977, where he is still a member today.

By 1978 Millar knew what he wanted and what was required to get it. With a professional career as his dream, he saved every penny he earned to finance a planned assault on the Continent. But first he had to prove himself at home. So that year he gave up an engineering apprenticeship to race in Great Britain full-time. Many impressive results later, the British Pernod series, followed by his 21st place in the Milk Race with his national title produced his passport to cross the Channel.

ACBB was not Millar's initial choice however. Were it not for a letter from Jones passing on the Parisian club's vacancy to him, then he probably would have headed to CSM Persan; a club bearing particular affinity with Scottish riders, as former professional Billy Billsland raced there, and Arthur Campbell – a long serving, influencial and still active member of the UCI. Nevertheless, Jones' letter was convincing enough to make Millar change his mind.

Without Millar or Anderson knowing it, both simultaneously packed their bags and headed off to ACBB having been told that it was 'the' place to go. When both arrived in Paris, though not together, it was quickly made evident to them that the rewards would not come easily.

It was less than an hour after arriving in Paris that Anderson realised the eager support from his long-time confidant Georges might be the last he would get for some time. 'I arrived at the airport not knowing what to expect. I thought there would be someone to pick me up. Wrong! All I had was an address so I caught a taxi and went there, to some far corner of Paris which I didn't even know' says Anderson, referring to the ACBB at Boulogne-Billancourt.

Meeting Escalon rekindled his hopes, but not for long. Almost immediately, Escalon showed a wide-eyed yet very jet-lagged Anderson his brand new bicycle, his racing equipment and then the apartment where he would live for the next ten months. 'I thought I was going to be set up pretty well. But eventually I had to buy a lot of my own clothing, training gear and tyres. I was under the impression that you would get pretty well looked after. Now when I speak to some of the guys who got salaries as an amateur I feel I got the short end of the stick, even though I was pretty naive then. But it made me harder in the end.'

Millar's upbringing and common belief that nothing came for free led the Scot to be more wary of what awaited him, or rather to be more realistic. But even he was caught on the hop when he arrived in Paris, looking for the address Rue du Sevres, how was he to know that there were two such streets? And easily enough he chose the wrong one. 'No one came to meet me, so I took a taxi. We drove to Paris and came to this place with huge doors. There was no sign, but I walked through to ask a lady there, who came up and asked what I wanted. I couldn't speak any French at all. But I

Paris–Evreux 1979: amateur classic wins like this saw Millar take the Merlin Plage series unchallenged

Anderson looked more like a rugby forward than a Tour de France contender when he joined ACBB in 1979

worked out that what she was saying was that the Rue de Sevres that I wanted was on the other side of Paris.'

Another taxi trip and more francs later Millar finally arrived at ACBB, met Escalon and unlike Anderson who lived in the ACBB apartment, was escorted to a nearby gymnasium where he was to sleep until 'finding quarters' later. At the begining of the season the club had pre-assigned the space it would need during the major races after the February training camp. The natural ACBB rationalisation of discouraging deadwood in the club would always take place at the end of February.

Basically, the club saw nothing wrong with making foreign riders 'grovel' for a few days and sleep where they were told, whether in the club apartment, the local gymnasium, or anywhere. If they wanted a racing career so badly, they would put up with the disciplines of ACBB club life.

'There were so many good riders that to survive you needed to be special. You needed something more which put you above the rest. You could race in England and expect to race up to ten guys of the same calibre, but in France every weekend there were up to 50 of the same class and you had to be better than them,' says Millar.

One year before joining ACBB as an amateur Anderson's flapping knees and elbows belied his potential as one of the world's greatest cycling prospects

The Class of 79: noted ACBB members include, *directeur-sportif* Claude Escalon (far left), Robert Millar (fourth from right), Phil Anderson (third from right), manager Mickey Weigant (far right)

Both Anderson's and Millar's transition into ACBB life continued. Neither exactly liked it, but then they didn't complain. They were aware of nepotistic barriers, but accepted them for what they were – as a part of a system they had to fit into. They accepted the feeling of loneliness, the suspicion from local riders and the ignorance of not being able to speak French and every consequence that followed.

By the end of the season when Anderson and Millar had signed with Peugeot and in French eyes taken two professional contracts from them, the French ACBB riders even rode against them. 'That never happened until the end of the year when the French were getting desperate for a contract themselves. But all along you never really mixed with them. You went to ACBB for a reason . . . to do the best for yourself. And their impression was that you were coming to take their places,' says Millar.

Anderson and Millar were two of four English-speaking riders at ACBB that year. Englishmen John Parker and Neil Martin were the others, although they did not meet up until the training camp near Weigant's, where they met 15 other team members, at Les Issambres near Frejus in the south of France.

In the early training camp races there, Anderson confirmed what was said about him by Georges at Noumea several months before. He was second in his debut race, the Grand Prix de St Maxime. Then in his next, the Grand Prix de Sanary near Toulon, he won on an uphill sprint against a local rider.

'Then people started taking notice of this strange Australian rider with floppy knees, from the other side of the world. Before they never called me by name, not Phil or even Anderson. All they could say was kangaroo, or the Australian. But after I won they gave me more respect,' recalls Anderson

Meanwhile, Millar struck victory after a hesitant start where he sensed straight away that unlike Anderson he wasn't Weigant's favourite. 'Weigant didn't like little guys like me,' recalls Millar whose personal allegiance unsurprisingly leaned towards Escalon. As a result of Weigant's tag and the fact he had yet to win a race, Millar sensed the prospect of being kicked off the team before the classics. 'If you didn't win one of the races on the Côte D'Azur you were sent home. That's it.' With little time to spare Millar managed to counter Weigant's doubts with a victory in one of the last training camp races, the Grand Prix de Grasse. In the same race Parker was second at 1:33 and Anderson fifth at 3:32. And with that result, Millar's ambitions were once more back on target.

Anderson's and Millar's confidence was buoyant by the time the team returned to Paris, fighting fit and eager for those important Spring races. Millar went on to win several big races before the summer and like Jones and Sherwen, found himself as ACBB's leading rider for the Merlin Plage series. Amongst his wins were the Paris–Evreux classic, the Grand Prix de Boucherie, the Grand Prix du Picon and the Route de France stage race.

Then in July the Scot returned to England bolstered by his success, and motivated to win his seventh race of the season, the British title in which he was defending champion. So confident was he of winning that he even brought his 1978 British champion's jersey with him to wear on the podium! And by winning he found good use for it. His run of luck was tempered during the summer: after finishing 12th in the ten-day Rheinlandpfalz Rundfahrt in Germany, there was a lull in the calendar. Victory in the Merlin Plage series was a strong prospect, as too were his chances of joining Peugeot.

The only blemish anyone could see, was that he had still to win a time trial. Doing so would help dispell Weigant's myth that only big riders could win time trials. And finally with much satisfaction, it came a week before the Grand Prix des Nations in the final lead-up event. Millar still savours the memory of seing Weigant's shocked face, especially as the ACBB chief followed a favoured Anderson and not Millar in the team support car. 'Weigant always follows the team number one. But then the next week at the Nations he followed me and Anderson won,' says Millar who was fifth and one minute 25 seconds behind Anderson.

Meanwhile, the seeds of ambition for a professional career had started to grow furiously in Anderson as well. It began in early March, after unpacking his bags on his return from southern France to the ACBB apartment he shared with three French riders and Martin. He took time out to see the prologue of the professional Paris–Nice stage race in Boulogne-Billancourt. He saw the crowds, the television crews, the back-up personnel and quickly realised that professional cyclists of the European genre were not 'poofters'.

'They were like Gods, real professionals. They had a real job in the sport, they didn't work on the docks or as postmen as well like in Australia,' he says. The next few months were very successful for both Millar and Anderson, who scored 16 wins in the season. He won several races before travelling to the US for the Coors Classic during the summer. He then returned to delight Weigant with a win the amateur Grand Prix des Nations, after which the Olympics became a forgotten dream.

By October, he had still to race against the top Soviet and East German riders

All three of Millar's Tour stage wins have been in the Pyrenees: this one is at Guzet-Neige in 1984

Phil Anderson's aggression carries him through the 1983 Tour de France in search of the elusive yellow jersey

Millar ploughs over the Col d'Aubisque in 1985

Tour de France 1983 a proud moment for Ireland when Roche in the white jersey of best young rider and Sean Kelly in yellow is race leader for one day. Both jerseys would finally go to the then little known Frenchman Laurent Fignon

who would be the ones to beat at Moscow. The debate of whether to turn professional or not in Anderson's mind was resolved during the world championships at Valkenburg, in the Netherlands. There he and Millar were offered professional contracts with Peugeot for 3,750 francs a month. Both signed up, but only after bargaining for a higher wage. For Millar it was all a part of meeting his destiny. Whereas Anderson saw it as an open door to a new world and definitely a solution to his Olympic dilemma.

'I wondered what my Olympic chances really were. And I thought I mightn't ever get a professional offer again. But I wasn't going to turn professional for that. Then I heard on the grapevine that Mercier were going to offer 5,000 francs. So I went back to Peugeot and said I wanted more. And in the end they offered us both 4,250 francs,' says Anderson.

Anderson and Millar rode out the season the best they could, troubled by a constant tendency for their French team-mates to form combines against any winning move they made. It meant little. Both had contracts for 1980 and Millar had a clear run for victory in the Merlin Plage series which would be the last by an English-speaking rider, for the organisers slapped a ban on foreigners competing because of growing Anglophile domination.

1980

With Anderson and Millar out in the wider and cut-throat territory of professional life, Weigant and Escalon once more plundered the store of English-speaking talent. And when Irishman Stephen Roche came along, they found a diamond amongst this apparent treasure chest. Lucien Bailly, the French Cycling Federation's technical director, brought Roche to Weigant's attention. To this day, Bailly still regards it as his best deed. Roche went on to win the amateur Paris–Roubaix, Paris–Reims, the Tour du Haut Languedoc, the Grand Prix de France, the Chrono Madelainois and the Tour de L'Ile de France.

Having won the 1979 Ras Tailteann stage race in Ireland the year before, Roche left Dublin on February 11, 1980, with two big suitcases and a shoulder bag, bound for Paris. He had the idea, as had Anderson, that ACBB would provide the top-line preparation he needed for the Olympic Games later in the year. There would also be a full-time job offer to consider from his employers Premier Dairies, who had supported his cycling while he worked as a fitter up until 1979.

There was no sign of how his life would change, certainly not of the fortunes that would come. Rather the nine-hour delay of his scheduled 8:05am flight was a sign of the struggles ahead. Unlike Sherwen, Jones, Anderson and Millar who flitted in and out of the ACBB ranks with little resentment of their presence, by the time Roche arrived the French riders were starting to get a little fidgety about foreign newcomers who kept stealing the limelight.

Typically when Roche eventually arrived in Paris there was no one to meet him at the airport. And when he got to the ACCB office at 10:30pm, there was not a soul to be found, no message or even a door left open for him to shelter from the biting Parisian night air! He slept on the cold concrete steps until he was awakened at 4am by a group of young cyclists sent to collect and drive him down to the ACBB training camp in the south of France.

It was there that he met the ACBB 'family' including experienced Anglophile

Parker. It was also his first encounter with Escalon and more significantly Weigant. With Weigant, Roche made the big mistake of trying to be too familiar with him. 'In one of my first attempts at conversation with him,' recalls Roche in his biography, *The Agony And the Ecstasy*. 'I referred to him as *tu*. He replied sternly, "Mr Stephen Roche, Mr Weigant is a colleague to you. When you speak to a colleague you say "vous", you say "tu" when you speak with a friend. Mr Weigant is not a friend."'

That put Roche in his place, for the most part, but he still lapsed into periods of over-familiarity, even up until Weigant's death in 1991. Behind Weigant's verbal armoury came punishing and selfless racing demands of Roche, as if to remind the Irishman of the seriousness in which ACBB approached racing. As he discovered in his first race, the Grand Prix de St Maxime, there were pecking orders to be respected in the team. And as a newcomer he was way down on the list of 'protected' riders.

Weigant made that doubly clear in the St Maxime race when, as Roche alleges, he rode the Irishman off the road with his car after Roche chased down a protected ACBB team-mate, named Blagojevic, even though circumstances would have seen the two away and racing for first and second place. 'After the race I was in shock, total shock,' said Roche.

The Dubliner, unsurprisingly, laid low for several races until the Grand Prix of Les Issambres – Weigant's home town race. Roche badly wanted to win. Just for the sake of making his boss happy. And while he did win from a break of five riders, which included three other ACBB members, he discovered that his greatest opposition was his team-mates. For the three ACBB riders in the break had worked in a combine with the other two to try and catch him. 'I could not believe that all three of my ACBB team-mates were riding against me. To them I was nobody. I didn't exist. I was so innocent. I didn't even know what a combine was,' said Roche. He would not be the first to be educated on the meaning of a combine. Nevertheless, that win did change things. Suddenly he **did** exist. Overnight his innocence was gone. He knew what a combine was. Furthermore he was now a protected rider with the very team-mates who had previously stood in his way.

Roche was not prepared for the bout of depression that would strike him upon returning to Paris for the classics – all caused by Weigant's order that he use ACBB's Le Coq Sportif shoes rather than his old and trusted Colnago pair. The change from a leather to plastic sole resulted in a severe tendon strain during the opening Paris–Ezy race where he was third. At the time he didn't know what had caused the injury and doctors continued to tell him to 'take another week off'. It was not until he resumed riding three weeks later that he realised the real cause.

In his autobiography Roche says he 'went back to zero when there was no problem with my knee'. He put his own saddle and handlebars on the bike and went back to riding with his Colnago shoes. *Voila!* His tendon didn't even hint at a strain. And soon enough, he was back to top form and thankful for having heeded the advice of his Irish mentor, Peter Crinnion, a former cyclist who had plenty of experience of racing in France, and kept badgering Roche to at least 'stick out the year'. Since then, the pair have been inseparable and Crinnion has stayed as Roche's manager throughout his career.

Despite Crinnion's attempts to calm Roche, the Dubliner questioned the fact that Weignant didn't provide an income whereas other French riders got about 2,000 francs a month. Roche did not. Even after he followed up Weigant's explanation that only winners were paid, he still didn't even after scoring an impressive tally of victories in the season.

Finally, Roche adapted to this, and nearly every aspect of French club racing
– including the cramped living arrangements in ACBB'S two-bedroomed apartment in
Boulogne-Billancourt, where he slept in the living room. In the years to come as a
professional Roche always kept in close touch with Weigant, staying at his house before
the Grand Prix des Nations. 'It is a good house for the cyclist. You eat at the same time
each day, the routine is never broken. He knows when to talk cycling and knows not to
talk cycling all the time,' says Roche.

Whatever the frustrations of that first year in France, Roche knew that the
secret of survival was to get along with the others. He didn't balk at trying to make
friends even though his French was non-existent at the time. François Hervo, the local
butcher, was one handy ally. He always saved Roche a prime piece of meat each day
and charged the same ten francs. Roche, in turn, would bring in more Anglophiles who
would be treated similarly. And before he knew it, Hervo's backroom was filled, on a
regular basis, with tea-drinking English-speaking cyclists watching television.

Once on the road and heading from race to race, Roche learned the serious
side of his job. The ACBB might have been an amateur club, but it was professionally
run. And no day was more serious than that of the amateur edition of Paris–Roubaix,
the notorious cobblestoned classic in northern France. Roche won his first encounter
with the *pavé*, outsprinting Belgian Dirk Demol whose name would hardly be heard of
again until he won the professional edition in 1988.

Roche had never seen cobbles or *pavé* before. And he still wonders how he
raced his first Paris–Roubaix so well. 'I rode in the gutter at the side of the *pavé*, on the
actual *pavé* itself. I went from left to right to the middle as if I'd been on *pavé* all through
my career,' he said.

Roche has a vivid memory of Weigant that day, his bulky torso leaning out
from the bouncing and rattling ACBB team car with a smashed front window. Wearing
a thick black jacket and a Peugeot cap, the ACBB patron roared abuse at Roche for
letting Demol sit on his wheel. 'Weigant told me that if I did not win I was going
home.' Quickly, Roche tried to get Demol to ride in front, but to no avail. As the
closing kilometres approached all he heard was Weigant yelling: 'You are going home!'
Fearing that Weigant would carry out his threat more than the disappointment of defeat
itself, Roche had no choice but to win. And he did.

Like Anderson six months earlier, Roche's Olympic dreams were starting to
fade. Before Paris–Roubaix he had already calculated the odds of getting a professional
contract. And while initially rebuffed by Weigant, his win at Paris–Roubaix and then
in Paris–Reims in a solo break over the last 40km turned the tables.

Roche still went to Moscow but his efforts fell short of expectation. His desire
to join the professional peloton had overridden his Olympic ambition. Upon his return,
Peugeot offered him a contract of 4,500 francs a month for the 1981 season, 500 francs
less than what he would have earned working as a fitter at Premier Dairies. Sensing his
own worth early, Roche asked Peugeot for 5,000 francs. He got what he wanted. His
spirit continued to show: he still raced hard for the remainder of 1980. His team,
ACBB, was rewarded with time trial wins in the Chrono Madelainois and the Grand
Prix de France and second place in the Grand Prix des Nations.

1981

Roche's success set a tough precedent for anyone to follow. There were seven hopefuls who crossed the Channel to join ACBB for the 1981 season, only three proved they were up to it.

Englishmen Sean Yates and John Herety would become the new ACBB headliners. Jeff Williams was another, but he elected to race only at selected periods of the season. He showed much promise but limited his future by committing himself to 'visiting' periods with the club. Whereas Roche's Irish friend McIlroy, and Englishmen Kevin Riley, Russell Williams and John Parker – the latter two on their third attempt at cracking the Continental scene – soon found themselves racing for other clubs or needing their return tickets home.

Sadly, Yates would be the only true survivor as Herety's professional career was cut short by a flurry of injuries and flagging health.

At first it seemed that 23-year old Herety had all the vital ingredients to become a success. He arrived with the stage win of the 1980 Peace Race to his credit and was reigning Manx International Champion. He was also wisely prepared for possible hostility from those French ACBB riders recently forced to take a step back as Sherwen, Anderson, Millar and Roche stole the limelight. 'I am looking forward to it, but I am a bit apprehensive. They might be getting a bit fed up with British riders in France,' he said a few weeks before going to France.

Joining ACBB for the 1981 season under Sherwen's recommendation, former chef Herety became an immediate star. With help from Yates, he won lead-up races like the Grand Prix de Peymenaide, de Sanary, and de Saint Maxime in the south of France. And while those wins placed Herety as the main favourite for the first Spring classic, Paris – Ezy, he never let complacency set in.

'The French have only started training while we have been stacking in the miles back in England. The true test will come,' he said before the team headed back north to Paris where 20-year old Williams was waiting to join them for his first five-week spell with ACBB. Expectation greeted ACBB and Herety at Paris – Ezy. 'Il Faudra Battre Herety' (It's necessary to beat Herety), read the headline to Robert Pajot's race preview in *L'Equipe*. And Herety's rivals took the tip: blocking by the peloton and four punctures during the race put paid to his chances. English honour – and ACBB's face – was saved by Williams who finished second after being pipped on the line by Frenchman Yves Beau. It was hard for Herety to miss a chance for a classic victory. He came to the Continent intent on becoming a professional. To have any chance of getting a contract he needed to prove that he could cope with the pressure.

Herety needed a win in the amateur classics. When he had still not claimed one by the time the British Milk Race arrived on the calendar in early May, he was forced to make a choice that would create a furore whichever way he chose. Williams faced the same dilemma: he had so far taken two second places in the classics, which would keep Weigant and Escalon happy – as well as any pro ambitions alive; he could scratch from the Milk Race to contest five French classics like Paris – Roubaix, which clashed yet had several professional managers watching. He could miss the classics and ride in the Milk Race for which invitations had gone out six months before.

Both Herety and Williams stuck to the French classics programme, fearing that future chances to impress the 'head hunting' pro managers would be scarce. 'If I'd won a classic I would have had no problem about the Milk Race. You've got to think about yourself sometimes. If I don't make it this year I'm back in England unemployed. It's

Yates in the 1981 Amateur Grand Prix des Nations. He was the true British 'tester' on the wrong side of the Channel

Herety, Yates' ACBB companion in 1981, here in a motor-paced race on the Champs Elysees in Paris

calculated but not a gamble as I think I am good enough,' said Herety.

Jim Hendry, the BCF director was naturally upset. He accused the pair of 'playing dirty' in *Cycling Weekly*. But Herety didn't flinch from his stance. It was not long before his conviction paid off.

In May, he won his first classic, Paris–Rouen, the world's oldest road race, which was first staged in 1869 and won by another Englishman, James Moore. Herety's win, the third ever by an Englishman was also the first since David Rollinson in 1971.

L'Equipe hailed Herety as having a great racing career ahead. 'He possesses a gift of velocity, a gift which will open up great opportunities for his future,' it said in a special feature two days later. And Herety realised the value of his win, calling it a 'downpayment on a pro contract.'

By early October and with 12 wins to his name, Herety was able to realise his dream: he turned professional with the CO-OP-Mercier team. Unfortunately for Herety the dream of a professional career would last only three years – until 1985 when injury and lost form forced him to return home.

Williams fared no better: after a promising start he had several crashes and the resulting injuries left his professional dreams hanging on the Grand Prix des Nations. But in that he disappointed with sixth.

Yates was very much a part of Herety's success at ACBB. The pair became a close-knit team professionally and socially. They shared an apartment at Boulogne-Billancourt. And later when Herety was with CO-OP-Mercier and living in Tours with the team owner's family, Yates was invited to live there as well.

Yates' joined ACBB after an introduction to Weigant by Roche. But when he first came to the Continent in 1979 to race in the Grand Prix de France he had not the slightest idea of where his destiny lay. It was nothing more than an attempt to gain some pre-Olympic preparation.

On an all-expenses paid trip by the BCF and dressed proudly in his Olympic jacket, the lanky Surrey rider embarked on the cross Channel journey to race the 1980 Grand Prix des Nations. The man who picked him up – the 1956 Paris – Tours winner Albert Bouvet – was the man who would whistle the *appel* [start] of so many punishing Tour de France stage starts in years to come.

Embryo celebrities were all around Yates, including a certain Laurent Fignon who would win the Tour in 1983 and 1984. 'I went training with him the day before the race, over the course. I didn't even know who he was. He was nothing special. He was just another amateur. I remember he kept attacking me on the climb. . .' he recalls, shaking his head.

It was moments after Yates finished sixth in the time trial that his career changed course. Roche, second to Spaniard Julian Gorospe, walked towards Yates. It would be the start of a new relationship for this Anglo-Irish duo. 'We didn't know each other, but he must have heard of me because he asked if I wanted to come to ACBB the next year,' said Yates. And, he just couldn't think of a reason not to take Roche's offer. He had been planning a move from his parents' home in any case. 'I wasn't that keen about racing abroad, but when Roche asked I said okay. I owed it to my parents really,' says Yates.

Yates didn't even have time to put together the personal resumé he was asked to send to Weigant. His second place at 0:05 to Roche in the Grand Prix de France, in Lyon was enough. Then a few phone calls and a couple of letters later confirmed the 1981 training camp dates and Yates was on the bus for Paris with John Parker. 'It was as simple as that.' Simplicity quickly went out the door. Like Anderson two years before, Yates was told he would be met by 'someone' at Paris' Gare du Nord. And like Anderson, he wasn't. Equipped with an address, a bicycle and a nine-month supply of clothes and personal items, Yates and Parker joined the sweaty, crowded Metro – the underground – and made their own way to Boulogne-Billancourt. For Parker nothing had changed.

'John said they were testing us, that it was all a test of character to see if we could find our own way,' says Yates. 'We got there, but if John hadn't known the address I don't know how we would have.'

After settling into the ACBB apartment where Parker, Herety and Kevin Ryan would all live, it was straight down to the south of France for training camp. It was there where Yates felt the first signs of expectation put upon him.

Until then it was all an adventure. He had still to discover the ambition that his new French team-mates had felt for years – to become a professional cyclist. He had not the slightest inkling of, or worry about the political nepotism that may be around the corner. Nor did he feel any pressure on him to succeed, other than what he created for himself.

But Yates' instinct told him he was regarded as 'special' as soon as he was told to sleep during camp at Weigant's house at Les Issambres where Escalon and another

French rider were bedding down. The others stayed in a hotel. 'Weigant must have thought I was the next protégé or something,' says Yates.

The esteem for Yates never waned, especially from Escalon who cooked and prepared so much food that Yates – with so much spare time in between training and resting – virtually took up eating as a hobby. 'We ate like pigs. Before I never had a problem with weight. But with so much spare time on my hands I took it up by eating,' says Yates who rocketed from 79kg in February to 88kg in May while still training and racing.

And as long as Yates could perform on the undulating courses he mainly raced on, there was no reason for him to worry. Or if there was, he never gave it much thought. 'I just got on with bike riding. I never thought about the end result. I remember once I packed 11 races in a row and I didn't think twice about it. They might have been pissed off at the time, but I didn't take much notice or they didn't show it.'

Yates' sheer strength seemed tailormade for time trials and the numerous winning lead-outs he gave to Herety. And he personally got off to a great start by winning his first race, the Grand Prix de Saint Tropez in February, where he was in a two-man break which finished 0:10 ahead of the Herety-led peloton. Yates' next win may not have been until May at the Grand Prix de Boulogne, but his investment in Herety's successes made him an invaluable team-mate. And before the year was out, he also boasted an impressive score of 14 victories which included the Grand Prix de France, and Paris–Connerre after a third in the Grand Prix des Nations.

The fact he eventually turned professional with Peugeot went without question. Yates was a natural choice.

1982

Allan Peiper was a superb replacement for the strong Englishman at ACBB in 1982. With him in the English-speaking fold were Englishmen Pete Longbottom and Alan Gornall and American Karl Maxon.

Peiper's door to ACBB was also opened by the Melbourne restaurateur who got Anderson to the club, Gerald Georges. While Peiper never became the champion Roche, Anderson or Millar did, as a 22-year old he was unique in that he arrived at ACBB with three years of European racing experience behind him.

Peiper's ACBB days marked a second start to a European racing career. His first began in Belgium in 1977 at the age of 17 and left him saying: 'I had aged ten years mentally and didn't feel so young any more'. At ACBB life was supposed to treat him better. The club prided itself on its professionalism. And it now had a record of success which made the club not only **the** club for French riders to get in, but any aspiring professional cyclist in world.

To all intents and purposes, Peiper was heading into an ideal arrangement which would justify the encouragement and support of his mentor, Peter Brotherton to make a return to racing after quitting in 1979 from racing in Belgium. Peiper learned the hard way to look after himself in Belgium. With his best 'mate' Brian Gillin, the pair flew to London, took the overnight ferry to Ostend before a train to Ghent. Arriving at midnight, their sole reference was an address for a certain Madame Des Nenk who had supposedly helped many English-speaking riders before them.

The 'reports' were true. She found them accommodation – in a butcher's shop where 20 or so other riders were also living. Giving them each a blanket, sheets, a pillow, a cup and cutlery she bade them goodluck and goodbye! Suddenly Peiper was in a chapter of his life which was often lonely and short on creature comforts. 'At night it was so cold. I had brought a beach towel with me, so I used that as a second blanket. In the day it became a towel again,' he recalled.

While tackling the Belgian calendar of junior races, Peiper hardly had a penny to his name. And as he had to pay for his own food, clothes, tyres and transport, his instinct quickly became one of survival. But he was boosted by a winning two-man breakaway with a local Belgian racer, Eddy Planckaert.

After Planckaert won the race, they chatted. And in weeks to come the Belgian picked up on Peiper's impoverished lifestyle. After seeing where he lived Planckaert asked his mother if Peiper could live with them. She agreed and Peiper moved in. The pair won nearly every race they entered with Planckaert mostly winning and Peiper happy to ride for second place.

Victory was never the be all and end all for him. He did win sometimes. But later on Peiper's generous nature meant he became one of the most hard working 'super' domestiques in Europe. He learned money was the key to his survival. Others scratched their heads in bewilderment as he rode on the front in breaks for race after race and picked up intermediate sprint wins along the way like a pauper would dropped pennies. Peiper's mind worked like a cash register. 'If I was second I had only £3 less than first place of £20. Sometimes I rode the whole race at the front with a rider on my wheel. He won the race but I won the sprint money,' he recalls.

Some riders fortunate enough to be in a Peiper-led break would even ask if they could win. He always agreed for the prize-money in return. But in the finale, he still always had a go. 'If I lost they paid. If I won, it was hard luck for them. I was a professional junior. I had to be hard. Money meant food and tyres.'

Peiper spent two seasons in Belgium, becoming stronger and wiser for it; that is, until early 1979 when a bout of hepatitis dealt Peiper's European ambition a threatening blow. He flew home, all he could do was sit back, recover and meanwhile watch his team-mate Anderson blossom at ACBB into the prospect he was 'meant' to be.

It was not until 1980 that Peiper's health and confidence returned for another crack at top-level racing. However Brotherton warned him not to be jealous of Anderson, now about to start his professional career. Brotherton told Peiper to get on with his own career. And he did.

In 1981 the rewards started coming. Peiper followed Anderson's path by winning the Dulux Tour of New Zealand. And the invitation from Weigant to join ACBB for 1982 took him to France. The experience of his first European assault, his heath problems and determined recovery would be important assets adding to his future resilience as a professional. But at ACBB he discovered another pressure which Belgium had not prepared him for – that of an unrelenting expectation that he had to win.

Eventually he grew to hate ACBB. Had Brotherton not convinced him to stay on, he would almost certainly have taken up an offer in May to turn professional with the Belgian Splendor team. But Brotherton hammered home the fact that if Peiper was to join the profesional peloton he **had** to go to Peugeot.

When the amateur Grand Prix des Nations came around, Peiper was happy to see the end of his ACBB experience – despite an all-out bid for victory to repay Weigant for his support

'I came to ACBB at the end of a line of so many great riders. And that was hard. Escalon was always comparing me to the others. As an Australian I was always compared to Anderson and as a cyclist, to Roche. But both of them, and all the others before me, had won so many races that I had to do the same if I had any chance of being regarded well,' he says.

Peiper never felt at home that year. He very rarely saw Weigant as health reasons forced the commandeering ACBB bossman to spend less time with the team and more at home in southern France. Had Weigant been present, Peiper's memories may have been happier because the Australian struck an immediate rapport with Weigant when, like Yates, at the February training camp he was a guest of the Weigant's household. Their bond would still be strong at the end of the year.

Once back in Paris, his outlook changed. Peiper did not gel with Escalon, who was also taking more control of the team as every week passed without Weigant looking on. 'He never helped with anything, not even when there was a problem,' says Peiper of Escalon. 'He wasn't very happy about Weigant either. He wanted to be boss, but couldn't be.'

Judging by Peiper's reflections, it was at this time that the barriers between French- and English-speaking contingents grew. Or maybe it was that Peiper was the first 'successful' ACBB rider to actually acknowledge the problem. After racing in Belgium, he knew too well what was a rip off and what was not. And Peiper sensed one when French riders like Philippe Lauraire were given wages of 3,500 francs a month – equal to Sherwen's first salary as a professional – and the English-speaking riders got nothing. And in Peiper's mind the last straw was when the 'paid' Frenchies would invade the ACBB apartment, where he, Longbottom, Gornall and Maxon lived. 'They were being paid, yet on the weekends they would stay over, eat all our food which we paid for and leave the place looking like a bomb-site. Longbottom and Maxon never cleaned up, but it was always me and Gornall who were left doing it. Boy . . . did I get sick of that,' says Peiper.

Peiper's woes never stopped him from winning. He matched the standard set by his predecessors, winning 14 races that year. By June he had won five races, including the Paris–Montargis classic. He then finished the season with a victory in the Grand Prix de Nivoplastic time trial, and a week later in the Grand Prix des Nations.

Winning the Nations – his tenth victory for the year – gave Peiper the chance to repay Weigant for what should have been happier times. It was not Weigant's fault he couldn't be as attentive to his charges as he had been in previous years. But in the short time he spent with Peiper he inspired the Australian far more than anyone in Europe – certainly Escalon.

Weigant accommodated Peiper in the week before his Nations victory. He enforced a strict daily regime: he was not allowed to walk or swim – they drained vital energy. He had to train hard and eat well, sleep more and focus on the time trial ahead. 'He banned me from swimming in his pool saying I could swim in it for as many hours or days as I liked after the race. And would you believe it? The day after it rained non-stop!'

When Peiper won, there was no hesitation over who he credited. In *L'Equipe* the following Monday, Peiper said he owed his win to Weigant. 'And that really put Escalon's nose out of joint,' adds the Australian with an avenging smile today.

Weigant lobbied for Peiper throughout his search for his first professional contract at the end of that year. Peugeot agreed to pay 6,000 francs a month, but then cut it to 5,500 francs when it came to putting pen to paper. But Weigant defended the loyal Australian to the hilt, pushing for the all-conquering French team to stick to its word and stump up the 6,000 francs it had agreed to. Such was the authority Weigant yielded, Peugeot stepped down and reinstated the 6,000 francs.

Anderson, with his yellow jersey rides in the Tour that year, may have become the 'Aussie star' in Europe. But Peiper, with two testing European amateur campaigns under his wheels, was waiting in the wings. After six years of trying, he was finally firmly set for a long and memorable professional career.

1983 onwards

In the years which followed ACBB continued to snap up English-speaking riders. Englishman David Akam was billed as the kingpin in ACBB's 1983 foreign line-up after an impressive two seasons in Holland. So impressive in fact, that it lead to the Dutch Federation slapping a ban on foreign recruits in 1983 and Akam's move south.

His 12 wins in races in Belgium, Holland and France in 1982, including the Grand Prix de France and the climber's category of the pro-am Etoile du Sud stage race attracted ACBB's attention. And when he joined the team he was told he had strong prospects of being contracted with Peugeot for 1984.

It seemed the English-speaking phenomenon was set to continue. Gornall and Neil Hunter who returned were never destined for greater success. But Akam's morale and confidence must have been helped by their presence in the team, together with that of English newcomers Peter Sanders, Tony Mayer and Australian Rick Flood who showed promise.

As always, the Anglophiles found early winning form as Akam won the Grand Prix de Sanary, de la Dadière, de Nice and de St Tropez in their February training camp. Then Flood took first place in the Circuit du Printemps Nivernais in March. And then in ACBB's home race, the Grand Prix de Boulogne-Billancourt in April, Akam was second and Sanders seventh. A week later Akam once more proved he still had that winning edge by adding the Tour de l'Essone to his credits.

The tide of glory turned when Akam was struck by hepatitis. 'I looked in the mirror and my eyes were yellow. I lost my strength and when I raced I lost a lot of weight. It took me three to four days to put my weight back on,' he told *Cycling Weekly*.

Ironically, out of such adversity came a stroke of luck. He still tried to race in the 'open' Tour of Norway but without success. The brightest moment was meeting Italian Francesco Moser. Moser was not ignorant of English talent: Phil Edwards had ridden on his team. And when he saw Akam struggling he was naturally curious to know what was wrong with him.

Helped by a mutual friend, a bike shop owner in Paris, they struck up a friendship. The owner had told Moser that Akam was a good rider. And Moser took his word, promising the red-headed Englishman a contract with his Gis team for 1984 should he do a good ride in the Grand Prix des Nations.

The chance was timely. Peugeot had been keen on Akam. But one suspects they would have been hesitant about taking on an English rookie possibly still ailing from the affects of hepatitis. It is impossible to guarantee a total recovery from this disease.

Inspired by Moser's challenge, Akam trained meticulously with the Nations in mind. His form returned. A fortnight before the Nations Akam won the Chrono Madelainois time trial, followed by the Grand Prix de Novoplastic a week before the big day. Overall he was second, and deserving in Moser's eyes, of a two-year contract with his 12-strong Gis outfit.

Unsurprisingly Peugeot was again thinking about taking on Akam. And they too came forward with a deal. But it was too late. Akam signed with Gis. Without knowing it, as he began a professional career that would never match his hopes, he broke Peugeot's long tradition.

The ACBB continued with its foreign recruitment policy, but in one of those inexplicable turns of fate, the stream of truly talented young professionals ran dry. In 1984 there were Irish brothers Paul and Raphael Kimmage, Sean Yates' brother Christian, the roll call goes on – Scotland's Brian Smith (1987, 1988), England's Deno Davie (1988), Ireland's Laurence Roche (1989), Australia's Clayton Stevenson (1990), England's Dave Cook (1990, 1991, 1992) and Matthew Stephens (1990, 1991, 1992).

Some turned professional in Europe. Paul Kimmage spent four years in France with RMO until he retired, disillusioned after the 1988 season. Davie and Roche spent two seasons with Carrera in Italy in 1989 and 1990. And when Davie returned to England for the 1991 season, Roche hung on to spend a season with the Belgian Tonton Tapis team before it disbanded, and he could find no other sponsor. Finally, Stevenson found himself floundering during two long seasons with RMO in 1991 and 1992.

None of them came close to the achievements of their predecessors. And it is probably no coincidence that the arrival at ACBB of a former Norwegian policeman, Dag-Otto Lauritzen in 1984 and his success, led to the club looking elsewhere for another goldmine in the late 1980s and 90s. More recently ACBB's focus has turned towards Scandinavia; then as eastern Europe opened up they looked to the cycling hotlands of Poland and Czechoslovakia.

By 1984 Sherwen, Jones, Anderson, Millar, Roche, Yates, Herety and Peiper were launched into their careers as professionals. But that same year may have seen the the all-conquering English-speaking Foreign Legion reach maturity.

4 PEUGEOT: THE RISE AND FALL

Peugeot was a traditional French cycling team. It was backed by a French firm, registered with a French federation, made up mostly of French riders, and run by French directors. And it had been involved in cycling since 1896.

It was meant to be **all** French, physically and philosphically – and proudly so. Up until its end after the 1986 season, it was a team that enjoyed a strict sense of loyalty – a rare quality in cycling today when sponsors and riders are chopping and changing even halfway through the season. Alas there were two painful realities in Peugeot's history. First, despite its strengths, it never won the number of races that its reputation deserved. Second, many of its greatest triumphs came via the leg and will power of its foreign team members.

Foremost of the great foreigners was Belgian Eddy Merckx. His first season with Peugeot was in 1966 when he won Milan – San Remo for the first of a record seven victories, finished second in the Tour of Lombardy and third in the Grand Prix des Nations behind Italian Felice Gimondi and French winner Jacques Anquetil. In his second and last year with Peugeot, in 1967, he won the world title, Milan – San Remo, Ghent – Wevelgem and Flèche Wallonne. He was also second in Liège – Bastogne – Liège and third in the Tour of Flanders. But the all important tour was still not his.

That same year England's Tom Simpson won Paris – Nice for Peugeot before his tragic death in the Tour. As a fellow Peugeot rider for Frenchman Roger Pingeon it took much of the polish off Pingeon's overall victory. Amazingly, Pingeon's Tour success was only one of ten by Peugeot riders since the Tour began in 1903. Since then Peugeot has also won the team category only eight times.

Peugeot's premier Tour triumph of 1905, came when Frenchman Louis Troussellier, on the rebound from his win at Paris – Roubaix in April, claimed victory. Peugeot quickly established itself when French team-mates Rene Pottier and Lucien Petit-Breton won the next three Tours. Pottier won in 1906 and Petit-Breton's successive wins in 1907 – when he also won Milan – San Remo – and 1908.

It soon became clear to the French car and bicycle manufacturer that it could not rely on local talent alone to bring success. It was this open minded approach that would belie the often held – and unjust – opinion that the French would only support their own. Of any team in cycling, Peuegeot has been at the forefront with their open recruitment policy. Such thinking was confirmed as right when Belgian Philippe Thijs, who won several classics in other years, gave Peugeot its first two Tour wins by a foreigner in 1913 and 1914. Further proof came after the First World War when another Belgian, Firmin Lambot who won the 1919 Tour for *La Sportive* cycles, rode for Peugeot in 1922 and won again.

There were various reasons why the momentum of Peugeot's early successes could not be maintained. Cycle racing was based on teams riding for one leader, and in the next quarter of a century Peugeot lacked the captain it needed. At the same time, other teams nurtured such champions for the classics and Tours as Alfredo Binda, Gino Bartali and Fausto Coppi of Italy; Louison Bobet, Andre Leducq and Andre Darrigade of France; and Rik Van Steenbergen of Belgium to name several.

In fact, the most impressive rider Peugeot seemed to nurture before Merckx, was Simpson who came from the French Gitane team. There he won the Tour of Flanders in 1961 and finished sixth in the 1962 Tour de France where he was also the first Englishman to don the leader's yellow jersey for a day. After joining Peugeot, his success continued: Milan–San Remo in 1964, and then in 1965 the world title and Tour of Lombardy crowns. And of course there was his Paris–Nice triumph in 1967 where he and Merckx clashed over the Peugeot team leadership.

If the team was to pride itself on being a champion French team then it needed a French rider who could win the Tour de France again. But it was not until the mid-1970s and the arrival of Bernard Thevenet that it would strike gold.

Other foreigners joined Peugeot: Scot Billy Bilsland spent his first three years as a professional there, Belgian Ferdinand Bracke, the 1962 Grand Prix des Nations winner and fellow nationals Rik Van Linden who won Paris–Tours in 1973 and Walter Goodefroot who beat Merckx in the 1972 Belgian championship. But when Thevenet finished second in the 1973 Tour to Spaniard Luis Ocaña it was thought Peugeot had finally found the Frenchman it had been looking for since Petit-Breton in 1907. Until then Thevenet had been riding in the shadows of Peugeot's 1967 Tour winner, Roger Pingeon. After his apprenticeship began, Thevenet won his first Tour de France stage – stage 18 from St Gaudens to La Mongie – in the Pyrenees of the 1970 edition, in which Pingeon did not ride. Thevenet rose as a true contender the next year, 1971, when Merckx won his third successive Tour. Thevenet took fourth place overall at 15:18. But he proved his consistency with ninth place in 1972, and second in 1973 after earlier winning the French championship and taking third in the Tour of Spain behind Ocaña and Merckx.

Eventually Thevenet, a big broad shouldered man with his distinctive bushy black sideburns, realised the hopes placed upon him by winning the Tour in 1975 and 1977. His reign at Peugeot was unquestionable, although he did have his share of critics. Some said he was too temperamental under pressure, and would crack when things went wrong – such as the 1976 Tour when he abandoned through exhaustion and saw the great Belgian climber Lucien Van Impe ride to his one and only winner's yellow jersey.

When asked to explain the fact that he won two Tours de France, other detractors suggest he was advantaged by the fact that his peak years came in the transition between the two eras of Eddy Merckx and Bernard Hinault. It was seen by many that Merckx's sixth place at 12:38 in 1977 was the great Belgian's 'adieu' to top line Tour racing. They were not wrong.

Nevertheless, for Peugeot it was still two Tour crowns. And that meant they were once again the leading team in France. Renault and La Vie Claire vied for the limelight with Hinault and Greg LeMond in the mid-1980s. More recently Spain's Banesto team came into the picture when their star rider Miguel Indurain won the Tours of 1991 and 1992.

In 1978, just as Thevenet enjoyed his hard fought status as 'patron', along came Hinault. Young, hungry to win and laden with immense ability, Hinault was to rise up and topple Thevenet from the top spot with the first of five Tour victories – equalling the previous bests of Anquetil and Merckx.

Peugeot and Thevenet would once more fall by the wayside. Thevenet eventually headed to Spain, joining Teka for a two year sabbatical after 1979. And Peugeot – then directed by Maurice de Muer – was left in need of a new star.

According to Jean-Marie Leblanc, then a journalist with *L'Equipe,* Peugeot's dilemma was not just caused by Hinault's success. It was also a result of several internal factors. In an article in *Cycling Weekly*, Leblanc once summed up Peugeot's slide from grace after Thevenet's departure saying: 'The climate in the team was degenerating (after 1977). De Muer was less attentive in his recruitment. His team lost its cohesion. Cliques formed. Doping scandals hit the team and for some two years De Muer lost his enthusiasm.

In the French Peugeot fold were many well-known names who would form the backbone of the team's image. Peugeot may have been studded with foreign riders, but it was always two-thirds full of Frenchmen. One Frenchman who inspired great hope was Michel Laurent. He was even given the chance to fill the void left by Thevenet before Dutchman Hennie Kuiper and many others came along. And one can't deny Laurent's rise to leadership. In 1975 Laurent was second in the Tour of Catalonia. Then in 1976 he won Paris–Nice, then a much bigger race than it is today. In 1978 he came back to finish second behind Hinault in the Criterium National (now dubbed 'International') and soon after won the Belgian Flèche Wallonne one-day classic.

However 1979 was the year that really saw Laurent establish his leadership. Coming as Thevenet's winning gloss started to fade, Laurent could not have timed the transition better: he began the year by winning the early season Tour of the Mediterranean, and four months later he suprised everyone with a fourth in the Tour of Italy. Was it too good to be true? Sadly for Peugeot it was. The team had little to show for that year's Tour. Not even their star sprinter Jacques Esclasson was able to pull off stage wins, as he had in 1975, 1976, 1977 when he also won the green points jersey, and in 1978 he won two stages.

De Muer was getting anxious. By now it didn't matter whether Peugeot had a French winner or not, like ACBB, it needed a winner. Hopes were placed in yet another foreigner, Kuiper who arrived on the team in 1980. The 1975 world champion was a strong bet: he had finished second to Thevenet in 1977 and proved – as he would so many more times in his career – that he had not lost his competitive edge by finishing fourth in 1979.

In any other team, Kuiper's second place in the 1980 Tour behind compatriot Joop Zoetemelk would have instilled an immediate vote of confidence in him. But for Peugeot the reality was that victory and only victory would do. And Kuiper had still to prove he could bring it home. So once more Peugeot looked for a new leader; they looked to Frenchman Jean-René Bernaudeau.

In the two previous seasons Bernaudeau had plenty of headline space in the French papers. In the 1979 Tour he was fifth overall, enjoyed a one-day spell in the yellow jersey, and was eventually best young rider. Even then, the reigns were pulling on him as he was on the rival Renault team of eventual Tour winner, Bernard Hinault. Bernaudeau was a popular figure in French cycling. His youthful good looks, tanned face and beaming smile won him many fans. Cycling aficionados, as well as the press, believed he would be a serious threat to Hinault, were he on another team and given his own chance. The scenario finally led to Bernaudeau joining the Peugeot black and whites for 1981.

From then on there was constant news of the new-found rivalry between Renault's Hinault and Peugeot's Bernaudeau. By the time the Tour arrived, Bernaudeau had won the Route du Sud and a second of four consecutive Midi Libre titles, while Hinault had won the Criterium International, the Dauphiné Libéré, Paris–Roubaix and the Amstel Gold.

Graham Jones a rider with immense talent
yet – in many people's eyes – overaced
by his Peugeot bosses

Moments before Paris–Roubaix, 1981, Jones'
uneasy look is not his alone

The battle commenced as *L'Equipe* confirmed with its June 23 headline: 'Hinault-
Bernaudeau. *Le Match est Lancé* , Hinault was favourite to win his third of five
Tours, but nothing ruffled De Muer's conviction that Bernaudeau would
be the winner.

'There is Hinault on one side and Bernaudeau, Laurent, Bossis, and Duclos-
Lassalle on the other. Our ambition is to make life hard for Hinault. We have the
baroudeurs [attackers], a leader who is in good form at the right moment with
Bernaudeau and a *collectif* which will help us put our battle plan into action,' said De
Muer in that day's edition of *L'Equipe*.

Such were De Muer's ambitions that Peugeot was going to take back its
ranking as the number one French team from Renault, and become **the** team to
defeat Hinault.

Well . . . that was the plan, until the 117km stage six of the Tour from St
Gaudens to the 1,680m summit of Pla d'Adet in the Pyrenees. Bernaudeau's loss of
4:30 against Hinault's second place at 0:27 left behind the dreams of De Muer and his
team comrades. An unknown Australian Peugeot rider named Phil Anderson, stunned
everyone by riding pedal for pedal with Hinault taking the yellow jersey. Confirming to
Peugeot and the entire cycling world that an English-speaking presence in the peloton
was no longer a curiosity, but a force to be reckoned with – and a much needed
reinforcement for De Muer.

Following this, there was an ill-fated bid by the talented Frenchman Pascal

Roche. . . about to make his professional debut in Paris–Roubaix

Roche and Duclos-Lassalle (left and right) protect team-mate Simon – suffering from a broken shoulder blade – during his doomed and painful spell in the yellow jersey

Millar's climbing flair still shines on the Alpe d'Huez in the 1990 Tour de France where he was a member of Greg LeMond's Z team

The Peugeot Team of 1980: Phil Anderson, Jacques Bossis, Bernard Bourreau, Frédéric Brun, José De Cauwer, Régis Delépine, Gilbert Duclos-Lassalle, Yves Hézard, Graham Jones, Hennie Kuiper, Michel Laurent, Roger Legeay, Hubert Linard, Robert Millar, Patrick Perret, Guy Sibille, Pascal Simon, Marcel Tinazzi, Allan Van Heerden

The Peugeot Team 1981: Phil Anderson, Jean-René Bernaudeau, Jacques Bossis, Bernard Bourreau, Frédéric Brun, Francis Castaing, André Chalmel, Gilbert Chaumaz Gilbert Duclos-Lassalle, Graham Jones, Michel Laurent, Roger Legeay, Hubert Linard Philippe Martinez, Robert Millar, Patrick Perret, Stephen Roche, Dominique Sanders Pascal Simon

Anderson, Millar and Roche (left to right) lead Peugeot to second place in the 1983 Tour de France team time trial. Also pictured, Pascal Simon (4th from right) and Gilbert Duclos-Lassalle (in polka-dot jersey)

Hinault storms past Anderson (foreground) in the stage 16 time trial of Mulhouse in the 1981 Tour. Rivalry between the two riders will continue for years to come

Simon to win the Tour in 1983, but Peugeot would never again find a Frenchman worth pinning its yellow jersey hopes on.

Still, Anderson's feat which must have left De Muer wondering whether to laugh or cry, was not the first remarkable event to save the day for Peugeot. Its significance could not be denied. The timing of his coup was critical – coming the day Bernaudeau's winning hopes evaporated leaving a doubly shocked De Muer saying with obvious understatement that his plans for the French leader's future was now 'a delicate subject'.

Hinault and Bernaudeau's battle had barely two and a half seasons to run before English-speaking Peugeot riders gained strength, acclaim and reputation. Even Greg LeMond was a target for De Muer. The American was offered up to 15,000 francs a month to join Peugeot for the 1981 season – as against the 4,750 francs a month deal Millar and Anderson were offered, or the 5,000 francs given to Roche. However as Samuel Abt explained in *Greg LeMond: The Incredible Comeback*, LeMond was wary of Peugeot's set-up and opted to join the reputed Cyrille Guimard's Renault team, led by Hinault, for 6,000 francs a month. Finally, to put Peugeot off, it took a demand from LeMond of 25,000 francs a month 'to even consider' joining.

'I knew there was no way I wanted to go to Peugeot because I heard that the team was lenient about drugs,' LeMond told Abt. 'To this day I don't whether that was true, but it was a rumour going around then. There were others about Peugeot. It was a bad-reputation team.'

Paul Sherwen also nearly joined Peugeot. But he left the legion by opting to join FIAT rather than Peugeot in 1978. ACBB wanted him to wait until after the amateur Spring classics before signing with Peugeot, whereas he didn't want to wait, and liked the terms of FIAT's offer. Another consideration was that in 1978 Thevenet was still team leader after winning the Tour the year before, and a rookie like Sherwen would be obliged to pedal every kilometre for Thevenet's sake alone. Although Sherwen was never going to be a Tour de France champion, generally Thevenet's tight command spread throughout the racing calendar.

Had Thevenet not been there at the time Sherwen may well have ridden with Peugeot. 'FIAT offered more opportunity to do something for myself. At Peugeot it was still in the era where Thevenet and his combines controlled everything. There would have been no opportunity for me at all,' says Sherwen who left FIAT in 1979 and joined the French La Redoute in 1980 for six years.

With Van Heerden, Jones the Manchester 1978 Merlin Plage winner joined up with Peugeot in 1979. And their combined presence ressurrected an English-speaking tradition at Peugeot which had been left dormant since Bilsland's final year there in 1973. However by signing with Peugeot they also opened up the door for those *Acebebistes* like Anderson, Millar and Roche to follow. And follow they did.

Millar and Anderson joined in 1980. And so to did Roche in early 1981 when Bernaudeau and his loyal French team-mates were anticipating with excitement their affray with Hinault. Yates would also join in 1982 and Peiper in 1983, their arrival came after the foreign legion had begun, however, their presence and ensuing results made them worthy team members in their own right, and did much to tip the scales of Peugeot's confidence in its legionnaires' favour.

Nevertheless, it was far from a fairy-tale rise to prominence for them, they earned every ounce of recognition. While they all knew that merely making it into the professional ranks was an achievement in itself, they also knew that life at Peugeot was not going to be easy, and never would be. And while each of them came under

A year later, Anderson responds to Hinault's domination of the Tour. On stage two of the Tour to Nancy, Anderson (leading) slips into the winning break and claims his first ever stage win and a spell in the yellow jersey. In the break with him are (right to left) Henk Lubberding, Bernard Vallet, Peter Winnen, Peugeot team-mate Michel Laurent and Marc Madiot

De Muer's wings with solid reputations, the fact that they were winners as amateurs far from guaranteed any favours. Luckily, they were for the most part prepared for such a challenge by their apprenticeship at ACBB.

Allegations of French bias and anti-English sentiment within Peugeot are founded to a degree; perhaps it seems reasonable to expect an element of that where a healthy attitude to competition is fostered. And naturally enough home riders were going to be protected as the favourites. Why shouldn't they? It's human nature to defend what is yours. That said, what fairness is there in trying to make newcomers to a team feel uncomfortable the moment they join? After all they were supposed to be on the same side.

Former French Peugeot rider Roger Legeay saw both sides of the problem. After turning professional in 1973, he joined Peugeot in 1979 and rode there until his retirement in 1983. He then became *directeur-adjoint* to Roland Berland in 1984. And ever since Peugeot made its retreat from cycling in 1986 Legeay has managed the team with the help of various sponsors. Led since 1990 by Greg LeMond, it rode under the colours of a French children's clothes manufacturer called Z from 1987 to 1992. In 1993, Z were replaced by the French insurance firm Gan which sponsored triple Tour runner-up, Raymond Poulidor's team in the 70s.

Legeay was not a great cyclist. His early days at Peugeot saw him hold the post of domestique. But in later years, when it became clear that his greatest attribute was to mix and communicate with anyone, he was captain on the road – an organiser of

Back in yellow in the 1982 Tour. No longer is Anderson the open-eyed chance claimant to Tour leadership. His defence doesn't last, but his label as a future contender stands firm

Anderson wins stage two of the 1982 Tour de France and takes the race lead as a result

Here with De Muer (centre), the burly French *directeur-sportif* can't believe what he's found in Anderson!

tactics. He was the link between hard-line French riders who resented an English-presence and the Anglophile contingent. It was a diplomatic task of sorts, and it's no wonder he found himself needing to sneak away and smoke the 'occasional' cigarette. 'Just one now and then,' he says today. According to Legeay there was never a problem of nationalities, despite claims to the contrary from some of the legion. New English-speaking riders were treated just the same as new French ones. Language difference was an obvious barrier which required a sometimes reluctant adaptation from both parties to overcome. But at Peugeot, the most sensitive issue was the pride of several French veterans on the team who didn't want to let go of their 'top-dog' status.

The talent of others would be their biggest threat, whether from a Frenchman or Englishman. But their authority in the French set-up always ensured support from younger French members of the team as their contractual future was often dependent on an elder's reference. Whereas Jones, Anderson, Millar, Roche, Yates and Peiper were individuals racing in Europe for their career and not someone else's. They all sacrificed for the team cause on numerous occasions; they always felt it fair that others should do the same for them. Experience taught them otherwise.

Apart from Bernaudeau and Laurent, the principal characters in the French ruling order were Jacques Esclasson, the team's number one sprinter; all-round *rouleurs* like Jean-Pierre Danguillame; Gilbert Duclos-Lassalle, and Jacques Bossis; and one of

The 1983 Dauphiné Libèré. Anderson (centre) and Berland (left) fall out over a doping scandal. LeMond (right) goes on to win overall

the most reputed and generous domestiques of the time in Bernard 'Le Petit Frère' Bourreau.

Their relations with the English would vary, some like Bourreau would become friends, others as close to enemies as permissible between team-mates. But they all bore a stoic French *fierté* or pride which cynics could label as dogged machismo. What else would prompt them to slip into the big chainring for annual group photos while pedalling uphill? Their leg muscles may have been flexing under the strain, at least their foreign team-mates riding in the small chainring didn't bear their strained and forced smiles!

'There were not a lot of problems really. In fact I have very fond memories of the English-speaking riders being in the team. The fact they came to the team from ACBB was important too. It was a club sponsored by Peugeot, so it was natural that they joined Peugeot. And because they came from a Peugeot-type club, run under our structure, they knew what to expect,' says Legeay

'The problem that you could have had at that time was from the different mentalities; not because they were Scottish, English or Australian or whatever, but because they were young riders coming into a team with a lot of old ones like Danguillame, Esclasson, Thevenet, Bossis, and ... Legeay,' he comments half jokingly.

'What was good for a French amateur was good for an English one. They had to earn their place in the team just like Duclos-Lassalle had to – by winning. It might have been hard for them because they couldn't speak French well, but it was never harder for them than for a French rider.'

In reality, there was little point in English-speaking riders fighting the working environment they themselves aspired to be a part of, and as Sherwen settled into professional life at FIAT and then Jones into Peugeot, the reported struggles became a part of the myth. Back home in England, Ireland, Australia and Scotland, tales of them putting up with the rigours of a European professional rider's life made what they were doing all the more impressive.

The thinking was that if Jones and Sherwen had made it, not to mention the 'pioneers before them', then complaining and quitting could be interpreted as a cop-out – even if it wasn't. On the contrary some English-speaking professionals in Europe would tell you that NOT trying to make it in the big league at all was the cop out.

While the fear of being labelled a failure back home pushed them all to stay on, impressing others back home was never the goal. All would find that no matter what they did in Europe, media interest mainly came from specialised cycling publications. While often running reports on the Tour de France, the mainstream dailies would never commit beyond a few centimetres of copy. And that was only when – and if – one of 'their' riders won.

The riders all knew that the only way they would succeed was to prove their value by one means – as a cyclist. And when they finally achieved that, there was little if anything for the French loyalists to do but stand back and accept that the Foreign Legion was indeed a fighting force for Peugeot to have.

Anderson, Millar and Roche would all become Tour contenders, and enjoy careers made complete by numerous stage wins. While Van Heerden returned to South Africa after 1980, and Jones left Peugeot following the 1982 season when he followed Bernaudeau who was to lead the new French Wolber team, Yates and Peiper would stay on at Peugeot to become very able and trusted super domestiques. Eventually each would ride down varying paths in their careers; their trails would often cross. And Sean Kelly and LeMond were carving out individual professional careers, away from the realms of Peugeot and its in-house politics, though as we will see, the struggle was just as hard and as noble.

5 ON THE FRONTLINE

The 1980 Tour was never to be rated as a great Tour. It was marred by the surprise middle of the night abandonment by race leader, Hinault after stage 12 from Agen to Pau. Tendinitis was given as the cause, but the mysteriousness of his departure led to unfounded rumours of him fearing the dope control because he had taken cortisone to remedy his complaint. The brouhaha raged, but eventually subsided as Hinault's closest rival, Dutchman Joop Zoetemelk of the Dutch TI Raleigh team, rode away to his first victory in ten Tour attempts.

For Peugeot it was a Tour which left them shaking their heads in despair. Their leader Kuiper was second at 6:15 to Zoetemelk. Not only was Peugeot's overall objective smashed by TI Raleigh, but so too was every other goal. They failed to win a stage, whereas TI Raleigh won 11 as well as the teams' and young riders' categories.

This was Graham Jones' first Tour, he was the youngest rider in the race and it was a major step in his career. Despite Peugeot's sorry performance, Jones managed to stir plenty of interest along the way. He was even placed as high as 12th overall after the first Pyreneen stage – stage 13 from Pau to Luchon. And were it not for a bout of bronchitis on the last day in the Alps, when he was still 13th overall, he would probably have won the young rider's white jersey which TI Raleigh Dutchman Johan Van der Velde claimed.

Jones (centre) leads his Peugeot team-mates in a 1982 team trial. Also pictured are (left to right): Frederic Brun, Sean Yates, Jacques Bossis (behind Yates), Jean-Paul Dalibard and Robert Millar

Ironically, while the Pyreneen 'triumph' is so remembered for putting Jones' name up amongst the best, it was also the first harsh reminder of how team tactics can close the door on a newcomer's ambitions. On a stage which included four 'Cols' and saw the field spread over 40 minutes and 11 riders abandon, Jones was an impressive 19th at 7:48. But the nett return for his efforts would have been greater had he not been ordered by De Muer to relinquish a solo chase of the winning break of ten riders which included Kuiper. 'I'd have got up to them and stayed with them. Then I would have been sixth overall instead of 12th,' a frustrated Jones said at the time.

As Jones and so many others quickly learned, that is all part of the professional racing package. Victories are what count and Peugeot had few of them. Their new member, Jones, was young and his career had only just begun. When Jones joined Peugeot in 1979 he quickly warranted the hopes put in him. A second place in the Grand Prix de St Raphael heartened De Muer and put the 21-year-old on line for a berth in Peugeot's team for Paris – Nice, the first major test of the season.

In the 'Race to the Sun', Peugeot may not have won, but Jones confirmed that his St Raphael placing was far from being a one-off, and that the sales banter of Mickey Weigant and Claude Escalon at ACBB was not empty talk. In Paris – Nice Jones rode a strong race, particularly on the hilly Lyon – St Etienne stage where his climbing qualities were given a chance to shine.

Such openings were rare for a new professional in that era, but then again the pecking order of leadership at Peugeot was starting to change there. Bernard Thevenet and sprint specialist Jacques Esclasson were no longer the powers they used to be. And that was made clear when Thevenet headed to Spain, and Esclasson retired at the end of the season to start his own cyclist's clothing company. Then Michel Laurent tried the leader's cap for size, with a victory in the Tour de Mediterranean and fourth place in the Tour of Italy. But it was not enough.

Jones hoped that the team's horizons might broaden in the light of the changes in Peugeot after 1979. Laurent was clearly not the man to fill Thevenet's shoes, so Peugeot recruited Kuiper for the Tour. Meanwhile Alan Van Heerden who turned professional with Jones in 1979, had his eyes on Esclasson's vacancy as the lead sprinter, while two new English-speaking professionals joined the fold, Millar and Anderson.

The prospect of early season success for Jones quickly collapsed as he crashed on the second day of pre-season training: tearing a knee cartillage he missed all of the early Spring season. After several weeks of therapy failed to improve his condition he had a knee operation in late February. Forced to recuperate at home in Manchester, Jones was not able to race again until April, although he scheduled May as the month for his return.

To make up for lost opportunities, there was no choice but to pencil in the Tour de France in July. After returning to his European base at Lille in northern France, where he lived with Sherwen, the Tour was all that rested on Jones' mind.

Climbing prowess is a valued skill amongst Tour riders, even if time trialling is just as important these days. So it was with a clean bill of health and a strong showing in the mountainous Dauphiné Libéré that 22-year-old Jones was selected for the Peugeot Tour team to help Kuiper.

Normally when a rider is chosen to help the team leader his efforts are recognised by the management. As a result he may be offered as many as 25 contracts to race post-Tour criteriums, these can be quite lucrative and give the rider the opportunity to boost his earnings. For Jones as support rider to Kuiper he could have expected to get 10 or 12 from a potential 25 contracts that year, but in fact the total was only five. And the figure would have been higher had he not fallen ill and lost his high placing; or had Kuiper lived up to his reported promise of securing contracts in the Dutch criteriums. But the fatigue he felt after the Tour was a warning to the dangers of over-racing.

In the months and years to come Jones tried to take heed of such inner warnings. He could feel when he was being over-raced, although frustratingly those who gave the orders and assessed his form card never agreed. That became clear as soon as he missed the world championships in early September. Won by a tendinitis-free Hinault on the tough Sallanches circuit in France, Jones missed the title race which many thought would suit him. Few wanted to hear his explanation that he was shattered from the racing demands already put upon him. 'The riders who did well hadn't finished the Tour,' he said in his defense. The sceptics, particularly the press, did not agree and it took an 11th place in the end of season Tour of Lombardy to assuage their doubts.

A belief that he was susceptible to stress-related injury was upheld that winter when his previously injured right knee swelled up again while running. He notified Peugeot of the problem immediately. And one must wonder whether it was because the 1980 season was only just over and a good winter break awaited that they were so open minded. 'I have got to get fit early, which means being ready, for Paris – Nice and the Spring classics,' he said addressing the British Cycling Federation dinner in Blackpool in late December. In reality, with Peugeot always being dominant in the early season races, they would would have told him the same thing, injured knee or not!

Not all eyes were on Jones in 1981 though. It was also time for Anderson and Millar to assume a little more responsibility as they now had a season of settling in behind them. And in the same season, Roche drew up alongside them after his year at ACBB. No longer would Jones be the novelty he was in 1979 and 1980. But then, having showed his potential in the Tour and at the Tour of Lombardy, he too had to move up a level.

After taking second place in the 1979 Grand Prix de St Raphael an older and wiser Jones was content with 17th in the 1981 edition. This year his season was planned. The first major target on his agenda was Paris – Nice, from the 18 – 20 Peugeot members eligible to compete only ten would be selected. Jones aimed to be one of them but he needed a big win and the Tour de Mediterranean was his goal.

His eventual second place at 0:16 to Switzerland's Stefan Mutter in the five stage race drew both applause and criticism. *Cycling Weekly* labelled it as an inspired performance. And while the *L'Equipe* headline read: 'Jones Opens Himself To Ambition,' and dubbed his class as a 'mixture of elegancy and efficiency' it said he needed to attack more. But then again, such scrutiny originated from the belief by the French press that Jones was capable of more.

The decisive stage in the Tour de Mediterranean was stage two from Frejus to Hyeres where Jones, Mutter and two others rode away in the blinding rain to finish more than 11 minutes ahead of the peloton, led by Peugeot's new-found sprinter Frenchman Francis Castaing. Mutter, third, took the overall lead and Jones moved up to second at 0:04 after finishing fourth. That wrote the script for the next morning's first sector of stage three, an 8.5km time trial up Mont Faron near Toulon. Mutter won the time trial, but signs that Jones was a veritable champion came via his second place at 0:11. There was significance in his place against Mutter who was a former TI Raleigh rider, but foremost was the fact that he beat third placed Hinault by two

Jones becomes Britain's brightest winning hope since Barry Hoban with his second place in the 1982 Het Volk. Here Jones ponders over a journalist's question

seconds, Roche by 0:07 and Peugeot's supposed leader Laurent by 0:11 on the stage.

One can understand the dilemma De Muer found himself in when faced with the team selection for Paris–Nice. Jones, Roche, Laurent and even Castaing and Anderson had all fared well. And when nine Peugeot riders finished in the first 19 of the Tour du Haut Var, won by Peugeot's Jacques Bossis it must have been even worse. Still, Jones – fifth in the same race – had earned his much wanted Paris–Nice place.

Jones started the six-day race well. Although in the 27km team time trial in which Peugeot was defending Laurent's overall lead and was finally won by 0:27, he was the victim of an ill-fated puncture at the start, costing the team at least 0:20. And on stage three he had to pull out because of an upset stomach. But as history shows, stage five saw Roche assume team leadership when he got into a winning eight-man break and end up with Laurent's white leader's jersey on his back. Roche lost the jersey for a day, but won it back for good two days later. For Jones, he may not have repeated his Tour de Mediterranean success but seeing another English-speaking team-mate succeed was a consolation.

All along, Jones may not have got the results he wanted, and the fact that Roche did, and to a lesser degree Anderson too, might have been frustrating. But then again, he was earning plenty of respect as a 'willing and gifted rider who will still improve,' De Muer claimed. And as the months passed, the Tour de France once more became Jones' goal.

Jones and Anderson were the two Anglophiles to be selected for the Tour. Roche and Millar would have to wait. And how the 1981 Tour saw Jones' loyalties split. Anderson would pull off a thrilling yellow jersey ride on stage six, on the same day that Peugeot leader Bernaudeau blew up. Jones was both happy for Anderson and sorry for his friend Bernaudeau, with whom he rode all the way to the finish in a bid to help him pull back time. The sacrifice was expected from Jones and it left him in 16th place overall, two places down on Bernaudeau. And it was a sacrifice which would be repeated time and time again for Bernaudeau and Anderson before finally arriving in Paris placed 20th and 41:06 down.

Jones was naturally looking forward to a rest after the Tour. Who wouldn't after having raced the Tour de Mediterranean, Tour of Corsica, Paris – Nice, the Spring Classics, Dauphiné Libéré, Midi Libre, British title race and the Tour de France? Few riders today would follow such a tough programme. But Jones was virtually an indispensable work horse for Peugeot's leaders when they were in the mountains. He also became a great race tactician. 'Graham reads a race very well and he knows the ropes. "Watch out for him," he tells me. "Watch out for that." He'll give everything to help you,' said Roche, in his first year as a professional.

It was odd that Jones was never given the chance to 'lead'. However the sudden and unexpected leaps to prominence by Roche and Anderson left him with little opportunity. And Jones never really argued the point. Another man who would 'steal' that chance was Frenchman Pascal Simon. Simon had missed the Tour de France because of a broken collar-bone. When Peugeot lined up for the start of the Tour de l'Avenir, Simon had only one professional win to his credit – the 1980 Tour du Haut Var. He was to have left Peugeot after the season and ride for La Redoute in 1982. Simon neither had the results nor the affinity with Peugeot to stay on. Basically, Simon was rated as a lazy and unpopular rider on the team with all but Millar. As Jones told *Cycling Weekly* then: 'Riders always complained that he was not giving 100% to the team.'

All that changed at the Tour de l'Avenir, where Jones was a last minute entry for Peugeot as one of the French riders had fallen ill. It began when Simon attacked on stage four, and finished with five minutes on the field and in overall leadership. Suddenly Simon was no longer deadwood to the Peugeot plan, but Peugeot's protected property for the rest of that race and many others to come. And just as suddenly Jones with Roche and Millar were once again relegated to workhorse duties.

Simon went on to a convincing win, showing a *genre de classe* that would propel Peugeot into thinking of him as a potential Tour de France winner. 'It didn't surprise Simon that he won, but I think it suprised him how well he won. He also gained in confidence,' said Jones.

Simon certainly earned the praise, especially after winning the mountain stage to Morzine and the mountain time trial to Avoriaz in the Alps. It was no shock to hear that soon after, Simon had renewed his contract with Peugeot for a handsome pay rise. Still Jones, Roche and Millar's efforts had not gone unnoticed; on the contrary their unity assured their future on the team. 'I am happy to be with Peugeot,' said Jones at the time, 'because I've managed to be a part of all the winning rides. The team has done so well and plenty of money has been coming in. So I have no complaints about the work I have to do as a team rider.'

After a season totalling 130 races Jones had no delusions about his place in the team. 'It dawns on you that you are never going to be a big star. I had the heaviest programme of the whole team. I think De Muer sees me as a reliable sort of rider . . . a

At Alcala des Hanares in the 1984 Tour of Spain, Millar is all smiles for pulling off the leader's *amarillo* jersey performance. By Segovia, he would be needing two fingers, not one

grafter. The better riders can be more choosy about their programmes,' he said on the eve of the 1982 season. Not everyone would agree with Jones. 'He had the ability to get in the top five of the Tour. He was just over-raced,' said his former flat-mate, Sherwen.

The 1982 season saw little change in Jones' role when it began in the south of France. If anything it had become second nature. His only concern at the time was, ironically, the increasing size of the English-speaking contingent at Peugeot. Hearing of Sean Yates' arrival in 1982 was not totally pleasing to Jones. 'When I first heard that there were more English riders coming I wasn't very happy with it,' he said. 'It's hard to explain but I supposed it would make us less of a Continental team. If there were just a couple of English-speaking riders, they would fit into the team better. They wouldn't be French but there wouldn't be too many of us. I thought if there were more we would end up with a team split – one half French and the other half English.'

It is easy to understand his fears. They were a reminder that life for an English-speaking rider in a French team was always less secure. Jones didn't dwell on the matter for too long: 'Really, it worked out well.'

He was on-form physically and mentally. And he proved it by finishing seventh overall in the the Tour de Mediterranean, after once more helping his Peugeot team-mate Laurent win for the second time in four years. But it looked like Jones' career would take a different direction in early March, when the team headed north to Belgium for the one-day Het Volk classic.

The race saw Jones ride for himself for the first time in his professional career. His second place in the 217km, race won by local Fons De Wolf, in a solo attack was his best individual result to date. And he was only 0:26 short of claiming Britain's first win in the race since Barry Hoban nine years earlier. Sadly the outcome didn't really alter Jones' role in the team at Paris – Nice. With Gilbert Duclos-Lassalle and Roche being the key players he was naturally relegated to a supporting role. Despite Peugeot's offensive tactics, nothing could stop Irishman Sean Kelly winning from Duclos-Lassalle.

Each month Peugeot's spring campaign had a focus. For the big leaders like Bernaudau, the months before July were preparatory phases for the Tour. For everyone else they were opportunies to earn their Tour selection. Jones had yet to win a professional race and despite having raced strongly early in the season it was still doubtful if he would make it to Peugeot's Tour line-up. 'I lack climbing form. I may be paying for last year's efforts,' said Jones once more conciliatory.

The 1,300km Tour of Colombia in May, in which Peugeot was one of only two foreign teams competing, was to have given Jones the climbing conditioning he needed. But the high altitude, Colombian combines and flighty style of racing, which Peugeot riders were not accustomed to, took their toll on him. He abandoned at the foot of a 40km mountain on the last day. When he returned to Europe to prepare for the French Midi Libre stage race, Jones knew that his Tour selection was in question.

It was when he was omitted from Peugeot's Midi Libre team that Jones realised that the Tour was out altogether. As he said: 'I got a letter saying I wasn't riding and that was that.' Jones, the rider who had so much natural class, was now a forgotten man at Peugeot. Ironically his first ever professional wins came during the ensuing period of low morale as Peugeot geared up for the 1982 Tour. Jones' first win came in the Tour of Delyn in north Wales, and his next, after abandoning the national title race, was in the Woolmark Grand Prix in England. But his heart told him they were not major victories – not for a rider of his calibre anyhow.

His morale picked up after the world titles in September at Goodwood, England. He had raced or trained very little and found himself off the back with two laps to go when the main group split in two: 'I chased up the finishing hill but across the top there was a cross-wind. I got caught, punctured and had a nose bleed. I just wish I had been fit,' says Jones who was 53rd.

Disillusionment was to flow alongside Jones for the season. He didn't finish the Tour de l'Avenir. And the more he tried to wonder what went wrong, the more a hidden resentment for having been over-worked the year before crept out from the shadows. On the other hand Peugeot believed Jones just lacked strength. There were too many lows to make the highs worthwhile. Finally they did not renew his contract, despite calls from Anderson and Roche to keep him on. Retaining Jones meant that Peugeot would have to do the unthinkable and sack a Frenchman.

Jones also needed a change, and quick. And it was probably at this moment that the alliance he had built with Bernaudeau in the past two seasons paid off. Bernaudeau flopped in the Tour after winning the Midi Libre for the third consecutive time and finishing second in the Dauphiné Libéré to Laurent, and again in the Route de Sud. By now Peugeot had its eyes on Anderson, Roche and Simon as their future Tour winners. Bernaudeau, like 24-year old Jones, needed a new start to his career, and he wanted Jones to come along in support. By the end of 1982 both had signed up with the French Wolber team for 1983.

Whether he liked it or not, Alan van Heerden was always destined to be an odd man out. The political wranglings over South Africa's apartheid policy at the time were one reason, but on top of that, as De Muer pointed out in early 1981, just after Van Heerden left Peugeot, he was very much the loner. 'At the start with Van Heerden and

Millar (left) was the strongest English-speaking ally of Pascal Simon (centre in the Peugeot jersey). Pictured at the back is LeMond, a rider whose wheel Simon and Millar would find themselves following in years ahead

Peugeot Michelin team prove
themselves a force to be reckoned
with in the 1983 Tour

Roche (centre and in pink) and his two greatest allies in the 1987 Tour of Italy — Millar
(left in green) and Eddy Schepers (right)

Peiper's greatest personal triumph –
victory in stage 14 of the Tour of Italy.
Days after beating Frenchman Pascal
Poisson, Peiper confirms he will leave
Panasonic and Post's 'spell'

After leaving Peugeot, Roche (second from right) finds English-speaking company at
La Redoute in Paul Sherwen (third from right) on the 1984 Tour de France

Anderson there was a sort of a clan and, as they spoke the same language, Jones and Millar joined it. But the South African and the Australian are adventurers, and their approach is not the same as the English. Now (after Van Heerden's departure) things are better. Jones and Millar no longer form a separate troop. They are part of the team,' he said.

People who knew Van Heerden say that when he joined Peugeot, he was poised to take over Esclasson's position as lead sprinter. He was not a pure sprinter as Francis Castaing was, far from it. 'He was someone who would like a clear run to the line. He didn't like anything too messy,' says Jones. In contemporary terms he could be compared to a sprinter of the Jelle Nijdam mould – one who would jump the pack early and hang on at the front right to the line. He was a talented rider, and as Sherwen recalls, a true professional: 'He was impeccable. Everything had to be right, his bike, his clothes . . . everything. He might not have been a champion, but he was strong, gave his best and did whatever was asked of him.'

Van Heerden's early results with Peugeot were creditable considering that he came into the team at the age of 25 at the tail-end of Thevenet's tight rule. In his debut season, Van Heerden tallied some impressive results – a seventh in the season opening Tour of Corsica and 12th in the National Criterium in France, in June he even won a stage in the Tour of Italy where he was 75th overall. But for Van Heerden they were not enough to keep his competitive spirit in Europe. As De Muer pointed out: 'Although he had certain qualities, he was not getting the results he wanted,' said the Peugeot boss.

When Van Heerden left Europe after 1980 and returned to South Africa he continued to race. And on home soil he got the results he wanted. He won South Africa's national stage race, the Rapport Tour, a record number of times after claiming his first victory in 1982. He also won many stages. The harsh lessons learned in Europe obviously put him on another level back home. He was to South Africa what Eddy Merckx was, in his heyday, to Europe.

Van Heerden's career was one that **should** have been more prosperous, but then he reportedly wanted 'out' as much as the political circumstances forced him. 'I think he had had enough of the racing life in Europe. It probably had as much to do with him going home as did all the apartheid business,' said Jones with whom Van Heerden made the jump from ACBB to Peugeot.

To his English-speaking Peugeot peers – particularly Phil Anderson – he was more than a good rider. He became a person to trust in a world full of doubts. 'He knew who was who and what you had to do where. He knew who you could trust and would help you out. He was probably one of the first guys I got close to on Peugeot,' recalls Anderson.

He certainly added a little spark to team life, even to De Muer's. Europeans still recall the 1979 Tour of Italy where Van Heerden won a stage, but left a greater impression on De Muer for his linguistic prowess – or lack of – than for his racing.

A break was away and De Muer wanted Peugeot to chase. And he came barrelling up alongside Van Heerden to get him to act – and quickly. *'Devant! devant!'* [Up front! Get up front!] yelled De Muer in a panicked rage, urging the South African to ride to the front of the pack. Van Heerden, an easy going good natured man, who was unaware of the change ahead, thought De Muer was simply making small talk about the weather.

'Oui, il y beacoup du vent aujourdhui' [yes, there is a lot of wind today] Van Heerden replied with a smile.

If you had to judge today, what had a greater impact on De Muer . . . Van Heerden's stage win or poor French . . . you might be inclined to think the latter.

Ask anyone in France today if they recall Alan Van Heerden and before you take a second breath, a smile will always light up followed by the words: 'Bien sur . . . oui!'

Phil Anderson was still very much the wide-eyed and innocent journeyman when he joined Peugeot in 1980. If there were big changes in his life in 1979 when he left Australia for Paris and the amateur ACBB club, then they were even bigger after jumping into the professional peloton.

'Things are so different riding for a professional team than at ACBB. The ACBB set-up was what I was used to in Australia,' said Anderson then in making a comparison. 'Now I know exactly what races I am riding, what the travel arrangements are and even who is going to meet me at the airport'.

But as the 22-year old would quickly discover, those were not the only changes. In his four years with Peugeot he would also learn the ropes, and by the time he crossed the border to ride for the Dutch Panasonic team in 1984, he was a seasoned professional – a hard headed and feared individual both on and off the saddle. Anderson's development was helped by his easy going outlook and loner's spirit. Like his English-speaking peers, he knew how to look after himself. And that was a useful skill: 'I was pretty much an individual. I was never really close with anyone. I was closer with the English guys than the French guys though,' reflects Anderson.

He went through the usual apprenticeship, performing first year 'domestique' duties in 1980. He finished eighth overall in the season opening Tour of Corsica and then 19th in Paris – Nice which were both won by Duclos-Lassalle then in his fifth year as a professional. He learned his craft and Peugeot was happy. In early 1981, he went about consolidating his place in a team blessed with an immense amount of talent which brought victory in the early season.

That February, Peugeot showed its winning self in the Grand Prix D'Azuria – then an unofficial series of season-opening events in the south of France of which only the Haut Var race exists today. In 1981 Peugeot claimed wins in the Grand Prix de Grasse, Grand Prix de Monaco and the Tour du Haut Var. And then in the Tour of Corsica five Peugeot men finished in the top six, with newcomer Stephen Roche winning overall. But Anderson, fifth overall, also won a stage.

Peugeot became used to winning so many races. That's what De Muer wanted. It was the norm, so Anderson's stage win was not as sensational as it may have been in any other team. Particularly in 1981 where they won a total of five stages and the overall individual, teams and points categories. The only person who created a stir was Roche, who took the limelight as leading *étranger* with his overall victory. Today, when Anderson recalls Roche's debut he confesses to being just a touch jealous of the Irishman's sudden rise to the top.

Meanwhile, Bernaudeau, their new-found gladiator to combat Hinault in the Tour was keeping Peugeot's aspirations alive with victories in the Grand Prix de Monaco, and then the Route du Sud and Midi Libre stage races. His support personnel continued jostling for their right to race with him in July.

Peugeot's best results that Spring came via Bossis and Duclos-Lassalle. Bossis won the Tour de Haut Var and was third in Milan – San Remo, and Duclos-Lassalle second in Ghent – Wevelgem. In the stage events, Jones and Bossis were the closest to victory: Jones was second in the Tour Mediterranean, as Bossis was in the Criterium International, won by Hinault before taking third place in the Four Days of Dunkirk.

Celtic aggression at its best . . . Millar and Roche drop Peter Winnen and Laurent Fignon (left to right in background) on the Joux Plane during the 1983 Tour de France

Millar: King of the Mountains and 4th overall – Tour de France 1984

Glory was very thinly spread and Anderson had barely touched it.

Still, the Australian's brute strength and willingness to attack at De Muer's slightest whim made him a key man in any team. De Muer loved riders with an aggressive instinct, riders like Anderson. His courage was quickly noted by many around him. And in Paris – Nice it brought him his first major win – the sixth stage to Mandelieu.

Jean-Luc Vandenbroucke felt the hair on the back of his neck stand up after challenging Anderson for that stage win. It was a double celebration for Peugeot as it also saw Roche retrieve the leader's white jersey. But for Anderson, as much as his win was due to strength, it was also thanks to fearlessness on a frightening daredevil descent of the twisting eight-kilometre Tanneron climb. The only words the Belgian could gasp after finishing at 0:22 were: 'I love winning, but I love my life as well. He's crazy, this Anderson.'

It was a week before the Tour that Anderson provided any clue to his form. Bernaudeau had already secured official leadership in Peugeot with another win in the Midi Libre. But Anderson's win in the four-day Tour de l'Aude in France was proof enough. The Tour de l'Aude was typically a race controlled by Peugeot, leading to Anderson's first ever professional stage race win. The team finished with two other riders in the top ten overall – Millar, fifth at 8:06 and Bossis, ninth at 8:48. It was a major boost for team morale and gave Hinault a preview of their likely strength in the coming Tour. It left Anderson on song and looking forward to the Tour.

The Tour came and on stage six from Saint Gaudens to the ski station of Pla D'Adet, Anderson, unsure of how to race that day, faced his first ever Tour mountain stage. He felt good, but didn't know how good. Hence he settled on following someone steady 'like Hinault' rather than trying to match the Colombians.

It was a champion climber who won the stage – Belgian Lucien Van Impe. But though he took the stage most attention was on the battle between two men following him at 0:27 – Hinault and Anderson. Hinault's contempt for the Australian 'daring' to challenge him was clear. It was even worse when Anderson just sat on his wheel. It was only when De Muer told Anderson that he could work 'a bit' that Anderson took a turn at the front. 'It was just as well, as Hinault was going off his block as I wasn't working,' said Anderson.

The Breton really lost his cool when Anderson naively offered Hinault a drink from his bidon 'I didn't even know who Hinault was. I couldn't even pronounce his name. But I was there with him and when I gave him my bidon I was only trying to be sportsmanlike. I figured something was really up with him when he hit it away,' recalls Anderson. 'I suppose I should have been intimidated by it all, but I wasn't. Heck I was Australian and couldn't even spell Hinault, let alone know who he was.'

Once rid of Spaniards Marino Lejarreta and Alberto Fernandez, and Belgian Claude Criquielion, Hinault Anderson and Van Impe were all racing for the stage win. But Van Impe settled that when he attacked with eight kilometres to go. While Hinault may have thought he had silenced Anderson's challenge by outsprinting him for second place by half a wheel, the reality of seeing Anderson with the leader's yellow jersey and knowing he was in second place overall at 0:17 rubbed more salt into the fiery Breton's wounds. And as everyone knows, *les blaireaux* [badgers] always bite back when they are wounded.

Hinault's immediate post-stage reaction revealed his anger. 'Anderson never wanted to work. It was not an indication of a champion. He never got off my wheel,' he scoffed after. But Anderson's gall to stand up to Hinault's wrath was an inspiration to a world accustomed to accepting 'the badger's' authority. Peugeot, having seen Bernaudeau lose 4:30 and virtually any chance of winning the Tour, was now undecided whether to defend the untested and relatively unknown Anderson, or whether to try and get their top star Bernaudeau back into contention. Opinions were mixed. Realising the sensitivity of his position De Muer remained guarded. Overnight, as Hinault's anger calmed to the level where he finally admitted that 'Anderson was a rider with potential' and Anderson tried to come to terms with his own achievement, all of sporting France was in a fever over what happened that day. One significant vote in Anderson's favour came from Tour de France *doyenne* Jacques Goddet. 'Peugeot should now play Anderson's card,' he boldly judged in his daily diary piece in *L'Equipe* the next day.

In the build-up to the next day's showdown between Hinault and Anderson – a 27.7km time trial from Nay to Pau – the 'Australian phenomenon' was analysed, questioned and judged in every way. One obvious question was how Anderson, as an Australian in a French team, had adapted to the system if at all. The response of Michel Laurent confirmed that even within his own team, Anderson was not the popular figure a yellow jersey wearer should be. When asked, Laurent told *L'Equipe*: 'Yes and no . . . Yes, because he is a guy who always smiles, is nice and happy when all goes well. No, because he hardly speaks French so there is a barrier. At the table in the evening when we talk about the race, he can't take part in the conversation.' Anderson was never confronted by such criticism from team-mates like Laurent. And one can only wonder how they would have fared on an English-speaking team if the tables had been turned. Certainly, Anderson sensed that official attitudes towards him changed after he took the yellow jersey. But he was readily aware of the 'barrier' Laurent was referring to. 'Roche could understand all the jokes and everything that went on. I used to kind of go along and laugh but then I would wonder, shit . . . what are they laughing about,' he says.

De Muer was never going to publicly condemn Anderson, but by the time he left Peugeot after 1983 the two were far from best friends. Of Anderson, at the time, he said: 'Once installed they [foreign riders] fit in quickly. The best example of this adaptability is Phil Anderson who, when he arrived had no understanding whatsoever of tactics. But he rode, made mistakes and learned. He watched the others and assimilated all the little tricks that go into being a true professional.'

If anything Anderson's first day in yellow – the first ever by an Australian – troubled him later: 'I didn't sleep too well because of the jersey. It was a dream, a dream come true. I never thought I would be riding in Europe let alone the Tour de France.'

Furthermore, Hinault didn't just want the yellow jersey back, he **had** to have it. And while Anderson was forced to surrender it, he didn't do so without a fight. Hinault won the stage and took the yellow jersey, but Anderson's third at 0:30 after leading Hinault until 11km and keeping the gap at only 0:03 after 14km was creating a welter of interest. And when he finally lost the jersey by only 0:13, even Hinault gave his 'blessing' to Anderson's new-found label as a star for the future. 'I thought he had ridden very well. After all the time trial is one of my specialities. He proved today that he is going to be a very good rider indeed,' he said. Hinault went on to consolidate his lead; Anderson confirmed his reputation and led in the young rider's competition which awarded him the white jersey.

The French race leader was not in any danger of not winning the Tour for the third time, but Anderson was proving to be a potential winner for future years as he was still

Roche and Berland (right). . . an uneasy alliance

second overall after 18 stages. Their feud remained fairly dormant until stage 16, the 38.5km time trial at Mulhouse where Hinault passed Anderson with 10km to go to win the stage. Anderson, who was fourth and then dropped to a 2:58 deficit, didn't let Hinault get away – despite earning the wrath of following commissaires for alleged slipstreaming. And fittingly the two finished near-enough together.

The following day, stage 19 in the Alps from Morzine to L'Alpe D'Huez brought Anderson back to reality. Not only did he lose his second place to Hinault after finishing 17:06 behind stage winner Dutchman Peter Winnen, but he also lost the white jersey to the victorious Dutchman. To be fair, Anderson was never a bad climber as was thought, but as for winning the Tour, his inability to follow the best on the climbs would be revealed as his biggest weakness and drastically change the odds. De Muer would have thought so, especially as Anderson's team-mates, Bernaudeau and Laurent lost only 4:16 and 4:27 respectively. But Anderson was young and as De Muer said, he knew how to learn from his mistakes. He never gave up hope of pegging back his overall place and claiming the white jersey. By the end of stage 23, after a series of strong stage placings he was back to tenth overall and the white jersey was his again. He held onto his claim to both victories right up to the finish on stage 24 at Paris, where Hinault won once more. Anderson's result was the best ever by an Australian since Sir Hubert Opperman's 12th in 1931.

Peugeot may have been disappointed in Bernaudeau's sixth place overall, but the team's victory in the team's category, and Anderson's in the young rider's competition were enough to keep De Muer smiling as he looked to 1982.

Anderson didn't join Jones, Millar and Roche for the Tour de L'Avenir. He was naturally a contender for the lucrative post-Tour criteriums. And his next objective was to be the world championships at Prague. But that goal and every other one pencilled in for the season were scrubbed when he broke his finger at the Chaam criterium in Holland in a crash which also killed a young spectator.

Two operations and the inevitable period of recuperation from the Tour and injury gave De Muer no choice but to give Anderson an early mark for the season. Anderson didn't complain about that. He locked up his Belgian residence, then at Lockeren, for the winter and returned to Australia where he married his American fiancé, Anne Robel. Returning to Europe in 1982 with 4,000km training kilometres in his legs he found that Peugeot had added to its English-speaking force Sean Yates. There were now five English-speaking riders in the 20-strong team with himself, Yates, Millar, Jones and Roche.

Anderson's main aim was again the Tour. And he wanted to do better than his tenth place in 1981. He felt the route was better suited to his talents – or comparative climbing weakness. With two seasons behind him, he knew 1982 was a year he had to show he could produce consistent results. He was religiously devoted to Peugeot and De Muer. 'The *directeurs sportifs* are pretty old fashioned, but they are the bosses and we have to do what we are told,' he said.

The Spring classics didn't see Anderson shine as expected. He was fifth in the Amstel Gold and in the leading 13-man break, which also included Roche. But once Roche got away with eventual winner, Dutchman Jan Raas, Anderson had little choice but to confine his ambitions to third place, and when that came down to a sprint Anderson stood little chance against the likes of Irishman Sean Kelly and German Gregor Braun.

Peugeot notched up many wins and top placings: Laurent won the Tour Mediterranean and Dauphiné Libéré, Duclos-Lassalle was first in the Tour de L'Oise and second in Paris – Nice, Jones was second in Het Volk, Roche was third in the Four Days of Dunkirk and Bernaudeau won the Midi Libre after finishing second in the Route du Sud. Meanwhile to secure his Tour berth, Anderson banked on his 1981 results and several early season appearances helping Peugeot riders to win races.

When July arrived and stage two of the Tour had finished, Anderson was established, backing De Muer's belief that the only way to harrass Hinault was to take the offensive. Anderson won the 246km stage from Basel in Switzerland to Nancy, and he did so by attacking five other breakaways with 10km to go. In the group with him were: team-mate Laurent, Frenchmen Marc Madiot from Hinault's team, Bernard Vallet, and Dutchmen Henk Lubberding and Peter Winnen. Anderson was full of praise for Laurent after. 'I was doing most of the work with Vallet and Laurent. But I owe him [Laurent] a lot because it was he who was doing a lot of the work at the end, and it was he who did so much to get the break away.'

Anderson would not win a Tour stage again for ten years. But more importantly, Anderson took the yellow jersey from Belgian Ludo Peeters. 'I intend to hang onto this jersey for a lot longer this time.' And he did. The yellow jersey was his for the next nine days, despite challenges from Kelly and imminent capture by Hinault who had won the Tour of Italy a month before. As Anderson expected, his fate arrived on the stage 11 time trial at Valence d'Agen. And it was Hinault who rode in to take the jersey back after he finished second, but still 2:47 clear of Anderson in the 68km test.

In a sign of the times, De Muer didn't hesitate to declare Anderson team leader, despite Anderson previously saying that he thought Bernaueau would assume his role once the Pyrenenees arrived. But then circumstances left De Muer with little choice, Anderson was still third overall at 2:03 when stage 12 from Fleurance to Pau began and it ended with Anderson finishing second to Kelly, and Bernaudeau being dropped on the Col de Soulor, finishing 3:53 down after injury. The choice to protect Anderson all the way to Paris was an obvious step – he was now second overall, still at 2:03, while Peugeot's next best overall was Bernaudeau in 22nd place at 11:34.

Anderson needed help the next day, the second Pyreneen stage from Pau to St Lary Soulan. Anderson took the race to Hinault by attacking the Frenchman twice. But then he paid for his efforts, blowing up as Hinault simultaneously attacked. And were it not for the support from his team-mate Laurent who had attacked earlier, Anderson may have lost more than the two minutes he did on Hinault. But 24 hours later, after Hinault won stage 14 the 32.5km time trial at Martigues, Anderson was unable to call on team support again. In the 'race of truth' he was 20th at 2:05 to Hinault and while still second overall was 5:17 down, with the Alps still to come, Anderson's threat was quickly diminishing.

Still, he had given the Badger a greater headache than anyone else in recent times. He lost time on two of the three Alpine climbs, but then on the third from L'Alpe D'Huez to Morzine – stage 17 – he was seventh at 2:28 to a victorious Winnen and only beaten for sixth place in a sprint against none other than Hinault!

That 17th stage included four mountain passes and Anderson belied his exhuastion and troubles of the previous two days by riding in the front third of the bunch all day. 'Once we were on the first Col I knew I was okay, but everyone else was suffering. Lots of riders were nervous as they fought to try and stay in the front,' said Anderson. In fact his only problem was an early puncture, nearby was team-mate Bernaudeau, and he could have asked the Frenchman for his wheel – and Bernaudeau would have given it – but Anderson amazingly couldn't bring himself to do it and rode five kilometres with a flat, having to wait for a team car to come and change bikes. 'He was a good guy and trying to get back in the reckoning. He had lost his team leadership in the Pyrenees and some pride. So I didn't like to ask him to give me his wheel,' recalls Anderson.

When Anderson rode into Paris and the finish, still in fifth place overall at 12:16, De Muer was once again rubbing his hands in delight. And on all accounts Anderson was doing the same. But it would be all for nothing. De Muer was victim to a purge within Peugeot and ousted as *directeur-sportif*. And in 12-months time Anderson would himself be facing a ruptured association with Peugeot and its new team director the former assistant *directeur-sportif*, Roland Berland.

Anderson had not paved the way for smooth negotiations for his 1983 contract. He horrified Peugeot by bringing a solicitor with him to the discussions – something that had never before been done in cycling. Peugeot were willing to increase his salary from 6,000 francs a month on the second year, but it was not to Anderson's liking or that of his legal advisers.

'They were offering me seven or eight thousand francs a month, but that was after all the races I had won, and having worn the yellow jersey for so long. It wasn't right,' recalls Anderson. 'I said I wanted a bit more, but they said I wasn't worth it. I couldn't read French and that was what the contract was written in, so I turned up with a solicitor from Paris. But he read the contract and said it was a piece of shit, that wasn't worth the paper it was written on.'

There were three points in the contract which Anderson's solicitor pointed out. 'There were no bonuses, it said Peugeot could fine me any time they wanted and that if I was sick for longer than a week I could be thrown off the team. Looking back it was pretty funny really . . . all these people around a table and me with my reps in suits fighting for a few extra dollars. But in reality, it was something the sport needed.'

Anderson's tactic hit the headlines the next day, especially as the firm he used to negotiate on his behalf was used by Formula One racing drivers. 'The papers started saying that I wanted a Formula One driver's salary which was totally exaggerated.'

Anderson's Spring campaign in 1983 marked the first stage of his eventual transition from a Tour to a classic racer. The Tour was his main objective, but after he finished second in the Tour of America and returned to Europe to take third in Liège – Bastogne – Liège and then win the Amstel Gold, a new direction became evident.

Winning the Amstel Gold was a major breakthrough for Anderson. It was his first classic win – a major hallmark in any racer's career – and the first for Peugeot since 1978. It also improved his self-confidence in the classics which would inspire him throughout his career, especially after winning the Tour became virtually impossible.

Anderson won the Amstel in a solo attack from seven breakaways: Dutchmen Jan Raas who was a five-times winner, Raas' TI Raleigh team-mate Adj Wijnands, Steven Rooks, Adrie Van der Poel and Joop Zoetemelk; Belgian Etienne De Wilde and Rooks' American team-mate Jonathan Boyer. Anderson made his winning move with 21km to go. 'No one was really working and Raas and Wijnands were waiting for their team-mates to come up. So I attacked and Zoetemelk came with me,' recalls Anderson. The pair got 0:35 lead but at the top of the Valkenberg climb with 15km to go: 'I turned around just before the top and they were 50m back. Joop sat up, but I attacked again and that was it,' adds Anderson who was clear away with a 0:31 lead.

Winning the one Dutch classic on the calendar aroused interest from many Dutch teams. Unlike Peugeot which just focused on the Tour, Dutch and Belgian teams often base their whole season on the classics. And when Anderson fell out with Peugeot later in the year, it was no suprise that the Dutch Panasonic team snapped him up.

His win did not shift his focus from that year's Tour. Anderson was set for undisputed team leadership, and as July neared, he justified the decision to his team-mates, with a second place to Roche and a stage win in the Tour of Romandy, and tenth in the Grand Prix of Frankfurt. But in the hectic final lead-up to the Tour, Anderson's position suddenly became rocky.

The Dauphiné Libéré opened Anderson's eyes to the fact that his future at Peugeot was not all that promising. After winning the prologue, he rode superbly to help Frenchman Pascal Simon win and then finished sixth overall. But then in a mandatory drug test, both were tested positive. Simon had the victory taken away from him and handed to American Greg LeMond while Anderson was also relegated. Both riders explained that the substance had been in a mixture to treat hay-fever and little was made of the scandal. Barely a paragragh in the French press, and as far as can be checked, it was never reported in the English, American or Australian press. However behind the scenes a fight erupted between Anderson and Peugeot. As Anderson recalls:

'It was kept pretty quiet, that Simon and myself were both suffering from hay-fever. The team doctor gave us something to help our breathing. Then three weeks later we got a letter in the mail saying we were positive. It ended up that what the doctor gave us, was something which had just been put on the list. It was all hush hush, although there was a blurb in the paper. So I asked the doctor to come out and say that he administered something to us. And they [Peugeot] said they wouldn't do it. So it looked like Simon and I took the shit. Luckily it never got a lot of publicity, but still, it was there.'

Having won the final Tour run up – the Tour de l'Aude – for the second time, Anderson was introduced in the official pre-Tour team presentation as leader. And Roche, making his debut, was a natural second-choice should Anderson find himself struggling in the mountains. In the light of Hinault's absence due to a knee-tendon injury, it was declared an 'open' Tour. 'Every team believes they have a winner in their ranks,' said Berland before the start. 'I have two. First Phil Anderson who will be ready to go from the off. Then there is Stephen Roche who will be looking for a surprise break.'

It seemed Anderson's status was secure as the Tour raced towards the Pyrenees with him nicely placed third overall. But no matter what argument any Frenchman was to give later, what happened on stage ten from Pau to Bagnères-de-Luchon, was interpreted as nothing but treachery by Anderson. It had nothing to do with Millar, brilliantly winning the stage. If anything Anderson was pleased for his former ACBB team-mate. Rather it was the successful bid by Simon to attack and take the yellow jersey. Anderson might have had an idea that something was up when he crashed earlier on on the Col d'Aubisque and lost his shoe. Not one team-mate waited to bring him back and the energy used to rejoin the peloton would prove costly when Simon went off. According to Anderson, he was race leader on the road and would have taken the yellow jersey had Simon not attacked as he did. But once Simon did go, Anderson was unable to do anything but watch him race away. Team ethics say you never chase down a team-mate. But Anderson had no idea Simon, eighth overall at 2:45 at the start, was actually racing for his yellow jersey.

'I was the protected leader. We had the last climb to go at the end of the day and I was going to get the yellow jersey because all the guys in front of me overall were dropped. I was leader on the road and working with Beat Breu, Johan van de Velde, Peter Winnen and Zoetemelk, but Simon was doing nothing. He was just sitting on. Then he attacked and I had to sit there.' says Anderson who then fell to tenth overall at 9:22.

After placing third on the stage Simon crashed the next day and sustained a hairline fracture of his shoulder blade. For the next six days until he abandoned in the Alps, not a soul attacked him as they knew he would never make it to Paris. Peugeot lapped up the publicity of having the yellow jersey. A French newcomer named Laurent Fignon, who was second overall, just waited until Simon dropped out before taking the lead, and his first of two Tours. Anderson on the other hand was suddenly bound to being a domestique.

Opinions still vary as to who was right or wrong. Frenchmen like Peugeot team-mate Legeay still believe Simon would have won the Tour had he not broken his shoulder blade. 'If Phil had it, then he should have been able to be stay up with Pascal. But where was he? No . . . Simon deserved to have the yellow jersey,' says Legeay.

Nobody in the French team thought any differently. Even Roche, although he confesses today that Simon's act was not the right thing to do. 'When we finished that day and I said: "Congratulations Pascal" I thought it was great at the time. But I found out later that he would do the same thing in other races too. So looking back, it wasn't fair to Phil really.'

Anderson took the insurrection against his leadership as a hint to find a new team. He would have no trouble doing that. 'There was nothing said but I think Simon knew I was pissed off because he knew I was going to be in the yellow jersey. Nobody said anything to me about it, nobody. But still I don't think I would have won the Tour then anyway,' says Anderson. 'That's the way it goes I guess. Two years before in 1981 when Kuiper was in the team I went with Hinault and got the jersey. But then I didn't attack. I followed Hinault. In 1983 Simon attacked.'

Anderson and Peugeot's feelings for each other were mutual. Anderson was not offered a new contract. And he didn't ask for one. A few days after the Tour, the news was revealed that he would join Panasonic in 1984. 'I was disappointed with what happened on the Tour and with the Dauphiné Libéré. But there were also too many leaders,' he said.

The Australian bided his time with Peugeot by racing the City Centre criterium series in Great Britain. It may have been preparation for the world champion-ships at Altenrhein in Switzerland, but he still won two of the five events and finished second overall in the series. Then in the worlds he was ninth at 1:36 to a 22-year-old LeMond who beat Van der Poel and Roche for the gold medal. But Anderson was the key aggressor in the race, having led an eight-man break for five laps before it was caught with two to go.

His career at Peugeot may have ended in disappointment, but Anderson had not lost his fighting punch. As the years ahead would show, his best was yet to come.

To most of us the biggest curiosity of Robert Millar's professional career was that it took him three years to get a place on Peugeot's Tour de France team. Ask him about it, and the reason is clear – *the directeur-sportif* Maurice de Muer didn't like him.

The hesitation to enter him in the world's biggest race does not seem justified considering his results to date, making him Britain's most successful stage racer in years, fourth and best climber in the 1984 Tour and second in the 1985 and 1986 Vuelta à España, and 1987 Giro d'Italia in which he was also best climber.

There were so many leaders at Peugeot when he joined in 1980, it was easy for a rider whose success may have been slow at taking off to be left by the wayside. And if you had personality clashes with Peugeot directors it was even easier. Even though Millar proved himself a gifted amateur at ACBB, it took a stunning 11th place at the 1980 World Championships at Sallanches, where Hinault won, for people to start talking about his 'potential' as a professional. Millar revelled on the Sallanches circuit which included the steep 2.7km climb of Domancy Hill and was covered 20 times. Many later labelled it as the toughest ever in a world title. But Millar was still with the leaders with five laps to go. 'I thought I could make a name for myself. I wasn't riding at 100%, but I couldn't attack. Then the 18th time up the hill Hinault attacked and that was it I couldn't hold it,' he said. But Millar admitted he found the first year as a professional hard – most do. 'It was very difficult at first. I was meant to ride many of the early season races, but I wasn't up to it,' he told *Cycling Weekly* at the year end post-mortem. He still finished two of the three classics he started: Milan – San Remo and the Tour of Flanders. Ghent – Wevelgem was the one he didn't finish. He also finished the Dauphiné Libéré. But his best result, apart from a third in the mountain stage of the two-day Criterium National where he was 12th overall, was 14th in the Midi Libre and third in the Tour de Vaucluse. The key missing element was stamina.

The success at Sallanches was a morale booster for the diminutive Scot. It at least gave De Muer something to think about for 1981. 'If you are riding well he's okay. But if not then he might not talk to you,' said Millar, not saying which end of the

Peugeot *directeur-sportif* Maurice de Muer (centre) with Roche (left) and Gilbert Duclos-Lassalle, stars from two generations and two vastly different cultures

scale he had sat for most of the year. Millar is blunt about his rocky relationship with De Muer. 'As a *directeur-sportif*, I respected him. But I know he hated my guts. Like Weigant at ACBB he liked big guys and I was small. I remember at the start of Paris–Nice in 1989, he came up to me and said: 'Millar . . . what are you still doing here', as if he didn't even know what I had done in my career or that I should have survived.'

It took until May 1981 before Millar revealed the same signs of form he showed at Sallanches. And that came in the Tour of Romandy with a seventh place overall at 3:06 to Swedish winner Tommy Prim. Earning a place in the Tour de France team was his objective and it seemed he was just hitting the right form when he finished fifth in the Tour de l'Aude won by Phil Anderson, and then seventh in the Dauphiné Libéré. But still, De Muer felt Millar was not ready for the 'big one'. Millar was kept on the bench.

His 14th place at the world titles in Prague proved his value for the Tour de l'Avenir where he, Roche and Jones all rode to help Simon win. Millar's role was instrumental, especially in the mountains where he kept the tempo at the front of the bunch. Finishing 11th overall, he was rewarded with the best team rider's award. Millar was disappointed at not winning a stage or finishing in the top three overall. But Simon was a friend and he was happy he won. It was also a message for De Muer. 'I hope that this Tour de l'Avenir has shown my bosses at Peugeot that I am worth a place in the Tour de France next year,' he said.

Sadly, 1982 was a similar story. He was clearly not a classics man at the time – unlike now where he is suited for hilly races like Flèche Wallonne and Liège–Bastogne–Liège. The big men of Peugeot in the A Team were up in Belgium and Holland, Millar rode in the 'Y team'. 'The Y team was the number two team, which in other teams is often labelled the B team. 'It was full of wankers really. And we called it 'Y' because Y is so far off from A, further than B, it's not worth worrying about. I always thought it was because when you got in the A team there was this attitude of why the hell are you here!' he says.

Racing in the Y team meant tackling events like the 'open' Circuit de la Sarthe: in that he was sixth overall and highest placed professional. Then in the Tour of Romandy he once more took seventh place. Then he accompanied Jones, Anderson and Simon to the Tour of Colombia where Simon was team leader. But Millar floundered in the high altitude peaks there. 'We went there more because of the money,' he says. He returned to France to ride for Bernaudeau in the Midi Libre. Bernaudeau won, but once more Millar was instrumental in the victory. And as a result Millar was told by Bernaudeau that he would 'probably' be in the Tour and had better get ready. 'I didn't ride the British championship because I was down as a probable for the Tour. The race was on a Sunday and I was to have been at a Tour meeting on the Monday,' he said then.

De Muer once more flicked Millar. When asked why he omitted Millar and put in Frenchman André Chalmel at the last minute, De Muer simply said: 'By taking Millar instead of Chalmel I risk breaking up the equilibrium of the team. Don't forget that with Laurent, Simon and Anderson we are already well covered for riders to help Bernaudeau.' Millar once more put it down to De Muer's personal dislike for him. 'As it was I only found out through a friend that I wasn't in the Tour team, he'd read about it. No one bothered to tell me,' said Millar.

It was not until six weeks after the Tour and at the Tour de L'Avenir that Millar had a chance to show his potential. While surrendering his place on the British world's team because he felt he lacked condition, he still finished second overall to LeMond in the French race. Finishing 10:18 down, his ability to defend second position against a number of challenges in the mountains was astounding. Millar was riding with new vigour – no doubt boosted by the news of De Muer's departure from Peugeot in 1983. Millar had greater affinity with Roland Berland, who would be promoted to number one director.

'The French riders have been afraid to say anything against De Muer,' said Millar. 'He treats us like animals. For instance he tells me to go with every break in the first hour of the race and then says he is surprised that I wasn't with the leaders at the end.'

By the end of 1982 Millar was desperate to ride in the Tour. 'Every year I fight for a place in the Tour. It's my burning ambition,' he said as 1982 came to an end. It was an ambition that 1983 would finally make a reality. And it was no coincidence that De Muer was no longer a part of the team either.

In the build up to the Tour Millar was in terrific form. He finished third in the mountainous Dauphiné Libéré; and was officially elevated to second three weeks later after Simon was found positive in a dope test. The Tour was fast approaching and Millar was ready. Crashes, several breaks and a general spell of settling to the big event were the characteristics of Millar's first week on the Tour. He knew when the moment would be right for him to make his mark – in the Pyrenees. And he took the opportunity as soon as it arrived – stage 10 from Pau to Bagnères-de-Luchon where Simon would also take the yellow jersey and set off a battle for team leadership with Anderson.

The stage included four giant mountain passes. On the descent of the first, the Col d'Aubisque, Frenchman Jacques Michaud began the drama with a solo attack, in pursuit on the next climb the Col du Tourmalet was Colombian Patrocinio Jimenez.

Millar was the only one who could follow: 'When I counter-attacked with Jimenez I knew I was going to win.'

At the Tourmalet's 2113m summit Millar and Jimenez had long passed Michaud and were four minutes clear of the nearest chasers. The two leaders stayed together until the final climb up the Col de Peyresourde where Millar attacked. Like a freed bird, Millar flew away from Jimenez and left behind three years of frustrating neglect to his talent. Once over the top, it was all down hill to the finish and his first ever professional win. What better race to claim it in. Yet his solo victory by 0:02 on a chasing Pedro Delgado of Spain was not only a personal triumph, but a historical one too. It was the first Tour stage win by a Scottish rider. It was also the first stage win by a Briton in eight years – Barry Hoban being the last with his eighth stage win at Bordeaux in 1975. It was also a great day for Peugeot as Simon's third had made him race leader – a position he would later lose in the Alps, when the agony of a broken shoulder blade sustained in a crash would prove too great to bear.

Boosted by the win, Millar set his sights on the King of the Mountains polka-dot jersey which belonged to Jimenez. He took the jersey from the Colombian three stages later, although stomach troubles cost him the lead on stage 15. 'It's inevitable in three weeks. You go through a cycle and your condition will vary,' he told *Cycling Weekly's* Martin Ayres.

Millar rode on to Paris where he finished 14th overall; the highest place by a British rider since Tom Simpson's 14th in 1964. But Millar has never liked comparisons; what was important to him was proving that he did have precisely what De Muer thought he lacked – winning potential. And while he raced the year out without any significant success, he wanted to drive the point home in 1984 even though De Muer was long gone.

A second place in Nice – Alassio in late February of 1984 confirmed he was still on the boil. He was one of five Peugeot members in the winning 13-man break, which also included a victorious Roche, now riding for La Redoute. Then in Paris – Nice a fortnight later, he took the overall lead on stage four (A) from Orange to Mont Ventoux.

Never before so strong so early in the season, Millar was the protagonist of all the action too: he attacked on the lower slopes of the Ventoux, then caught by a chase group including Hinault, Kelly, Roche, Laurent, Germany's Raymond Dietzen, and Frenchmen Eric Caritoux and Jean-Claude Bagot, he attacked again with three kilometres to go and would have won the stage had not Caritoux fought back in the last kilometre to take it by a second. Millar may have been angry about the loss, but he had done enough to move up from 15th place to first overall and take the leader's jersey.

His reign as race leader ended 24 hours later in the fifth stage from Miramas to La Seyne-sur-Mer. The result was dubious. Worker protests in French cycle races are not uncommon. And naval dockmen from the town of La Ciotat saw Paris – Nice as a prime vehicle to publicise their cause. With 35km and one climb to go they blocked the route, and consequently the passage of an 18-strong breakaway group yet to be joined by Millar. He should have been there, but for his poor descent, he would have been a threat to Hinault's lead.

While the Scot and his Peugeot charges tried chasing the break down, up front at the protest site a fight broke out between a furious Hinault and some of the dockers. It took a good 20 minutes for the pandemonium to settle down, in which time the main field was there. And while organisers allowed the break to start again with its original

0:53 lead, by shortening the course by eight kilometres to make up for lost time, they drastically minimised the chance for Millar and his Peugeot team-mates to reel them in for good.

All he could do in the ensuing 27km was watch Kelly, then placed second overall at 0:30, ride off into the horizon and take the lead and eventual third successive victory. Millar, finishing in the main bunch at 2:18, fell to sixth overall at 1:53. That margin increased again the next day to Mandelieu where Millar tried to attack on the climbs, but was duped by the descents where Kelly and Roche formed an Irish alliance to try and outwit Hinault. At 2:26 to Kelly going into the final Col d'Eze time trial, Millar didn't stand a chance even though his fifth place on the stage at 1:13, was good enough to hold on to sixth place overall.

The Tour of Romandy three months later, gave Millar another opportunity to show his form. He was confidently leading again after winning the mountainous stage two from Vevey to Crans-Montana. He won the stage with flair and panache. But he went into the final stage five (B) time trial over 26km with a slender lead of 0:10 on Roche, 0:11 on his team-mate Simon, and 0:26 and 0:27 respectively on the Swiss pair of Jean-Marie Grezet and Niki Ruttimann. All four would beat Millar who in turn finished fifth overall at 1:14 to a victorious Roche. He was definitely a great climber and full of gusto, but just as descending proved a weakness at Paris–Nice, so too did time trialling at Romandy.

He was still a natural selection for Peugeot's Tour de France team. Berland named him as the team's number two man behind Simon. That was fine for Millar whose primary goal for the race was to go for the King of the Mountains title and win a stage. The second of his two goals came prematurely. As in the year before, Millar rode off to win the very first Pyrrenean leg, the 228km stage 11 from Pau to Guzet Neige. His win was all the more incredible as he was no longer the unknown and underestimated Tour neophite in 1983. He was a marked man yet he still managed to finish 0:41 clear at the mountain top finish after attacking from three other breakaways on the final ascent. He also moved up to seventh overall but conceded team leadership to his friend Simon. 'I am not a Tour winner. Simon still has more of a chance,' said Millar who had better chances of winning the KOM jersey worn by his old Peugeot leader, Bernaudeau one of Millar's fellow breakaways and fourth on the stage. 'I'll let Bernaudeau look after it for now. I know the Alpine climbs and that's where I hope to take it from him,'said Millar.

That is exactly what he did on stage 17 from Grenoble to L'Alpe d'Huez which saw Frenchman Laurent Fignon take the yellow jersey from his Renault domestique, Vincent Barteau who had worn it since stage five. Millar was fourth at 3:05 to the Colombian stage winner he beat at Guzet Neige, Luis Herrera. And that was enough to beat Bernaudeau, as well as move up to fourth overall at 8:25. His team-mate Simon was now 11th at 13:33, but Millar's priority was still the polka-dot climber's jersey. Was he being loyal to Simon or realistic about his own overall chances? 'It's more important to win a jersey than get a high placing,' he said after the stage. 'I scored on all the high mountains today. I wanted to prove I can climb not only in the Pyrenees but in the Alps too.' Millar proved that without a problem.

The next day he was fifth to La Plagne, ninth at Morzine and fourth at Crans Montana. He may not have won another Alpine stage there, but his consistency was without reproach. He eventually won the King of the Mountains by 72 points from Fignon, and was fourth overall at 14:42 to the yellow-jerseyed Fignon. LeMond was third overall, Kelly fifth and Anderson tenth.

Millar was still noncommittal about winning the Tour. 'I could not win, but I could go one or two places higher,' he said then. And he still believes it was so. 'I thought then that the best I could ever do was to get in the top three.' The 1984 winner, Laurent Fignon agreed: 'He's limited in the time trials and hasn't the power that is needed to be a Tour winner. I think the climbers' prize is enough to keep him happy.'

One other ambition of Millar's though was the world title. He had proved twice that given the right course, he could get in the running. He just needed that extra kick and strength to go the distance. The 1984 world titles at Barcelona, Spain seemed a prime opportunity considering his strength in the Tour. But once more the rainbow jersey eluded him. He was one of the most aggresssive but finished sixth at 1:08 to Belgian winner, Claude Criquielion.

By now the Scot, who Berland once described as 'a small car with a big engine' had developed a reputation as a true individualist and a gifted climber. Surprisingly his vegetarian preference survived in a world where the thinking was still that bloody, rare, T-bone steaks were the best fuel for any cyclist. But that didn't worry Millar who actually admitted: 'I am an individualist. I have my own personality. And I am a vegetarian. I have the impression that I bore everyone with my cornflakes, wheatgerm, my honey, my pollen. What do you expect? I have always had to make my own way in life. That's why you end up thinking of yourself first. Phil Anderson is the same.'

In any case he thought he was settling down nicely in France. He had moved from Troyes to Lille in northern France after the 1983 season. And he was engaged to Sylvie, a relative of Pascal and Jérôme Simon. Millar knew what he wanted and really didn't mind what others thought, as he said, it was his life, not theirs. But 1985 would prove the value of having a few more friends in the peloton besides the Simon brothers.

In the 1985 Tour of Spain in May, Millar was beaten in the major three-week tour by Spaniard Pedro Delgado. But the Scot's defeat was a result of one of the greatest combines ever seen against any one rider. To this day, any Spaniard will simply look at you in defensive astonishment if you even mention it! When the penultimate stage began, the first of 200km from Alcala de Henares to Segovia, Millar was still the race leader. The only danger, or so he thought, was from Colombian 'Pacho' Rodriguez of the Spanish Zor team who was second overall at 0:10. Delgado, then on the Spanish MG-Orbea team, was at the normally unretrievable margin of 6:13. Despite there being three climbs *en route* to Segovia, the only man Millar really needed to mark was Rodriguez – even though Delgado may have tried to win the stage as Segovia is his home town.

Peugeot, the only French team in the race, were expecting a tough time: Berland had curiously told all the men, who Millar would need as support, to race as hard as they could on the previous day's time trial. 'The whole team was knackered as a result,' recalls Millar. From all accounts, Berland had generated much ill-feeling from the very influential Luis Ocana who was then *directeur-sportif* of the Spanish Fagor team. The crux of that dispute was that Berland had reportedly refused an offer from Ocana to buy his team's services to help defend Millar's 'amarillo' leader's jersey. Berland, overly proud of his team's efforts to go it alone, allegedly boasted to Ocana of Peugeot's supposed invincibility. Sources say Ocana was furious, humiliated and swore to prove to Berland how wrong he was. If it were true Berland might have just as well put a match to Millar's jersey.

On the road to Segovia the next day, attacks began almost immediately on the first climb, the Col de Puerto de la Morcuera. And one by one Peugeot riders started to drop from Millar's side, leaving only Simon and Ronan Pensec in his

The good and the bad for Yates at Fagor. There were many falls (lower) but some high spots such as his 1988 Tour of Spain victory at Jaca (upper)

Back on home soil and racing for the British Raleigh-Banana team. The climax of Sherwen's last racing season is a victory in the 1987 National Road title

company. Sean Yates, then in his fourth year at Peugeot, even abandoned.

Rodriguez gave Millar a shock with his attack on the descent. But it was brought back, although just as quickly followed by more accelerations. And simultaneously, just before the feed station at Raseafria, Millar punctured. Simon and Pensec waited to bring him back, but by that time they were too exhausted to stay with him.

Another attack followed near the top of the second climb to Los Cotos, were Delgado, Rodriguez, Vicente Belda (Kelme), Delgado's team-mate Pello Ruiz-Cabestany and French exile Eric Caritoux (Skil-Kas), and Millar once more dug in and chased them down. His attentive measures to stop the Colombian were clear to all. And when Delgado, Caritoux and another Spanish-based Frenchman Pierre Bazzo (Fagor) attacked again, without Rodriguez alongside them, they hoped Millar would not respond; and the Scot unwittingly obliged.

The final 69km to Segovia saw the Tour of Spain results turned upside down. Delgado caught the surviving member of an earlier leading break, Spaniard Jose Recio (Kelme) before the Los Cotos summit. By the summit of the third climb, the Alot de los Leones, they had 3:15 on Millar who was long without any team-mates or in any proximity to Berland and the team car. 'I didn't even know how far ahead anyone was. I never got a time check,' says Millar.

The worst news came with 23km to go when Millar discovered that their shortfall on Delgado was 4:54. Millar suddenly became aware of Delgado's threat and that virtually the entire peloton was racing against him. And Millar was in a 20-man group which simply wouldn't chase. It included three riders from Delgado's and Recio's teams, Frenchman Jean-Claude Bagot (Fagor), one Dutch Panasonic rider who didn't feel up to riding tempo and other Spaniards – including Rodriguez – who were happy to see Delgado win.

Millar tried vainly to get the others to work. 'But there was no chance. They all knew what was happening. They just sat there, pedalled along and laughed at me. They knew all along what was going on and they thought it was a bloody joke,' he recalls.

Millar had no choice but to ride like fury to the finish and hope that Delgado's lead had not passed the 6:13 mark, never knowing exactly where Delgado was, or if the stage was won. But a huge cheer from the partisan crowd counting the minutes and seconds as Millar was 400m from the finish line heralded his fate. He didn't know it until after finishing, but he had lost the amarillo jersey to Delgado by 400m or 0:36.

When Millar looks back at the 1982 Vuelta, the pain of such a defeat returns. He admits it. Who wouldn't feel cheated? 'I don't have anything against Delgado, nothing at all. He was just the poor sod stuck in the middle. But some of those others guys . . . they are not worth pissing on. The core of the problem was that the organisers wanted Delgado to win, although I think Ocana in the end wanted Ruiz-Cabestany to, as he was trying to get him on his team the next year.

Spaniards are genuinely horrified when it is suggested Millar had the jersey stolen from him. And the fact that Delgado became a hero as a result vindicated their belief. Meanwhile Millar tried again in 1986 without Peugeot's colours. Riding with Panasonic, he still managed to finish second behind Alvaro Pino.

He came into the Tour de France with a ninth place from the Dauphiné Libéré won by Anderson. And then in the Tour which was won again by Hinault – he may not have fared as well as in 1984, but he was still 11th overall and third in the King of the Mountains. In September he won the Tour of Catalonia in Spain. Finally, he decided the best thing he could do was to get out of Peugeot, and the best way, was by attracting interest elsewhere with results. This led him to follow Anderson's move and sign with Panasonic and Peter Post. Although, as he would find, life was not any more pleasant there either.

Few riders ever made the breakthrough into the professional ranks with the triumph that Stephen Roche did in 1981. Early season victories in the Tour of Corsica, Paris–Nice and the Tour de l'Indre et Loire stage races quickly elevated him to celebrity status. Few riders have achieved like Roche. He has suffered much heartache in his personal and professional life, and welcomed applause and praise. In his first year at Peugeot he experienced both and learned quickly that being a champion was not easy. Early on, it was made clear to Roche just where he stood in the pecking order of team protection – at the very bottom!

The day he arrived at the Peugeot training camp at Seillans that February with Millar, he earned De Muer's immediate wrath for being overweight, as he had at the end of his year with ACBB when De Muer reportedly warned: 'You will see, next year the pros will ride so fast that you will lose your fat cheeks and stomach.'

In Roche's very first race, the Grand Prix de Monaco, where he was in a winning break with three others, including team-mates Bernaudeau and Bernard Bourreau, Roche felt he could win and he let De Muer know. The response was that may be true, but 'Bernaudeau must win.' And every time Roche tried to convince De Muer, he got the same reply. Then much to Roche's surprise, came Bourreau's declared wish to take second place. 'In the sprint I braked on the line to let Bernaudeau win. There was a millimetre between me and Bernaudeau. But poor old Bourreau wasn't going to get second,' recalls Roche.

It was a bitter pill to take, but then Roche understood that Peugeot had just signed up Bernaudeau as team leader, and De Muer wanted to give his sponsors a quick return for their investment. Today Roche feels the sport is poorer for not having *directeur-sportifs* like De Muer or Mickey Weigant. 'Today's directors have to deal with sponsors, administration, publicity and everything. Then, guys like De Muer believed that the best way to promote the team and its sponsors was with results. That is what counted. And that's the way it should be,' he says.

An example of De Muer's tight control was to forbid wives and girlfriends around the team. It was not an uncommon policy in any European team, and Roche for the most part heeded the rule. Although as he recalls when he wanted he didn't shy away from telling De Muer what he was up to: 'Once, with Phil Anderson, we told De Muer that our wives were coming during training camp and that we were going off for a day to Cannes. Off we went. Later on though De Muer told me that he appreciated that because he knew darn well that other guys like Gilbert Duclos-Lassalle were climbing out the window every night to go down to the hotel where his wife was. When I told De Muer what I was doing he said: "Well what can I do, you can't say no to men," whereas climbing out the window is what a kid would do. It's childish.'

In the weeks leading up to Roche's amazing run of success, he settled into his team role. His second at Monaco was followed by a seventh at the Grand Prix de St Raphael where Peugeot's top man Jacques Bossis did no better than fifth, and then a fifth in the Tour Mediterranean where Jones was second overall, and in the Tour du Haut Var Roche was 18th. Roche was faring okay, but not brilliantly. Certainly no one was prepared for what was to come at the Tour of Corsica – especially Roche.

It started with Roche joining team-mate Bossis in a break on the penultimate day. Hinault was race leader and his Renault charges tried to chase the two down but failed over the next 120km. As Bossis finally took the leader's jersey, he let Roche win the stage. What Bossis or anyone didn't count on was that Roche would then beat his French team-mate in the final stage time trial. Peugeot's Michel Laurent won the stage from Hinault, but Roche's third was enough to take the overall victory from Bossis.

A Peugeot line-up including Anderson, Jones and naturally Roche, went to Paris – Nice with the hope of helping Laurent win. The 1981 season was important for him and as he was a long-standing member of Peugeot, there was no squabble about his protected leader's status. It seemed Laurent was set for the victory he wanted, taking the leader's jersey from Italian Silvano Contini of the Bianchi team, on the second sector of stage two, a 27km team time trial at Bourbon Lancy. However, Laurent lacked appreciation for Roche's help and conflict looked inevitable.

'Laurent got the jersey, but I was the one who got it for him indirectly in the team time trial. He punctured at the foot of the climb early and we were 0:20 down on the Bianchis. Then on the hill I led all the way and going over the top we were leading by a few seconds. I still led all the way to the finish. We won the stage and Laurent the white jersey. Laurent was there kissing and hugging everybody. And I was there and got nothing at all. Later on the lads spoke about how I drove them over the climb. We saw the photos. They knew I was the one who got the time back. But for me the time wasn't important, it was that I was part of the exploit. And Michel didn't even say thanks,' he recalls.

It was not an intended rift on Roche's behalf, even though the next day's third stage from Bourbon Lancy to Saint Etienne saw Laurent's dream end and, of all people, Roche took over the white jersey. He began the day with every intention of defending Laurent's lead, proving it when he stopped to help Laurent get back onto the peloton when he punctured. 'I was the only one who stopped for him,' says Roche. But as soon as the pair reclaimed their places near the front of the bunch, Belgian Fons De Wolf attacked and then Roche and several others went after him. Peugeot didn't chase, even though everyone expected them to. And by the end of the day he was in the white jersey while Laurent was in tears. Still, De Muer was by now happy to play Roche's cards. He may have felt the 21-year old still had a lot to learn. But Corsica, the setting for the Paris – Nice team time trial offered Roche a chance to hold on to the white jersey; it was a pretty sound prospect. At dinner that night the team pledged their support to Roche.

Roche couldn't sleep that night, and at the start of the fourth stage from Bollene to Miramas he felt ill. When the stage hit the foot of Mont Ventoux, Roche was powerless to stop an attack from Dutchman Adrie Van der Poel – the previous day's stage winner – who took over race leadership thanks to winning the time bonus at the summit. Roche was now back in second place overall at 0:14.

De Muer ordered the Irishman to win the white jersey back at all costs the next day La Seyne to Mandelieu. Every rider was ready to help, including Laurent. It is always a testing stage, perhaps more difficult for its winding, narrow descents. So De Muer suggested he 'go mad' on every one. The tactic had the desired effect. On the final descent, the Tanneron, Van der Poel crashed as he tried to follow the speeding Roche. With his team-mate Anderson riding in a similarly daring fashion to try to win the stage, Roche buried his head to the finish to keep the 0:20 lead on Van der Poel. He did and by the end was back in white, with a slender 0:06 lead on the Dutchman.

With a stage to Nice and the Col d'Eze mountain time trial to go, Roche as good as had the keys to final victory in his hands. He made more time on Van der Poel in both stages and wrote the Dutch rider's epitaph with a victory up the Col d'Eze. With a 1:19 victory to his credit, his Tour of Corsica win no longer seemed the fluke some

French detractors thought it may be.

Even before the Spring classics, people were talking of Roche riding the Tour de France in July – even as team leader, despite Bernaudeau's presence. Although some were not so supportive, including Laurent. He quashed the idea when asked by *L'Equipe* soon after if he would ride for Roche if ordered. 'No I would not. And I don't think De Muer would ask me to. Our strength is in the collectiveness of the team,' said Laurent. And when asked if Roche at least deserved a 'protected rider's status', Laurent added: 'I don't believe so. Will Roche beat Hinault in a time trial? If we were sure then there would be no problem to put ourselves at his service.'

Perhaps the question was academic as Roche didn't want to ride the Tour in his first year. He was exhausted after such a tough and successful start, followed by Spring Classics like Milan – San Remo, the Tour of Flanders, Paris – Roubaix and Flèche Wallonne. He wanted a rest. But De Muer thought otherwise. 'I know he is only 21 but he has nothing more to learn from the professionals. He is healthy and solid. And if he is looked after from now until June I believe it is a sensible project,' he told *L'Equipe*

Roche took a week's break with his girlfriend Lydia before Paris – Roubaix; De Muer was furious – he called him a tourist. On the eve of Flèche Wallonne the next weekend De Muer asked each rider how he was feeling for the coming race, when he got to Roche, the Irishman jokingly responded: 'I'm taking a camera with me. I am going touring.' The ensuing row between the two was watched by all at the dinner table. It had never happened before: 'You just don't do that to Monsieur De Muer,' Roche was told.

Despite his differences with De Muer, the pair developed a mutual respect. After De Muer was deposed from Peugeot Roche still visited him at Seillans, and he proudly recalls the day when De Muer said: 'You're a great guy Stephen. All these guys like Duclos-Lassalle, Bossis, etc. They were my mates at Peugeot and not one of them ever come to see me. They can be 500 yards down the road and none of them come to say hello. We were supposed to be the ones who didn't get on but you come. I respect you because you are the only who stood up to me. That showed in the way you raced.' It did, and still does.

De Muer was determined to get Roche into the 1981 Tour. And it seemed almost certain he would succeed when he won the Tour de l'Indre et Loire that May. But Roche's performance in the mountainous Dauphiné Libéré finally convinced De Muer to think otherwise. Roche did nothing but lose time in his first experience of racing the tortuous Alpine passes of the Tour a month later.

He knew there would be pressure on him to perform in the second half of the season. He may have been a new professsional and normally granted a year's grace to learn. But Roche was a star, like it or not. At the Tour de L'Avenir he rode brilliantly to help team-mate Simon win. Roche won the Etoile des Espoirs stage race, took second place to Switzerland's Daniel Gisiger in the Grand Prix des Nations time trial and an end of season 14th in the Italian Tour of Lombardy won by Dutchman Hennie Kuiper, in which he and Gisiger were in a 104km attack. In the space of 12 months Roche had gone from being an overweight, under-raced and inexperienced novice to a veritable champion who had earned the respect that many great professionals take years to acquire.

It seemed too good to be true. And as 1982 and 1983 proved, it more or less was. Roche's professional career has always been scarred by a frustrating syndrome of 'one year on, one year terribly off,' and the cycle began after a magnificent first year

Roche's greatest moment. He wins the 1987 World Road title at Villach and claims the
'Triple Crown'

'on'. But when 1982 began, Roche had not the slightest inkling that his fortunes would tumble as they did. He was confident and hungry to win. He also knew that with him was a bolstered Anglophile contingent which included himself, Jones, Millar, Anderson and now, Yates.

As Roche then said of the French: 'I get on well with everyone, but it's hard to know who your friends are. They invite you here, there and everywhere, talk to you about this and that, but you're thinking all the time that they are wanting something.' Then asked if there was a conflict or brewing resentment of the English-speaking force at Peugeot, he simply replied: 'At least they've got someone who can win things for them.'

Roche was particularly ambitious to tackle the 1982 Tour now. And he was not afraid of Hinault who had won the Tour in 1978, 1979 and 1981. He may have never raced it, but pundits were tipping Roche as the man most likely to worry the burly Breton. 'Hinault has two arms, two legs just like I have. Last year the choice was between Laurent and Bernaudeau for team leader, but I can beat Hinault in a time trial. The only thing I am not sure about is the mountains,' he commented then.

Only one thing was forgotten – a solid winter training programme. As he said in his autobiography, he 'lived the life of a star' and went to reception after reception. And then he went off to training camp he had only 500km in his legs – the average was three times this amount. The season did not go so well for Peugeot, or for Roche. Laurent won the Tour Mediterranean for a second time and Jones was second in Het Volk. But something was missing, some said Peugeot had too many leaders and quoted the old adage: Too many cooks spoil the broth. The March 26 headline of L'Equipe summed up the problem saying: *Peugeot: Une Harmonie Perturbée*'.

Roche was particularly concerned about his results. His worry grew at the Criterium International where he could not keep up with the leaders. This worried De Muer too, although he simply laid the blame on Roche's fiancée, Lydia who he married later that year, unfairly saying she was a distraction. Roche showed some sporadic signs of his 1981 form: a second behind Jan Raas in the Amstel Gold, ninth in Liège–Bastogne–Liège, and third in the Four Days of Dunkirk. But then in the Dauphiné Libéré in June, Roche was once more struggling until he found himself in one winning break and took fourth place. De Muer, eager to put Roche in his first Tour labelled this as a good sign.

Roche again saw otherwise, especially when the next stage to St Etienne left his legs like dead weights again. Roche saw a doctor that night, abandoned the race – 'the first race I have packed in for five years' – and went to Cologne, Germany for medical tests. They diagnosed chronic fatigue, and finally convinced De Muer that Roche should not race the Tour. 'I have never felt like this all my life. I make an effort and it's as if my legs are burning,' he said then. So once more Roche was on the sidelines for July, although he didn't mind in the slightest. He was desperately in need of recovery before the post-Tour season. In the meantime, English-speaking interest in the Tour was well catered for with Anderson's ten-day spell in the yellow jersey.

Roche never really got back to top form that season. He rode well at the world title road race in Goodwood, England to help Kelly win the bronze medal. For him the goal was the 89km Grand Prix des Nations. But it was a goal clearly beyond his dreams: he finished 19th. Before he had even showered he was looking ahead to 1983; a year which would also see De Muer replaced by Roland Berland as *directeur-sportif*.

Berland was never liked at Peugeot. For a while Millar was the exception. Berland secured his place on the team as De Muer's number two only because he could lure Bernaudeau to the team from Renault-Gitane. Many riders felt he spent most of 1982 trying to lay the foundations of an end of season purge against De Muer. He succeeded.

Roche tried to think positive, and the Tour de France was his only goal. He may have felt he was too young for it in 1981, and too fatigued in 1982. But he was desperate to compete no matter what shape he was in in 1983: 'I am determined too, even if I don't find the form I had two seasons ago.'

A fourth in the Tour Mediterranean and second to Zoetemelk in the Tour du Haut Var proved his winter base was solid enough. Paris – Nice was no longer the objective as in the year before. Peugeot had enough leaders for the 'Race to the Sun' – perhaps too many. In any case, he raced it and was in eighth place, and was Peugeot's highest placed rider up until the sixth stage. He was was forced to quit the race with a day to go because of a knee injury. Berland was furious with Peugeot's poor results there, calling all his charges 'A bunch of tourists.' But Roche wanted nothing more than to keep his resources for the Tour in July.

By May, Roche was back on the road to success: he won the six day Tour of Romandy ahead of his team-mate Anderson, he took the lead on stage three from Fribourg to Loeche-Les-Bains – he and Anderson finished second and third in a winning five-man break. For Roche it was his biggest win in 18 months and the fifth stage race victory of his professional career. It also put his name alongside Anderson's as a likely leader for Peugeot in the Tour. Another win in the Grand Prix de Wallonie in Belgium a few days later reinforced his claim.

Roche was finally ready for his Tour debut after a rest and training camps in the Alps and near the French Atlantic coast. He made his return to competition with several lucrative criteriums at Baltimore in the US followed by the Midi Libre in which he was fifth, and the Tour de L'Aude. It should also have been the lever to greater contractual clout. His was not the only contract up for review, and Roche had thought about leaving Peugeot and going elsewhere before the Tour. However Berland convinced him that by the time the Tour was over and several others like Anderson had been culled, staying with Peugeot would be the best thing to do. Berland needed a new potential winner. Anderson had proved he wasn't up to it and was clearly intent on leaving. Millar was suited only for the King of the Mountains category. And Simon, while breaking his shoulder blade was unfortunate, had shown that putting all of Peugeot's hopes on him was a risk.

No one will know how Simon *would* have fared that year. As it was, once he was in yellow and bandaged up, no French racer was going to attack him. The overall race was virtually neutralised. 'They were all over Simon. They were practically holding his dick while he was pissing. For seven or eight days, there was not even one attack. The mountains were coming up. It was just a question of time. And they knew it was going to explode there. Fignon was back there too, lying in wait. But if Simon hadn't broken his shoulder blade it would have been a completely different race. If it was thought Simon was okay, they wouldn't have waited. A group might have got away. . .'

For Peugeot, Roche was seen as the best chance for the future, even if he did lose time in the first Alpine stage and two Pyreneen legs. That was due more to inexperience than inability, for he was still sixth on the Alpine stage to Morzine, second on the Morzine to Avoriaz mountain time trial, and third in the Dijon time trial as well. But for his massive time loss at L'Alpe d'Huez he would have finished far better than 13th overall at 21:30 to a victorious Laurent Fignon.

As soon as the Tour finished Roche and Berland fell into a bitter dispute over his proposed contract for 1984. Roche agreed to all terms except the fee and bonuses and wanted it increased should he do well in the world titles at Altenrhein, Switzerland. Berland agreed. And his bronze medal there naturally led him to believe that Berland would follow through with the agreement.

Until this point Roche had only signed one of three pages in the contract. 'The first was between Peugeot and Stephen Roche saying they agreed to give a car and a loan for one year etc. The second said they would give me so much per month and so much for bonuses and what have you. And the third just read: *lu et apprové* [read and signed]. I signed the first page, but the second and last pages I didn't sign. I gave him back the three pages and the next day I finished third in the world championships.'

Roche spoke to Berland who reportedly agreed to increase the fee. But when Roche discovered it was only a marginal increase and not comparable to his bronze medal efforts he confronted Berland. The two couldn't come to terms and finally, as Roche recalls: 'Berland said: "Anyway, that's your contract and I'm holding you to it". I said you can't as I haven't signed. Then he says: "I'll hold you by it."'

That angered Roche to looking elsewhere and he was quickly snapped up by La Redoute where Sherwen was still racing. Part of his deal with the French mail order firm was to pay for his legal costs against Peugeot, who had threatened to claim £400,000 compensation.

A battle of different sorts began and Roche had no idea it would follow him for years to come. Yet Roche's conviction was steadfast and it was amazing that in such a crisis he still pulled off several strong end of season results – victories in the Etoile des Espoirs and Paris–Bourges stage races, his fifth place in the Grand Prix des Nations being the most notable. He also played a significant and loyal role in Kelly's first ever classic victory at the Tour of Lombardy.

Meanwhile, Berland sent Roche a solicitor's letter from Peugeot together with a copy of the supposed contract that he signed. 'But only the third page was signed. I hadn't a copy. Anyway at the courts Berland said that I signed it in the office on a certain day. I said no way as he had left it in a hotel for me to collect,' recalls Roche.

'So I got a letter from the secretary of the team saying that on that day Berland did not come to the office and that she never saw me signing a contract. But my solicitor went to court and didn't give anything of this information. I had to get all this myself. I was sure I was going to win, but in the end I lost because of lack of evidence. But then I heard later on that this person used to work for Peugeot.'

At the end of 1985, La Redoute was pulling out of cycling and Roche, headed for Carrera. He was equally as disillusioned with his last team's management. The Italian team agreed to put Peugeot logos on their shorts in 1986 and 1987 as part of the deal in having Roche. For Roche it was a way to soothe Peugeot's claim for compensation.

Meanwhile he and his new legal counsel built a case for an appeal. It took a year, but he finally won. Roche declared his bitter divorce with Peugeot settled.

His memories of Peugeot are more of a reflection on Berland. He believed that Peugeot's reputation suffered as a result of having Berland in command. Sadly the best team members had gone before anyone realised.

Peugeot had once more reached the end of an era. Roche was not the last Anglophile recruit, but he was the last of the big champions that Peugeot let go all too easily.

6 THE PEUGEOT GUARDSMEN

Sean Yates and Allan Peiper never achieved the same glory as their predecessors, but their contribution to the foreign legion story is just as valid. When the domestic bickering between Peugeot administrators and Anglophile riders had died – with the resultant departure of its English speaking corps – Yates and Peiper found themselves with a different role in the team. For them – the rear guard of the foreign legion – triumph was for the team. Their services as domestiques were sacrificial, but neither complained. And for that conviction they were, in their own way, two of the most valuable assets ever to ride for Peugeot.

Sean Yates was the longest serving member of the foreign legion. He has seen both the rise and the fall of this exciting chapter of cycling history. He came in 1982 when Graham Jones, Phil Anderson, Robert Millar and Stephen Roche were all there. He has also ridden under both Maurice de Muer and Roland Berland.

But when he left after 1986 – one year after his 'soul mate' Allan Peiper and Millar had departed – he was the only one holding the fort. He was the only English-speaking rider on the team. And even Berland was gone as *directeur-sportif*, to be replaced by the former rider and former number two, Roger Legeay.

It was an irony that the beginning and end of Yates' career at Peugeot was in the company of Legeay. After leaving his Ashdown Forest home in Sussex, Legeay was the first person he met up with in France. The pair met at the team presentation in Paris which Yates attended by travelling to the French capital on an overnight bus from London. He was still a week away from getting his first car which he used to return to France the next time. Yates arrived in Paris at 6am and sat outside the presentation site for four hours until it began.

At the time all that Legeay wanted was a lift to the training camp at Seillans. 'I was a bit in awe I guess and Legeay asked me if I had a roof rack. I said no, and he said he knew someone who could make one for my car,' said Yates recalling how Legeay arranged to be picked up by the British new professional, who was on a 5,000 francs a month salary. 'When I look back it was a bit lippy of him. I had just turned professional and he was a long standing pro. And here he was trying to hitch a lift off me.'

What Legeay didn't know was that Yates' car was an old model Ford Taunus, so old that the exhaust pipes had to be held on by toe-straps. 'It was an old car with these huge side pipes. It was a V.6 which made a bloody racket. It was really old but I had it resprayed.' Today, Legeay still remembers that trip down to Seillans in what the Peugeot camp jokingly nicknamed *le bateau* [the boat]. Yates arrived at Le Mans as scheduled, with Legeay and another French Peugeot professional Jean Paul Dalibard. The trio headed south to the the Cote d'Azur.

'We put the roof rack on and away we went,' recalls a grinning Yates today. 'But it was always questionable if it would start once I stopped. Couple of times we had to bump start it. It was a bloody long way. I was in my first car. I think they were regretting it, but they asked me for a lift. After training camp we went back to Lille for Het Volk and I gave them a lift, but Graham Jones came instead of Dalibard.'

Yates' first significant result came before Het Volk, at the Grand Prix de Cannes where he was in the winning eight-man break, but finished seventh after crashing and puncturing in the final kilometres. Training camp was an introductory period. Results counted and certainly helped to pay-off the mandatory daily fee of 80 French francs that each Peugeot rider had to pay for accommodation and food – unlike today's professionals who have every expense paid for them. But adapting to the team was vital. And as Yates simply put it, he just 'got on with it.'

Once back to northern Europe and the classics, the reality of professional racing struck hard. He abandoned Het Volk, his first classic, with 50km to go. And that cost him a place in Peugeot's Paris-Nice team. But at the end of April, Yates finally scored his first win: the time trial stage of the 'open' Circuit de la Sarthe in which he was also fourth overall. He then rode the classics, but as a servant for riders like Roche, Anderson and Bernaudeau. And in the Four Days of Dunkirk he was 19th after losing 17 minutes in one day.

His confidence improved as the weeks passed, so did his results: he won a stage in the Tour d'Indre et Loire and in helping Bernaudeau win the Midi Libre, he was fifth in the prologue and fourth on the final stage. He didn't ride the Tour that year, but the British track and road championships gave him enough work to be getting on with.

Yates took second place in the road title behind fellow professional John Herety who joined CO-OP-Mercier after ACBB. Herety and Yates were close friends even though they were on separate teams. They shared a house in Tours, which was owned by the parents of CO-OP-Mercier *directeur-sportif*, Jean-Pierre Danguillame who was a former Peugeot rider.

After the British road title, Yates then won the Great Yorkshire Classic. It was a significant win to Yates as it was in the final time trial where he caught England's Tony Doyle – his greatest rival for the British track title a fortnight later. And Yates won that by five seconds.

'That was the best ride of my year,' reflected Yates after the 1982 season. 'People say Doyle was faster than me in the qualifying ride, but I just rode around without pressure while he was on the rivet.'

His career slumped after his victory over Doyle, following a three-day delay in Paris to wait for a new road bike. His naivity led him to believe that he should make up for what he lost, resulting in him overtraining. His daily regime consisted of three to five hours of cycling, 200 sit-ups, 200 push-ups, two hours gardening and the occasional flurry of football! 'I didn't have to do the gardening. I just did it to fill in the time. I thought it would be good for me. But I was completely knackered for the world titles,' he said after. He was.

Knocked out of the 5000m pursuit in the quarter final by Italy's Maurizio Bidinost, he headed for the road circuit at Goodwood to rediscover his road legs. With an awesome programme of 1,000km training before the race, his reward was a poor 41st at six minutes.

It was unsurprising that he didn't finish the Tour de L'Avenir soon after. 'My heart rate was 36, so I was fit but tiredness would creep into my legs,' he said. When the 1982 season closed, that tiredness showed. 'I didn't think the jump would be so big,' he said when asked about the change to professional from amateur ranks. 'I thought it might compare to the difference between ordinary amateurs and the top amateurs. But it is far greater.'

Yates cut down his winter training programme, enjoyed life a bit and even threw much of his interest into motor-cross racing – one of his favourite non-cycling pastimes. However, 1983 saw a much similar story. There were few results and for the most part he helped others to win, thanks to his 'incredible turn of speed', as everyone referred to it. The year did see the begining of his friendship with Peiper who came to Peugeot from ACBB.

Yates raced strongly in Het Volk and impressed a lot of observers with a solo chase of an eight-man break. At Paris–Nice he spent most of the week struggling. It was a disasterous race for the entire Peugeot team, which saw their leader Roche pull out with knee trouble on stage six while placed eighth overall. Team morale was at its lowest because of brewing discontent in the team for Berland. Relations between Berland and Yates were so strained that Berland gave the Englishman a public dressing down after being dropped in the team time trial. 'I'm in charge of a load of tourists,' said Berland. 'Yates was supposed to be one of the strong men in the team time trial yet he was one of the first to go off.'

His fatigue, and size, made that year's Milan–San Remo an unbearable marathon. He failed to finish the near-300km 'Primavera'. His most noted achievement there, was to ride straight through the feed station without taking his musette. The press was not the only party puzzled by Yates' inability to hit the form he had enjoyed at ACBB. He had trained better than the year before, he had rested more and even raced less. But the results never came, or when they did a failure followed soon after.

Was it a subconscious block caused by increasing speculation that Englishman David Akam – then racing at ACBB – might join Peugeot in 1984? For Peugeot would then have to sack one of its current legionnaires, Yates was aware that it could be him – he had yet to sign for another year.

Even as a neo-pro Yates' wheel was one of the toughest to follow. Here even Anderson (second from right) and Francesco Moser (third from right) are heads down during an English race

Peiper in the bunch during the 1984 Four Days at Dunkirk. Far left is Johan Lammerts who won the Tour of Flanders a month earlier

It was a hard time for Yates. He had ridden so well at ACBB and so much was expected of him. And it wasn't made easier when other Anglophiles rode so well. Roche, Anderson and Millar all had tight grips on affairs at Peugeot, Jones then at Wolber was an established name too, and elsewhere riders like Kelly at SEM, Sherwen at La Redoute and Herety at CO-OP-Mercier were keeping the English-speaking side alive. It was not suprising that he wasn't confident of riding the Tour that year – or that he would be selected. Confirmation that he wouldn't start came at the Midi Libre where he abandoned on the last stage.

Perhaps it was because Yates and Peiper were in similar circumstances that the two 'black sheep' of Peugeot became closely knit. The two went to England that July, and there he helped the Australian win the Great Yorkshire Classic, while he finished third. Yates knew that racing well in England counted for nothing in Berland's eyes. He always raced well there but needed results on the Continent. His only season successes that year were in the national pursuit title where he once more beat Doyle, the Isle of Wight Classic and the 'open' Milk Race where he had the leader's jersey for a day and finished fifth overall. The most important plus from racing in Britain was that the successes there boosted Yates' morale. 'Coming back gave me good motivation. I felt on equal terms. I was quite reserved when I started riding as a professional,' he says.

On the Continent, he had yet to score until the Etoile des Espoirs stage race in France that October. He finished fifth overall, third in the final stage and won the best young riders' award after helping Roche to second place overall.

The fact that Yates kept his place on the team for 1984 was thanks to that Etoile des Espoirs result, and a word in Berland's ear from Roche and the French Peugeot sprinter Francis Castaing who naturally valued Yates' power. Also the departures of Anderson and Roche to other teams kept the allotment of English-speaking places open. And finally, when French stalwart Gilbert Duclos-Lassalle accidently shot his hand while hunting in 1983, Peugeot needed to fill the void with another strongman until Duclos' expected return in May. Yates fitted the bill.

He has never had the wrong idea about his place in the peloton. And these first years at Peugeot showed it. 'I knew it was every man for himself. I was just a worker,' he says.

At the time Yates didn't believe that he would be kept on, hence the surprise of his 'reprieve'. 'When I turned professional I never had any objective about staying a pro for ten years or whatever. My second year was terrible and at the end I got an official letter saying that my contract was not going to be renewed. So I was ready to go back home,' he recalls today.

It was not until January of 1984 that Yates resumed training after the winter break. 'I started on January 2 with three-hour rides building up to six hours, on 42 x 16 (gearing) most of the time,' he said at the Peugeot team presentation in Paris. He knew that the Tour was on the cards this season and didn't want fatigue to play a part in a failed attempt.

After the Tour Mediterranean and Paris–Nice, Yates rode the classics. And then came events like the Tour de L'Oise and Post-Giro in Sweden where he played crucial roles in Peiper's eventual overall wins. He was particularly strong in the Post-Giro where he finished third. Even Peiper later said: 'He could have won it, but he doesn't have my confidence. But just having him there boosts my morale.' Other season highlights included a victory in the Four Days of Dunkirk prologue, second in Nice–Alassio and third in the Tour de Vendée.

Yates and Peiper both made their Tour debut that July. And both fared strongly at the start, Peiper finishing third in the prologue and Yates fifth at 10:02 to Bernard Hinault. It was the best prologue result in a Tour ever by a Briton. Both were the strong men in the team time trial – perhaps too strong as their French team-mates were unable to keep up with the pair's tempo. And as a result Peugeot finished a disappointing fourth and 0:28 behind Hinault's Renault team.

Still, it was clear that Berland felt Yates was at last coming of age. During the second week he signed another one-year contract for 10,000 francs a month with Peugeot – and not without time to spare. A day after announcing his deal, the demands of the Tour dug deep into Yates' strength. It was a baking, hot day which took the Tour to the foothills of the Massif Central. 'The tar on the road was so soft, it felt like I was sinking in it up to the rims. It's murder, there's no force left in my legs,' he groaned after finishing last on the 220km stage 13 from Blagnac to Rodez, just one place behind Sherwen and at 9:47. Yates made it to Paris, placed 91st from 124 arrivals and 2:26:24 behind a victorious Fignon. It was a result that might have been clouded by the success of Millar who was fourth overall, the winner of a stage and the King of the Mountains title. But at last Yates had broken through a barrier that in the last few

Peiper in the 1985 Isle of Wight classic. The experience and hardship from years as a professional already shows

seasons he had thought impassable. And the value of finishing the Tour was clear when he signed up for 25 post-Tour criteriums.

The final two years of Yates' career at Peugeot were not happy. The 1985 season brought no results, although he did compete in the Tour and finished 122nd. Yates tackled all but the last one and half stages of the earlier Tour of Spain where Millar was second. He abandoned on the fateful penultimate stage and just before the Spanish combine went into action to rob Millar of his leader's jersey. 'What a disaster that day was,' says Yates shaking his head.

That same race brought the politicking over Berland's future in the team to a head as well. And the in-house problems didn't help Yates' morale. Perhaps the stress was compounded by knowledge that his friend Peiper was committed to leaving the team for Panasonic. Whatever, Yates just didn't have the results and his contractual future was once more on the line.

'They were umming and aahing as to whether to hire me for 1986. And this was when Berland was getting ousted and being taken over by Legeay. Berland said I was going to be signed up and Legeay was taking over. He said Legeay would have the contract ready to sign at the Grand Prix d'Isbergues. I got to Isbergues and Legeay didn't know anything about it. I rang up Berland and asked what the hell was going on.

He said he didn't know. So one of them was bloody lying,' he recalls.

Yates' career was overshadowed by a giant question mark which only got bigger. He was called up to race Paris–Brussels, but when he arrived he discovered he wasn't meant to be there. At the same time he was given a contract to sign for the 1986 season. 'I think Berland convinced Legeay to sign me, but if I hadn't gone there they might not have signed me, right there and then. It was my last race for the year,' he says.

Such weak communication had become a hallmark of Peugeot's administration and when De Muer stood aside for Berland at the end of 1983 it was at its worst. Yates was secure for another 12 months but nonetheless felt uncomfortable. He didn't want to be be left hanging around again, and almost as soon as the 1986 season began he started thinking of moving elsewhere.

Frustratingly, results wouldn't come. And as the only English-speaking rider at Peugeot, Yates needed a break if he was to keep his place on the team. His chance came when Jérôme Simon, the brother of Pascal Simon, crashed in a race before the Tour and broke his wrist: 'I only rode the Tour at the last second because Jérôme broke his wrist'

It was during that 'ride' in the Tour that Bernaudeau, the former Peugeot leader who was then with the Fagor team, heard of Yates' problem. The pair had already struck a solid friendship and Bernaudeau felt he could use Yates on his 1987 team which also included Irishman Martin Earley. Yates didn't take much convincing and as he rode to an eventual 112th place he signed up. 'I was lucky Simon broke his wrist. Had he not I wouldn't have gone to the Tour and got the offer at Fagor,' says Yates.

Legeay didn't discover Yates had signed with Fagor until after the Tour. And the news came second hand, even though Legeay told him he would be kept on if he could find a sponsor to replace Peugeot who had also announced their decision to quit cycle sponsorship after 1986. Yates feels no regret for having not let on about his plans. The team had given him no guarantee and he had learned too well that verbal promises meant little in this cut-throat world. When asked why he didn't tell Legeay, he simply said: 'I didn't want to get flicked.'

As in ACBB, Allan Peiper arrived at Peugeot at the wrong time during a delicate period, marred with inside politicking. His first season in 1983 saw him in the background trying to get his professional career off the ground. Yet how could he not be influenced by the problems Anderson, Millar, Roche, and even Yates were having?

Dilligence and loyalty were long-standing hallmarks of Peiper's cycling career – but he was only human. He quickly realised that the aspects of French life which he hated at ACBB would only be more prevalent at Peugeot. Still, he stayed at Peugeot for three years, despite the further collapse of the team's structure with each.

Peiper's first year at Peugeot was quiet. He had the perception to try and take things in his stride, observe what was going on around him, and perhaps things would go well. A thoughtful man, he observed the growing barriers between the French and English-speaking riders, and tried to regard things objectively. But he did share Roche's opinion of Berland. 'He had no personality. He was not strong enough and he was a bad communicator.'

There were no devastating results from Peiper in 1983: in Paris–Nice he was 63rd overall at 50:28; in the Four Days of Dunkirk his fifth place in the prologue confirmed his time trialling ability was good; then before July and the Tour he went to the USA with 13 other European based professionals for the championships at Baltimore. He never expected he would be selected for the Tour. Peugeot had enough good riders and Peiper, in his first year, was understandably inexperienced. He certainly hadn't given Berland the 'headache' Roche gave De Muer in 1981! Instead Peiper raced in England that July, winning the Great Yorkshire Classic from local star Malcolm Elliott, and fellow European riders Yates and Sherwen who had both missed the Tour. It was not a major win for Peiper on an international scale, but it was a significant step for when he would become known in England. It certainly helped boost his image for the post-Tour Kellogg's City Centre criterium series where Anderson, Roche, Yates, and even former world champion Francesco Moser had all raced.

Peiper threw himself into helping his Peugeot leader Anderson in the City Centre series. He was almost always in Anderson's shadow, and just as proud to be on his team, and a part of his winning efforts. Anderson did not win the series coming second to local Briton Phil Thomas. However the performance by the team to help Anderson worked well. It was repeated in the world titles at Altenrhein where LeMond won. Anderson was in a lead break, but was reeled in by a combined effort by Roche, and Kelly.

His wanting to be part of a major win by Anderson was a driving force in Peiper; even though deep down he never really felt his efforts were appreciated. 'As a neo-pro, Phil sort of looked down on us a bit. He was never really interested in the fact that we were neo-pros trying to work hard. It was like that at the Tour de L'Aude. After he won he just rode off. We said congratulations but he just sort of said: "oh . . . yeah."'

Like Millar, he quickly earned a reputation for his health-food fetishes. 'Allan came along and immediately started giving us his ideas on diet. We started getting the muesli in for breakfast and since then it's taken off with everyone,' says Yates of Peiper's impact.

Perhaps the best development that year for Peiper was his friendship with Yates. The friendship came close to brotherhood in 1984, when the two became known as the 'Siamese Twins'. Unlike Anderson, Roche and Millar, they didn't have the star status to help them through the year. They were pure workhorses.

However when Peiper returned to Europe for the 1984 season, he wasn't exactly relishing the idea. He was committed, but the rigours of the previous season had given him nightmares while he was back home. 'I dreamt I was begging Berland to let me go home and quit. People think it's all roses over here but it isn't. I know one thing though, I don't intend to have any nightmares at the end of this year,' he said at Peugeot's team presentation in Paris that February.

Peiper was always sensitive to what he felt was a current of resentment towards English-speaking riders in the team. Why him and not so much the others? Probably because he was at the tail end of a line of winners. They might have put up with Anderson, Millar and Roche winning – it brought them money after all – but when Peiper and Yates came along it started to leave several team members agitated. Another possible explanation was his not being an established star like his predecessors. So his contribution was open to question. And by 1984, Peugeot Frenchmen were probably still bitter about the circumstances of Anderson and Roche's departures.

Equally, Peiper started resenting French attitudes. He thought they were lazy, took their places on the team for granted, and that English-speaking riders were regarded as second-class citizens. Yates just accepted the situation and 'got on with it.' It was Yates who had to calm Peiper down when he lost his temper after a race when non of the French riders offered to lead out Peugeot's sprinter, Castaing. 'We did all the work, we always would. The French just wouldn't,' he recalls.

It was always Peiper's dream to help Anderson. Here Peiper gives Anderson a push-off, surrendering his wheel during the 1987 Tour de France

Peiper (left) and Yates (right) left everyone in their trail during the 1984 Isle of Wight Classic

LeMond and Hinault, mid-way up the Alpe d'Huez in the 1986 Tour de France – an epic day which saw them finish together and 'supposedly' put an end to their feud for team leadership

Jonathan Boyer: pioneer and maverick, riding here in US colours for the French Renault-Elf team

Two particular incidents stand out in Peiper's mind. One involving Duclos-Lassalle and the other Laurent. Peiper's run-in with Duclos-Lassalle came in Paris – Nice when the Frenchman rebuked him for speaking English and not French, he stormed out of the room in fury. 'We were both being massaged one night after a stage,' recalls Peiper, 'My soigneur spoke English and we were talking, while at the same time Duclos was getting his masssage from a French-speaking soigneur. Then suddenly he jumped out yelling "This is a French team and we speak French in it". Then he walked out the room, slamming the door after him.'

Laurent's chauvinism at the Tour Mediterranean was less dramatic, but the sentiment was tipped with the same poison. 'I was riding in the bunch and then Laurent rode up alongside me and said: "It used to be bad with the Flahutes (Flemish) in our races. Now it's worse with all you English-speaking riders." It was no wonder I had bad memories of France and feel more at home with the Belgians today.'

It's ironic that Duclos-Lassalle and Laurent are two of several former Peugeot stalwarts whose current employment – as rider and public and relations manager respectively – have recently relied upon the talents of English-speaking champion LeMond who led Z, then Gan in 1983.

Peiper rode with more success in 1984: 'With Anderson and Roche gone, Sean and I were coming of age,' he says. Peiper enjoyed a short spell of leadership in the Tour Mediterranean thanks to a second place in the prologue and a better placing than Dutchman Bert Osterboosch who won the prologue on stage one. By Paris – Nice a bout of tendinitis had struck and he pulled out on stage six. It was not until May and the Tour de L'Oise that any success came his way.

Peiper's win in the three day Tour de L'Oise was once more thanks to his victory in the opening 3.1km prologue. He won that by 0:04, and that stayed with him to the end. The win was especially pleasing as the man he beat was Roche who was then with La Redoute. Afterwards he credited his win to two things, first was the criterium skills he developed in the British City Centre series: 'After racing over those circuits the prologue course here was made for me.' And the second was due to his friend Yates who worked tirelessly as Peiper's domestique and even reeled in several breaks from Roche in the last stage.

The Peiper-Yates duo were definitely a one-two production who repeated the team work in late June, when Peiper won the eight day pro-am post-Giro tour in Sweden. It was his victory in the last 16.2km time trial which saw him clinch the win by 0:13 on Swedish favourite, Alf Segersall of Bianchi, and 0:59 on Yates. However his one tenth of a second loss in the prologue played on his mind. 'I was really depressed to have been beaten in the prologue. I couldn't sleep that night. So on the day of the first stage I decided I would win this race,' said Peiper.

During that first stage Peiper and Yates attacked, but Segersall went with them and took the leader's yellow jersey by a second. The margin stayed until the stage eight (B) time trial. Being team leader was a new and rare experience for Peiper: 'When you've been conserving your energy all week, which I had to do as team leader, it's negative riding and I don't like that. But you have to, and then in the time trial be positive and somehow explode. It's difficult,' he said then.

For Peiper, winning a stage race was the boost he needed for his career: 'I've won four prologues this year but this is the first real race I've won.'

Peiper's form, confidence and time trialling qualities made him a vital component to Peugeot's Tour de France team. But they certainly didn't expect that he would repay their faith so well. Third in the opening 5.4km prologue at Noisy le Sec, he was beaten by Frenchmen Hinault who won, and Fignon. When he finished third on stage one he held his third place yet came within 0:08 of the yellow jersey. Stage two saw the Peiper-Yates duo in action again. He wanted that yellow jersey and they pencilled in an intermediate sprint as a way to get it. But Peiper messed up the sprint which Yates led out. As Peiper recalled: 'His lead-outs being what they are, I lost the wheel, and when I finished fifth or sixth he said disgustedly "I'm not leading you out anymore."'

Peiper and Yates were in their element in the stage four team time trial. Peugeot was fourth, but for Peiper making the 'Frenchies' grovel in their slipstream was a personal victory. 'Sean and I did all the work with those French weaklings glued to our back wheels.'

By the end of that Tour, Peiper was 95th from 124 finishers and 2:31:28 behind a victorious Fignon – a far cry from the five-second margin he had after the prologue. But as he was to say like many Tour finishers: 'Just making it to Paris and winning the finishers' medal is a victory.'

He had also done enough to impress prospective teams elsewhere. During the Tour, Carrera approached Peiper, but the Australian would only go if they would take Yates too. He also asked for 20,000 francs a month. 'He was like a big brother to me. They wouldn't take Sean, so I stayed at Peugeot for 15,000 francs a month.'

Peiper and Yates travelled together for the post-Tour criteriums in Europe, tackling a schedule of 25 events. Then he travelled back to Britain for the City Centre Series once more. There, he and Yates were stars, no question about it.

In 1985 the team was in disarray, riders lost all confidence in Berland. And Peiper just didn't have the same form or morale that he had enjoyed the year before. He often wondered if he should have taken the Carrera offer in 1984, but as he didn't, he set himself the target of finding a new team for 1986 as soon as possible. He did at Panasonic, where Anderson had experienced two glorious years in 1984 and 1985 and he would hopefully do so again in 1986 with Peiper playing a major role as his guardsman!

7 LIFE AFTER PEUGEOT

When the curtain fell on the 1986 European cycle racing season, so it did on the Peugeot legend – for both French and English-speaking cyclists. The Peugeot firm pulled out of sponsorship, thus ending one of the most significant and lengthy chapters in the sport. But even had it stayed on, Sean Yates' departure from the team – announced well before Peugeot revealed its intention – would have still been regarded as the epitaph to the foreign legion story.

Yates was the only English-speaking rider for Peugeot in 1986, and his move to Fagor in 1987 ended what had been an intriguing seven-year contribution from cycling talent operating in Australia, Scotland, Ireland, South Africa and England. Jones, Anderson, Van Heerden, Millar, Roche, Peiper and Yates had all made an impact, even if the individual and parallel rise to stardom by Greg LeMond and Sean Kelly independent of Peugeot was as impressive. But the collective force of Peugeot's foreigners was unmatched.

It was unfortunate that each legionnaire's adieu to Peugeot was marked by one controversy or another. But it is very rare that any rider will leave a team under his or the director's wishes in a congenial atmosphere. Why else would he leave? Money perhaps? If so, that means there was obviously some dispute over the negotiated sum and inevitably that leads to trouble. Professional cycling is a vicious world. The environment breeds a selfish drive to survive. Nice guys never last very long.

Peugeot's team enviroment not only prepared riders for competitive onslaughts, but for a variety of hurdles ranging from blatant chauvinism, nepotism, and domestic politics to the simple and challenging necessity to adapt to a foreign lifestyle and language. Despite the troubles, each English-speaking rider experienced at Peugeot his share of success; without doubt being on the team strengthened their resolve for the years ahead and carried them through their careers when they would sign up with other Spanish, French, Italian, Belgian or Dutch teams – occasionally even crossing paths and teaming up with one another in various line-ups.

It was probably in those years after Peugeot that each legionnaire became aware of the ties between them. They were all different characters, all individuals, but they shared experiences which no other walk of life can provide. As Stephen Roche says: 'We were all different in our own way. But in the peloton we all talk to each other and help each other. And when I think about it, I guess it's because we all went through the same system. I didn't know any of the others before I or they joined. But when I met them, it was always as if I had known them for years. And that feeling is still there today.'

Life after Peugeot was no easier for the legion despite their experience. For Kelly, LeMond, Sherwen and any other maverick who tried making a career for himself away from Peugeot the terms were the same, and the conditions gruelling.

Jones' future years were still troubled by injury, as when he rode for Peugeot. His friendship and natural class made him a valued asset for Frenchman Jean-Rene Bernaudeau when he left Peugeot after the 1982 season. Without a contract for 1983, Jones didn't hesitate in going with Bernaudeau to ride for Wolber in 1983 and Systeme-U in 1984, But after 1984, Systeme-U shelved its sponsorship interests.

Jones, the first Peugeot legionnaire, left the 'black and whites' to join Wolber in 1983.
Here he turns the big ring in the Dijon time trial in the 1983 Tour de France

Jones had no choice but to return home to England where he rode in what was then a developing British professional scene. He was not alone in packing his bags: that same year saw Chris Wreghitt pack his bags after 12 months on the Continent, leaving the Italian Bianchi team because of an unrelenting sciatic nerve complaint. John Herety former ACBB amateur also went back after three hard seasons on the French CO-OP-Mercier team left him physically and mentally broken and saying: 'Obviously, I'm not up to it'.

Jones, then 28-years old, would later feel he quit the Continental scene too soon. He certainly wasn't too old, but the run of injuries and failures after early shows of promise at Peugeot clouded his judgement. In April 1984 a calf muscle injury dogged his Tour preparation; he finally abandoned with four days to go because of stomach trouble. In the second half of the season, the news of Systeme-U's temporary exit turned his interest to racing on home soil instead. When he did go back, he had no idea that three years later in 1987 he would return to the Tour in the ill-fated British ANC team.

Anderson and Millar, who joined Jones at Peugeot in 1980, looked to northern Europe when their interest in sticking with Peugeot ended because of various and separate controversies. Both went to the Dutch Panasonic team, although Anderson signed up when he left Peugeot after the 1983 season and Millar at the end of 1985.

Since his days at Peugeot, Anderson has been hailed as both champion and 'has been' on numerous occasions. When he led Panasonic down the winning trail in 1985, he picked up 17 victories, Post claimed him the greatest professional he had ever seen, but when he struggled in the 80km time trial in the 1987 Tour de France, the same man told Belgian and Dutch journalists Anderson was cycling like a 'retarded human being.' Since then, his career after Peugeot has seen mixed fortunes.

It was at Panasonic that Anderson earned his reputation as a classics rider, rather than a Tour winner. After winning the Catalan Week in Spain he still finished ninth in the 1984 Tour, but his wins in the Grand Prix of Frankfurt and Championship of Zurich, second in Liège–Bastogne–Liège and marathon three-hour solo break in Milan–San Remo set new records for him.

His prospects became clearer in 1985, his greatest ever season, he kept the flame of Tour ambition alight with an incredible fifth place overall. It was also in that Tour where his rivalry with Bernard Hinault smouldered again, when the Frenchman accused Anderson of pushing him off his bike in the bunch sprint to Saint Etienne and breaking his nose. That rift has never been healed.

In any case, Anderson's stage racing qualities were confirmed before the Tour with victories in the Dauphiné Libéré, the Tour of Switzerland and the Tour Mediterranean. His all-round skills led to second place in the Tour of Flanders where team-mate Eric Vanderaerden won, and again in Ghent–Wevelgem where Anderson was 'meant' to have won but botched up the sprint and saw Vanderaerden win despite almost braking on the line!

By this time Anderson was adding revolutionary dimensions to professional cycling. He pushed for higher wages. He had already 'Americanised' contractual deals while at Peugeot by taking a solicitor with him to the negotiations. His reputation for driving a hard bargain was renowned. 'A lot of the team directors are pocketing money that should be going to the riders,' he said then. 'The riders have no rights. There are no unions, well there are, but they are corrupt anyway. What the unions should do is set up a system to help the riders, such as a manager's representative, lawyers and an insurance system. All riders should have representatives when they sign contracts so that they aren't taken for a ride by the teams.'

At Panasonic Anderson created another uproar by demanding his own personal doctor instead of relying on the team's. After his doping scandal at Peugeot he was wary of having others he didn't know or trust administer to him. 'In the beginning you are a little green. You don't know exactly what is going on all the time. You don't know who to trust, but you don't have a choice. After a while you get a little wiser and you see that you do have a choice and can buck the system if you want. And when I didn't abide by the system I was ostracised. I wasn't thrown off the team but I thought I had certain rights,' he says.

'I always felt it was important to come out of the sport healthy. Others wanted to live for the moment. They wanted to risk their life, and be famous. I wanted to know exactly what the *soigneurs* were giving us. But they said: "no, that's a *soigneur's* secret. That's why they are paid so much". It was my body and I wanted to look after it the way I wanted. So I wanted my doctor, someone I could feel confident with.'

It was after that year's Tour that physical cracks appeared in Anderson's armour. His hereditary rheumatic back ailment plagued his post-Tour season, and while still leading the year-long Super Prestige series, the pain grew so bad that by the Tour of Lombardy in October he could not race. His last minute 'scratching' opened the way for a victorious Kelly to take the title from him.

Anderson was not the same: his back troubles saw him miss the first half of 1986 and race the Tour 'only for training'. Then he appeared to come back to his best with season closing wins in Creteil–Chaville, the New York City Tour and a stage of the Nissan Classic. He was also third overall in the Coors Classic – behind Hinault and Greg LeMond. But in 1987 poor form and the rigours of a divorce battle, in late 1986 saw him back down again. Post didn't hold much mercy. He had already tried to cut his salary. So it was not a shock to hear of Anderson's intention to leave at the end of the year.

His spell at TVM from 1988 to 1990 was equally troublesome. There were glimpses of the Anderson of old – especially in 1989 when he won a stage and overall classification of the Tour of Romandy, as well as stages in the Tour of Italy, Kellogg's Tour of Britain and the Nissan Classic. And he came close to avenging his second place in the 1987 Tour of Flanders to Belgian Eddy Planckaert with a third place in the Belgian Liège–Bastogne–Liège classic.

Personal differences with *directeur-sportif*, Cees Priem, got in the way of a long career with TVM. The crux of their many arguments was the presence of American *soigneuse*, Shelly Verses, on the team. She was also Anderson's girlfriend and it was part of his contract that she accompany him with the team. While she was arguably one of the best – if not the best – in her field, Priem was always against having her on the team. He was always poised for the first chance to dispose of her and Anderson knew it.

Eventually the relationship deteriorated to such an extent that Anderson left TVM without having a team to go to after 1990. A year highlighted with his brilliant Tour of Italy: he won a stage and the blue-jersey Inter Giro category, which was the second most lucrative classification after the overall competition. On top of that he finished second to Italy's overall winner, Gianni Bugno, in the points category and spent four days in the green jersey as best climber. Anderson's aggression was another reminder that he still had the fighting spirit in him which once scared Bernard Hinault and so impressed Post. But it disappeared soon after.

The lull following that year's Tour of Italy was almost too long. Anderson knew it was a risk to leave TVM without having signed elsewhere. But he felt he had little choice even though his concern grew as the weeks passed well into the winter break without any deal being finalised. It was not until December 24 that Anderson managed to settle a new contract with the American Motorola team. And after he said: 'I'll never let that happen again.'

He took a big pay cut, but had a lucrative bonus scheme to provide an incentive. And it obviously worked as he stormed through the 1991 season to win 12 races – his best season record since that most glorious 1985. And that included his first ever Tour de France stage win since 1982 when he wore the yellow jersey for ten days. Once again his detractors were silenced. Anderson was back.

Millar's career has been far less problematic, although he has been with four teams since leaving Peugeot after 1985, Panasonic, Fagor, Z and finally TVM.

When with Peugeot he hoped that he would find a more understanding *directeur-sportif*. He once more fell into conflict with Post 'He was just like De Muer. He didn't like small guys like me. He liked big 80kg types who were good for the classics. It didn't matter that I could climb,' recalls Millar.

One of the Scot's objectives in 1986 was to race the Tour of Spain again. He did but once more finished second, this time to Spaniard Alvaro Pino. However, his result was far easier to come to terms with. 'It was simple really, we just didn't buy the teams or help we should have early enough. Everyone was snapped up too quickly,' he says.

After the Tour of Spain, Millar was second in the Tour of Switzerland at 0:53 to American Andy Hampsten and went into the Tour as a real favourite. But he fell ill in the final week after finishing second to eventual winner, LeMond in the decisive 13th stage to Superbagnères and was forced to abandon. It was a huge disappointment for Millar and one not made any easier by Post's apparent lack of understanding. He merely regarded Millar as weak.

While Millar didn't like Post, he still respected him. 'Like De Muer, I respected his ability as a *directeur sportif*. He was one of the best. I just didn't like him and he didn't like me because I was small,' he says. However, Millar didn't let his personal feelings get in the way. In 1987 Millar wanted to prove he had what Post thought he lacked. For Millar, it was Weigant and De Muer all over again. The opportunity was made harder by the presence of rising Dutch star, Eric Breukink who was declared team leader. Millar regarded the 1987 season, the second of a two year contract with Peugeot, as 'hard labour'.

To prepare for the Tour de France, Panasonic this time missed the Tour of Spain and raced the Tour of Italy instead. Millar was still in good form. He was fifth in Liège–Bastogne–Liège six weeks earlier. And in the Tour of Romandy he was fourth overall at 2:04 to Roche. Finally in the Tour of Italy, Millar won the climber's green jersey and was second at 3:40 to Roche who fought his legendary battle against Carrera team-mate Roberto Visentini and most of the Italian peloton. Millar was one of Roche's few allies, even though the Scot today says he didn't ride for the Irishman. 'I didn't ride for him. It was just that on the opportunities when I could have attacked him, I didn't,' he clarifies.

To Post's chagrin, Millar's second was one position better than Breukink who was third at 4:17! 'That messed up his plans. He was pissed off with me half-way through the race when he knew I was going well. I didn't do anything to stop Breukink from trying, but in any case Breukink wasn't going to beat Roche,' he says.

As Millar fell out with Post, he just as quickly fell 'in' with Roche who invited him to Fagor in 1988. It was not surprising considering Millar's 'help' in Italy. Ironically, Millar's one year with Roche would be one of the most disruptive. The team, then registered as a French team, was heavily bulked with Roche's hand-picked men. Yates was already there, but joining Millar as a new recruit was English sprinter, Malcolm Elliott who was one of four Tour de France survivors in the beleaguered British ANC-Halfords team.

Mismanagement, deception, false promise and a much publicised feud between Roche and the team's director all played their hand in a disastrous year for every member. Millar wanted out as quick as he could. And thankfully he had some results – third in Liège–Bastogne–Liège, sixth overall in the Tour of Spain at 3:22 to triumphant Kelly.

The team Millar signed for was ironically a new-look Peugeot team. Millar's old team-mate and the successor to Roland Berland as *directeur-sportif*, Roger Legeay, found a new sponsor to replace Peugeot in the French childrens clothes manufacturer, Z. 'I had been everywhere trying to find a team. Going back to Z was sort of like going back home,' said Millar who spent three enjoyable seasons there.

It was clear he was happier. His results proved it. He was second overall in the Dauphiné Libéré, 0:18 behind Frenchman Charly Mottet and 10th at 18:46 to LeMond in the Tour de France which saw Millar win his third Pyrrenean stage – stage 10 from Cauterets to Luchon-Superbagnères. He then finished the season off with a victory in the Kellogg's Tour of Britain.

His next season was also successful. He won the Dauphiné Libéré. And while he didn't finish the Tour due to illness, he played a key role in newly recruited LeMond's third success, and Frenchman Ronan Pensec's effort to defend the yellow jersey which he wore for the day to L'Alpe d'Huez. And again he rode the season out with a second in the Kellogg's Tour and fourth in the Tour of Lombardy.

It was much the same story in 1991 – second in the Tour of Romandy and the Classique des Alpes, fifth in the Tour of Switzerland and Grand Prix of Americas and fourth in the Kellogg's Tour. And TVM, needing new talent to help Dutchman Gert-Jan Theunisse in the mountains, saw the value of taking him on.

Legeay could not match the big budgeted TVM's price. The team had reportedly only just agreed terms the year before when negotiating with Millar. This time, Z had no choice but to let Millar go to TVM.

Roche has arguably had the most turbulent career of the lot. He has also been the most successful, with 1987 and his 'Triple Crown' triumph in the Tours of Italy, France and the world road title at Villach in Austria. Only the retired Belgian legend, Eddy Merckx had ever accomplished the same feat in 1974.

However his contractual wranglings and spate of injuries have earned as much headline space as his race results. Since leaving Peugeot after the 1984 season, Roche has ridden for six teams – La Redoute, Carrera, Fagor, Histor, Tonton Tapis and again Carrera, riding out his intended final season in 1993.

Things started going wrong for Roche right from the start, in his first year out from Peugeot. It had nothing to do with his attitude or performance. On all accounts, 1984 was not a bad season with wins in Nice–Allasio, the Tour of Romandy and Subida Arate in Spain. He was also second in Paris–Nice, third in the Criterium International and Grand Prix des Nations. His biggest let down was a 25th in the Tour de France where he crashed two days before the mountains and injured his calf muscle.

The atmosphere of La Redoute was not a happy one created by former Peugeot men, Maurice de Muer as general manager and dual Tour champion Bernard Thevenet as *directeur-sportif*. Thevenet was clearly a better rider than director, proving the theory that champion cyclists don't always make great bosses. His apparent

Millar returned to the Tour of Spain in 1986 – this time with Panasonic. In the leader's *polka-dot* climber's jersey. Millar once more would succumb to defeat by Alvaro Pino (in yellow right)

Tour de France, 1985 (left to right) Anderson, LeMond and Roche

1985 brought headaches for Roche at La Redoute. But that year's Tour de France renewed his hope and sees him ride alongside LeMond on the 17th stage

downfall was because he let De Muer walk over him. According to Roche, even De Muer's wife Jacqueline tried to turn his own riders against him. Thevenet was always being outdone by De Muer and the rift between the two had a nasty affect on team morale. Finally, both men lost and it was announced that they would be replaced in 1985 by Raphael Geminiani, a former professional who finished second in the 1951 Tour but had built himself a reputation as a *directeur-sportif* as well.

Roche was wary of Geminiani at first. There was little communication between the two in the lead up months to the 1985 season. And it took a face-to-face argument during the Tour Mediterranean where they both aired their suspicions and doubts about each other before the relationship really started making progress. But when it did, Roche and Geminiani got on fine. The season was eventually Roche's best since 1981.

After taking third in that Tour Mediterranean, Roche won the Criterium International and the Tour du Midi Pyrenees, finished second in Paris – Nice, third in the Tour and seventh in the world titles. It was his Tour result which helped Roche realise his racing ambitions. Winning the 52km first sector of stage 18, from Luz Saint Sauveur to the summit Col d'Aubisque. It was in that stage that Roche wore a one piece suit under 'Gem's' instructions. Because it was so short a race, he wanted Roche to race it like a time trial – and he did before eventually winning alone and with 1:03 on Sean Kelly.

The honeymoon between Roche and Geminiani ended after 1985 when La Redoute pulled out of its sponsorship, and Roche signed up with the Italian team Carrera unable to take Geminiani with him. Still, the loss did not affect Roche too badly. In fact his two years with Carrera elevated him to near-immortality. But his glory didn't come before the one year 'on' one year 'off' routine came down on Roche.

Roche crashed in the Paris Six-Day event in which he teamed up with Englishman Tony Doyle. He injured his knee badly, damaging the cartilage, and endured a painful season culminating with an operation that October. During that time Carrera and Roche had received much publicity with many people believing Roche was washed up. But in 1987 he proved otherwise.

His second season with Carrera may have been highlighted by his 'Triple Crown' triumph, but there were other wins like the Tour of Valencia and the Tour of Romandy. He was also second in the Criterium International and Liège – Bastogne – Liège and fourth in Paris – Nice and Flèche Wallonne. It was hard to imagine that a rider of such calibre could fail amongst his team-mates. It began in the Tour of Italy with his much publicised fight for leadership with 1986 winner Roberto Visentini.

Roche's battle against the Italian, all his team-mates bar Belgian domestique Eddy Schepers and the Italian peloton and 'tifosi' was an epic. Visentini and the rest didn't want Roche to win and they did everything they could to make Roche's bid difficult. It led to Carrera riders racing against Roche. Their dispute made the headlines in every paper, and Visentini's fans showed their dislike throwing objects and spitting at Roche. His experiences in Italy made his eventual victory all the more impressive. And it certainly helped to instill an inner psychological toughness for the Tour de France a month later. No other rider could have staved off the verbal and phsyical abuse and still won like he did. Then again no other rider than Roche could have got himself in such a situation. Merckx may have been 'the Cannibal', but Roche could certainly be thought of as a veritable tiger.

It was that tiger's spirit which led to an amazing and most unexpected victory in the world championships later. The image of Roche pedalling like fury with his head buried between his legs, as he attacked in the final 400 metres, must surely remain in the minds of anyone who witnessed the occasion.

Roche still left Carrera after 1987. The domestic turmoil there required it. And so he signed up to lead a new-look Fagor team to which he was also given license to hand-pick the men he wanted around him. Nobody expected Roche to repeat the success of 1987, but then nobody expected he would have so much misfortune over the next two years. Disputes and injuries once more threatened his career. The issues created major rifts within the team; especially between Roche and his English-speaking allies in Fagor – Yates, Millar and Elliott. They were clearly unsettled by the wave of uncertainty which struck the team and they left after 1988.

Troubles continued to follow Roche, when he rode for Histor in 1990 and then Tonton Tapis in 1991: Histor was a Belgian team that never really adopted the French clan that Roche brought with him, and it was more or less the same at Tonton Tapis. Although his clash with former professional and Tonton Tapis *directeur-sportif*, Roger De Vlaeminck, was the cause of his headaches there.

The trouble came to a head in the Tour de France when Roche missed the team time trial start because he was on the toilet. Roche still completed the course alone, but was eliminated for finishing outside the time limit. For the 1987 'Triple

Crown' winner, such an incident was as humiliating as anyone could imagine. There were accusations and counter claims of what actually went wrong from both sides. How could such a mistake occur in such an important event? It was insinuated that Roche even missed the start on purpose because he wanted 'out' from the team, but such claims are hard to believe. Roche hotly denied them to the the press, public and the team's administration. One thing was certain though – he had to leave.

Returning to Carrera in 1992 was the answer to a prayer for Roche. As in 1985 when he rode for La Redoute, Roche once more found success. It was not the sort of success he had in 1987 or 1985 and he rode through most of the season with a back injury. But his old tiger's spirit returned, and in the circumstances his 15th in the Tour of Spain, and ninth and stage win at La Bourboule in the Tour de France were as significant to Roche as any other victory in his career. They proved that Roche could still emerge a winner.

He declared 1993 would be his last year. But that did not stop the threat of misfortune testing Roche once more. He hit his left knee in a fall while leaving his house early one January morning for a training ride and was unable to train for weeks. He could see his season was facing disaster and even hinted that if need be, he would not race at all rather than bow out struggling like an invalid. If Roche wanted anything, it was to be remembered as a fighter, and if 1993 could not prove that then the memories of 1992 would have to suffice.

Roche, Millar and Anderson were all champions. And naturally their achievements and itinerant publicity, deflected interest from the developing careers of Yates and Peiper.

Yates was already at Fagor when Roche came along in 1988, his 1987 season there being highlighted by wins in the Grand Prix de Cannes and stage three of the Nissan Classic. While 1988 was riddled with problems for the team, ironically it was a great one for Yates.

It was a policy for Yates to 'get on with the job and don't worry about the others' which helped him to win for himself for a change. He won the first stage of Paris–Nice that year, and spent three days in the leader's white jersey. Then he won the 12th stage to Jaca in the Tour of Spain, stage five of the Midi Libre and finally the stage six time trial from Lievin to Wasquehal in the Tour de France – in what was then the fastest ever time for a Tour time trial. His victory at Wasquehal stunned everyone. 'It just came together on the day. I knew I had good form and just wanted to do better than my previous best in a Tour time trial which was 15th,' said Yates who was 59th overall.

Besides a reluctance to get involved in the politics going on at Fagor, Yates was also a much more mature rider. He knew when and where to apply his strengths, rather than ride like a furious bull from the moment the season began to the time it ended: 'One of my secrets was setting myself goals. I didn't go into every race thinking I had to hammer myself.'

Yates had no trouble in finding a new team after the Fagor debacle. The American 7-Eleven team snapped him up eagerly for 1989. He has never looked back, since then the American Motorola firm took over sponsorship, and Yates rode with new-found confidence in 1989. He moved to the south of France where he still lives in Nice. His bodyweight down to 74kg instead of 80kg – an inevitable result of training on his local hilly terrain. As he says: 'I'm now serious about my racing, even though I thought I was before.'

His first year with 7-Eleven saw him win two stages, and the overall classification of the Tour of Belgium, the Grand Prix of Eddy Merckx time trial, and the prologue of the Tour of Holland in which he was fourth overall. He was also second at the rain-sodden Ghent – Wevelgem classic, after being in a day-long two man break with eventual winner, Dutchman Gerrit Solleveld. He was also 45th overall in the Tour de France.

There was never any doubt that he would be kept on the team by *directeur-sportif*, Jim Ochwicz when 7-Eleven withdrew from cycling at the end of 1990. Yates may have only had a third place overall in the Nissan Classic and a 119th in the Tour to his credit, but his experience and sheer strength in so many attacks, chases and in particular the team time trial was irreplaceable. Engine power like that of Sean Yates is hard to find.

Since 1991 and the arrival of Motorola, Yates has become a sturdy backbone for the team. He wins less, but stills wins on occasion as he did in 1991 with stage victories in the Dauphiné Libéré and Nissan Classic, and in 1992 in the British road title. As with ACBB and Peugeot, he puts the needs of the team first: he revels in helping others to win rather than himself. When he does retire – a question which he leaves open at the end of every season – he will be a definite loss to his team.

Peiper was the last legionnaire but nevertheless the first to retire. He called it quits at the end of 1992, although he may have deferred longer had his final two seasons at Tulip been more fruitful.

He left Peugeot after 1985 for Panasonic, or rather for Peter Post, Phil Anderson and the dream that he was going to the biggest and best team in the world. His old friend, Eddy Planckaert was the one who convinced Post that signing up Peiper was a shrewd move. It was all Peiper could dream of, or so he thought. Peiper became a disciple to Post's thinking. 'I went on my knees to Post and was thrilled to get a two-year contract,' recalls Peiper. And he stayed on his knees, or under Post's wing for six years.

They were hard years. He was quickly pushed into a secondary role, but had no trouble adapting to those around him. It may have been a Dutch team, but the Belgian influence was as strong as the Dutch. It was home from home being married to a Flemish girl, Christine, and he speaks fluent Flemish and lives in Belgium – at Ninove, just 400m from the finish line of the Tour of Flanders!

Like Yates, Peiper loved riding at the front of the bunch, being part of a powerful Panasonic chase or leading out sprinters like Eric Vanderaerden for great, historic wins. However, Peiper never won as much as Yates – perhaps he lacked the sheer strength.

In fact, the taste of victory was scarce for Peiper, but such were a domestiques duties and position in a star-studded team like Panasonic. In 1987 he failed to finish the Tour de France, but recovered from illness to win the first stage of the Kellogg's Tour of Britain and spent a day in the leader's yellow jersey immediately after. It was not until 1990 that he found a podium again: in the winning Panasonic team time trial in the Tour. He abandoned that Tour due to sickness, but earlier won a stage of the Tour of Italy and then the Nissan Classic.

Peiper did have several winning opportunities given to him though, the 1987 Milan – San Remo was one, where he was with eventual winner Eric Maechler of Switzerland before being dropped. Then in the 1988 world title race he took tenth place after leading out the sprint for the bronze medal being caught with 75 metres to go. In the 1989 Tour of Flanders he was also in the winning seven-man break and took seventh place, followed by a second in the two-man Barrachi Trophy time trial where he rode with 1988 world champion Maurizio Fondriest.

Eventually his love for Panasonic was quashed by domineering and relentless pressure from Post. Peiper always felt Post thought less of him than the others. He wanted to match Post's expectations, but then again few riders ever have: Post is always one jump ahead and ready to increase his expectations.

It was mid-way through 1990 that Peiper decided to leave Panasonic. Against many people's advice he opted to sign up with Tulip for the 1991 season, although he would dearly have loved to ride with 7-Eleven/Motorola and his friend Yates, had the opportunity arisen at the right time. It didn't.

Peiper's two years at Tulip were unproductive. The team lacked inspiration, discipline, and was riddled with conflicts. Its designated leader Dutchman Adrie Van der Poel neither produced the results promised, nor the spirit needed to induce a collective team effort. In 1991 it didn't even qualify for the Tour de France.

Team morale was never high and by early 1992 it was more or less split into destructive cliques. The final nail was hammered into the team's coffin when Tulip announced it would stop sponsoring. But by then Peiper had decided it was time to stop racing altogether.

8 THE MAVERICKS

The ACBB and Peugeot teams undeniably formed a major lifeline to the English-speaking force in Europe. After Paul Sherwen crossed the Channel to race as an amateur in France in 1978, the score of successes snowballed as rider after rider went through the same schooling, proving the adage: Success Breeds Success. The ACBB-Peugeot connection was not solely responsible. In the same era – the late 1970s to 1980s – two principal characters paved their own glorious, if maverick, way. Their names: Sean Kelly and Greg LeMond. Between them they won nearly every major race on the calendar.

Other names rose to prominence, although they were far less successful than the Irish-American pair, who arguably with their victories did more to promote the English-speaking cause abroad than the whole foreign legion combined. But the number of mavericks is significant for it proved that going the ACBB-Peugeot way, was not necessarily the **only** way. No one could deny the phenomenon of so many great riders passing through the same doors to success, but the presence of such mavericks certainly prompted questions as to whether it really was the Anglophile riders who were making the system and not the system making them.

Some became established professionals and earned reputations as great riders – some as protected riders, others as domestiques. Some lasted barely a year in Europe and fell victim to physical and mental problems. The causes of such failure were numerous: injuries, lack of ability, homesickness, disillusionment and even drugs. Those who survived were possessed of a deep, inner steel which would have found success in any other walk of life.

Sherwen, and Englishman John Herety experienced life on both sides of the fence as legionnaires and mavericks. Both left ACBB full of confidence and ambition for further success. Neither really fulfilled that, but contrasting fates awaited each of them.

Sherwen rode for FIAT and then for La Redoute after leaving ACBB at the end of 1977. By the time he returned to England to race with the Raleigh team, he had ridden seven Tours, he finished all but two – 1980 and 1981. Sherwen was a winner at ACBB, but once he turned professional he soon accepted his destiny as a worker. That is not to undermine his achievements, the peloton's regard for him was as high as any champion could ask. Many incidents illustrated this, but none better than on stage ten from Epinal, in the Vosges, during his last Tour in 1985, when he crashed 1.5km to Pontallier, just a week into the Tour as it approached the Alps. He was off the back and chasing the peloton from the gun. Three team-mates came back to help get him back – Alain Bondue, Ferdi Van den Haute and Regis Simon – but as the gap increased his team saw the prospect of having four riders eliminated for finishing outside the time limit. Sherwen, struggling with pain from his injuries, told the others to go; he rode on alone to the finish, some 200km away, and arrived well outside the time limit.

Sherwen knew he would be eliminated but was determined to finish rather than live with the stigma of abandoning his last Tour. 'It was my last Tour and it was so important for me that I finish. The ironic thing was that I actually began the Tour thinking I was in the best shape I had ever been in,' he says. Sherwen's pride and determination that lonely, painful day summed up the spirit of the Tour, according to

Kelly and LeMond in world titles and one-day classics, the pair were often neck and
neck in battle. Together they have amassed victories in nearly every race there is

Kelly, riding for the Spanish KAS team in the Valladolid time trial of the 1986 Tour of Spain where he was third overall. Two years later he won

Kelly (in green) on Jan Raas' wheel during the
1982 world title road race at Goodwood, England.
Hours later he would win the first of his two
career bronze medals

Tony Capper. . . the man behind the ANC-
Halfords pipedream

ANC riders in the thick of it, on the climb to La Plagne in the 1987 Tour (left to right)
Malcolm Elliott, 'Omar' Palov and Adrian Timmis

the Société du Tour de France. And as a result of his sportsmanship he was reinstated as race rules allow in extenuating circumstances.

Sprinter John Herety also left ACBB with an astounding reputation as a winner. But he didn't have the recuperative powers to put up with the rigours of professional racing. In 1984, a year where illness followed him from the start of the season, he announced his intention to return to England. 'During my first year I could do it. I got through no problem. In the second year I got as far as August before things broke down. This year I got as far as Paris – Nice before everything went wrong. I pulled out with bronchitis and have been ill ever since.'

They were not the only English mavericks though: there was Phil Edwards who etched his place in English-cycling history by riding as Francesco Moser's right-hand man on the Italian Sanson team for five years until 1980; another was Bill Nickson who spent 1977 and 1978 riding on the Peter Post directed TI-Raleigh team; then there was Steve Jones who rode for Splendor after racing as an amateur in the Dutch Van Erp team; five times British cyclo-cross champion Chris Wreghitt, who spent a year on the Italian Bianchi team; and Gary Dowdell who lasted a year on the Systeme U team of Graham Jones in 1985. From the United States in 1984, Olympic road champion Alexi Grewal lasted one season with the Dutch Panasonic team and short-lived spells with 7-Eleven and RMO before heading home. Another was Doug Shapiro who was on the Dutch Kwantum team in 1985 and finished 74th in the Tour before signing with the American 7-Eleven team for 1986. And Andy Hampsten entered the picture by riding with La Vie Claire in 1986 before joining 7-Eleven in 1987. He was a vital ally for LeMond in the 1986 Tour de France, and proved his potential by winning the white jersey for best young rider, finishing fourth overall as well.

Canadian Steve Bauer, signed for La Vie Claire after taking silver in the 1984 Olympics, and bronze at the world professional road race title a few weeks later. He was again alongside LeMond in the 1986 Tour and finished 23rd overall. Yet yellow jersey glory would come his way in the years ahead with Weinmann-La Suisse in 1988 and 7-Eleven in 1989 when he would wear the yellow jersey for a total of ten days.

In addition to riders from the US and England, Ireland's Martin Earley rode for Fagor, then for PDM and then Festina. Earley, who raced as an amateur in France, has often been left in the shadows of Kelly and Roche, but in between fulfilling his team duties he has also shown flashes of brilliance like his 1989 Tour stage win to Pau. His niche may not have been as defined as Kelly or Roche's, but it was a more secure one than say, that of two other Irishmen Paul Kimmage and Laurence Roche.

From the Antipodes, Australian Michael Wilson was arguably one of the most talented. He won stages in the Tours of Italy and Spain while racing on the Italian Alfa Lum team. But his career ended after 1990 following a three-year spell on the Helvetia-La Suisse team. New Zealand produced a crop of European-based professionals in Paul Jesson, Eric McKenzie, and Nathan Dahlberg who were all Tour riders. Jesson, who rode the Tour in 1979, had his career tragically curtailed when a car accident necessitated the amputation of his leg. In 1982, when McKenzie finished first in the Championship of Zurich he was found positive in the post-race dope control and disqualified. He'd turned professional from being an amateur track rider. New Zealand joined the Olympic boycott in 1980, and McKenzie rode for Capri-Sonne. But for the doping scandal, his result at Zurich would have been the first European classic victory by a New Zealander. He did go on to ride the Tours in 1983, 1985 and 1986 then returned home.

It was a slim chance that any records would be broken by Nathan Dahlberg –

who was nevertheless a courageous rider despite his limited ability. His best achievement was when he reached the top ranks in the 1988 Tour. Called up to race with 7-Eleven on the eve of the Tour, just after finishing a 200km Belgian kermesse, Dahlberg drove overnight from Belgium to the start at Pontchateau in Brittany. He arrived at 5:30am and was racing towards Paris a few hours later. His finish secured a contract for the next year, although after 1991 when the team was called Motorola he was released and moved to America to race.

Kelly outsprinting Anderson to take stage 12 of the 1982 Tour de France at Pau

Kelly and LeMond: the Guiding Lights

Greg LeMond

Date of birth: 26 June, 1961

Place of birth: Lakewood, USA

Teams: Renault (Fra), La Vie Claire (Fra),
    Toshiba (Fra), PDM (Hol), ADR (Bel),
    Z (Fra), Gan (Fra)

Turned professional 1981

Not yet retired

Sean Kelly

Date of birth: May 2, 1956

Place of birth: Carrick-on-Suir, Ireland

Teams: Flandria (Bel), Splendor (Bel),
    Sem (Fra), Skil/Sem (Fra), Kas (Sp),
    PDM (Hol), Lotus-Festina (Sp)

Turned professional 1977

Planned retirement for 1993

However the fates of most mavericks varied, Kelly and LeMond were by far the star attractions. They still are today as they both reach the latter end of their careers. Looking back we can wonder at what made them such brilliant riders. Was it luck, ability, money, or ambition? Maybe it was all of these.

The careers of Kelly and LeMond are as different as their characters and upbringing. The fact that Kelly is Irish and LeMond is American shows immediate social and cultural differences which probably form 90% of the explanation.

Kelly's bearing, of a stoic rural resilience, shows a toughness which is reflected in his stony expression and piercing blue eyes. He suffers fools lightly, is always ready to speak his mind and spends little if any time making up or hearing excuses. Kelly is also regimental in everything he does, from diet to training, to pre-race preparation; he is the ultimate professional who lets nothing get in his way.

Kelly and Moreno Argentin at Milan – San Remo in 1992

LeMond on the other hand is far more open to the distractions of the world around him. Cycling is not the only thing that interests him. He may not always like the wave of press attention which follows him at every race but it hardly shows. The regimentation pronounced in Kelly's outlook on life, is a sharp contrast to LeMond's, whose passion for Mexican food, McDonalds' hamburgers, fly-fishing and golf has been known to leave Kelly shaking his head on several occasions. However, when required, LeMond's determination to win is every bit as resolved.

The contrast between the two continues over the winter months. Kelly and his family (wife Linda and twins Nigel and Stacy) reside in the north Brussels suburb of Vilvoorde. During winter, when October heralds the end of the season, the Kelly's pack their bags and return to Carrick-on-Suir where they live at the modest yet cosy hillside home of Gerald Grant, the son of Kelly's brother-in-law Dan Grant.

The LeMonds – Greg, his wife Kathy and three children Geoffery, Scott and Simone – lock up their Belgian home in Kortrijk and head for Medina, 40km out from Minneapolis. There awaits LeMond's retreat, a 45-room Georgian mansion valued at $3.5 million.

Sherwen said 'No' to Peugeot. Instead he turned professional with FIAT, before signing up with La Redoute. Here he claims his biggest Continental win, stage three of the 1983 Four Days of Dunkirk

Kelly's training ground was in the amateur VC Metz club in Belgium. The Irish farmer's son joined the club for the 1976 season. His natural brilliance led him to victory in the Tour of the North, Tour of Majorca, Tour of Lombardy and stages of the Tour of Ireland and Britain. That in turn attracted the interest of Jean De Gribaldy who travelled all the way to Ireland to sign Kelly up for the 1977 season and the Belgian Flandria team. On the verge of his retirement 17 years on, in 1993, Kelly is thought of as one of the most influential figures in world cycling.

Kelly became a classics' man even though it took him until the 1983 Tour of Lombardy to claim his first classic crown. But his ensuing ten wins up until the beginning of the 1993 season firmly earned him the title 'King Kelly'. His victories include Milan–San Remo (1992 and 1986), Paris–Roubaix (1984 and 1986), Liège–Bastogne–Liège (1989 and 1984), the Tour of Lombardy (1991, 1985 and 1983), Blois–Chaville (1984) and Ghent–Wevelgem (1988).

So steadfast is Kelly's reputation for the classics, that it would be easy to overlook his achievements in other races. His winning style has also met with success in the 1988 Tour of Spain, the 1983 and 1990 Tour of Switzerland, a record seven wins in Paris–Nice from 1982 to 1988, and the Nissan Classic of Ireland from 1985 to 1987 and in 1991. And of course there are his bronze medal wins in the 1982 and 1989 world championships and his results in the biggest race of them all – the Tour de France.

Kelly never won the Tour. But as his many fans will testify, he was always a strong contender. His unfailing willpower fuelled his early career ambition of winning 'La Grande Boucle', but the closest he got was fifth in 1984. Although in 1983 he also wore the yellow jersey for a day, as history shows, the jersey that Kelly has best fitted is the green jersey – and not that of Ireland – awarded to the winner of the points competition. Kelly's record of four green jersey triumphs stood going into the 1993 edition.

Kelly was starting his fifth year as a professional, and his third and last with Splendor, when LeMond pedalled his way into the peloton in 1981. He spent his first two years with the Flandria team where he was signed up to be the lead-out man for the 1976 World Champion Freddy Maertens. He left Flandria for Splendor when a more lucrative offer came up, plus the chance to race for himself.

At the end of 1981 De Gribaldy offered Kelly a contract to join and lead Sem for 1982. And Kelly agreed. He made no bones about the fact that money was a consideration in any move he made. Like LeMond Kelly saw his cycling as a job, and he had to earn the most he could. Kelly was not as flamboyant about money and its use as LeMond but he was just as motivated. And even today, anyone thinking about a business arrangement with Kelly had better be prepared to make a good offer. He is ever the businessman.

The next five years from 1982 saw Kelly's career take off as he rode with Sem for 1982 and 1983, then Sem-Skil for 1984 and 1985 and then the Spanish soft drinks manufacturer Kas, from 1986 to the end of 1988. Kelly spent his apprenticeship under De Gribaldy, and they stayed together until his death in 1987. In that time, as the pair grew close, the cycling world became enchanted by Kelly. He did so much on the bike, yet spoke so little and at first appeared reluctant to accept his role as a much adored public figure.

Since pedalling out from under De Gribaldy's wing, Kelly has established himself as one of the sport's most prolific winners on the European circuit. And in the years after leaving Kas, when it disbanded at the end of 1987, Kelly has shone in the public spotlight during his three-year spell with PDM and the 1992 and 1993 seasons with Lotus-Festina.

His gritty determination on the ancient, muddy cobblestones between Paris and Roubaix perfectly reflects his dogged consistency, and sheer strength that has left team-mates behind and amazed his fans. In addition to his successive Paris–Nice victories between 1982 and 1988, and his participation in every Tour de France bar one since 1978, there is his five-year reign as number one on the FICP world rankings between 1984 and 1988. Then in 1989 when the World Cup began, he won that too.

To silence the inevitable tag of being 'past it' as retirement closed in, Kelly bounced back with a renewed vigour winning the 1990 Tour of Switzerland and Nissan Classic, the 1991 Tour of Lombardy and 1992 Milan–San Remo. Even when the 1993 season began, 36-year old Kelly was once more talking about racing in 1994 and that famous 'one more season' we have so heard so many times before.

What drives Kelly on? The need to earn money cannot be ignored, neither can the basic desire to race. Is it that Kelly simply doesn't know what he will do when he retires? Kelly's career has followed a golden victory trail, but for two exceptions and one can't help but feel that he believes he has unfinished business to settle before he hangs up his bike. Two dossiers on his desk are labelled 'The world title' and 'The Tour of Flanders'.

A win in either race – or both would be a fitting end to Kelly's racing career. Why? Because they are two of the greatest one-day races in the world and he has yet to put his name on the trophy. His record to date shows that he was third in the world professional road race, in 1982 at Goodwood and 1989 at Chambery. In the Tour of Flanders he was second in 1984, 1986 and 1987. He was fourth in 1988, and abandoned in 1991 with a broken collarbone. Being so close to victory has left Kelly nearly as upset as when he abandoned the Tour in 1987 and 1991.

Those who think tough men like Kelly don't cry, think again. There are no stronger images of Kelly's disappointment than of him crying on the shoulders of his Kas *directeur-sportif*, Christian Rumeau, in the 1987 Tour. His toughness made his tears all the more poignant.

An even stronger image was seeing him forced to attend the post-race press conference at Chambery. Unlike the 1987 or 1991 Tour where circumstances beyond his control, crashes and injury, led to his fate, the bronze medal that 'could have been' gold was of his own doing, simply because he selected the wrong gear and was out-raced. He knew it and so too did everyone else when they looked into his big eyes, almost bulging with tears as he raised his head slowly to so professionally explain to journalists how he lost the world title to LeMond. Riders may feel journalists are free of emotion and heartless in their criticisms, but there was no one in that room who enjoyed his interrogation. Kelly's dream of one day being world champion is appreciated by all.

One common denominator both Kelly and LeMond have, apart from their formidable record of success and such daunting pure ability, is that both made sure they had plenty of European experience before turning professional.

LeMond, a former downhill skier born in Lakewood, California, raced in France in 1980 with the UC Creteil amateur team based just outside Paris. Before moving to France that year LeMond had already made a name for himself, and not just by winning the 1979 World Junior Road Championship at Buenos Aires. In 1978 he came over to Europe and raced in Belgium and Switzerland and won several races. The experience also gave him a sound and early education in European race tactics and style. His eventual signing as a new professional with the French Renault team for 1981 was almost inevitable. He caught the attention of Cyrille Guimard while racing with the US Olympic team in Europe in 1980.

Sherwen (right) and Herety (left), two mavericks on rival teams, but friends nonetheless

LeMond wore the World Champion's jersey into his 1984 Tour de France debut

The US finally boycotted the Moscow Olympic Games, but LeMond's results in Europe unveiled a potential champion. He won a stage in his first race. Then he was first overall in the pro-am Circuit de la Sarthe from Peugeot's Roger Legeay who would later become his *directeur-sportif* at Z and Gan. As Samuel Abt pointed out in *The Incredible Comeback*, that win was the first by an American in an international stage race. It was after taking a top five place in the Ruban Granatier race that Guimard's interest was kindled and it was not so much by the result, but by the way LeMond lost his temper, when a sleeping French mechanic delayed a wheel change after LeMond punctured during a vital chase. To Guimard his anger mirrored a winner's determination. And to LeMond, despite offers from Peugeot, Guimard mirrored cycling success.

LeMond was not the only American who joined Renault. Jonathan Boyer had also been recruited after his great performance at the 1980 world title in Sallanches, France which Bernard Hinault won. Jealousy led to the two 'imports' clashing rather than helping each other. And the feud came to a head at the 1981 and 1982 world titles where the team was split over who should lead the US team – LeMond or Boyer who left Renault in 1982 and joined the Belgian Sem team.

LeMond's silver medal at Goodwood, England in 1982 was a landmark in American cycling history, even if it came at Boyer's expense – he was chased down by LeMond himself. It was the first medal by an American in a professional world road title. And when LeMond won the Tour de L'Avenir from Robert Millar a few weeks later, it was also the dawning of LeMond's true status as a champion. Press demands of his and Boyer's problems were becoming forgotten – at least for all but LeMond and Boyer.

As with Kelly and any cycling champion, how LeMond measured up to the hopes put in him has been well documented time and again. In the world titles he pulled off wins at Altenrhein, Switzerland in 1983 and at Chambery, France in 1989, as well as another silver medal at Giavera Montello, Italy in 1985.

LeMond made his Tour debut in 1984, a year which had seen Hinault leave Renault and join a new team owned by French businessman-cum-politician, Bernard Tapie, and called La Vie Claire. Despite Hinault's departure though, Renault's main hopes were still in Frenchman Laurent Fignon who won the Tour in 1983. LeMond was naturally deserving of his rank as number two leader, following his Tour de L'Avenir win in 1982 and Dauphiné Libéré victory in 1983. And in a race which saw Fignon win a back-to-back title, LeMond repaid Guimard for his faith with a third place overall. Sadly for Guimard LeMond's potential was too great, and Tapie poached the American from Renault in 1985, after negotiating what was then a historical $1 million three-year contract.

It is his Tour results that have built LeMond's reputation. It is the race he has not only won three times – in 1986, 1989 and 1990 – but controversially rates as the only race that matters apart from the world professional road title. Yes . . . he has won that twice, in 1983 and 1989. But those are not the only events he has fared well in either.

It is hard to say how many more times LeMond would have won the Tour, world title or any other race had he not been accidentally shot while out hunting in May, 1987. For LeMond his near fatal accident reshaped his entire cycling career and outlook on life. He had looked death in the face. And while he has always been a family man, when he survived, the priority of his family took even higher precedence. LeMond still clung to a dream of rediscovering his best racing form. Although the agonising 1988 and early 1989 seasons led up to an incredible 0:08 victory over Fignon on the last day of the 1989 Tour de France, they left the American on the verge of giving up on several occasions. Lesser mortals would have given up, but not LeMond.

It may seem hard to understand why LeMond can't race all year round and win other Tours and classics. He has the sheer ability. But who can truly measure the physical and psychological toll of being 25 minutes away from bleeding to death in 1987 and then going on to win the Tour in 1989 and 1990? What would Miguel Indurain, Tony Rominger or Gianni Bugno do in a similar situation? I hope the answer will never be demonstrated. But given his history LeMond's impact on the sport is arguably the greatest of any rider's in the 1980s.

Next to LeMond's competitive triumphs and impressive come back from his near fatal shooting, it was LeMond's 'Americanised' bargaining and push for higher wages which made him the name he is today. When he signed with Tapie, he almost simultaneously opened the floodgates to demands for higher wages from every cyclist in the peloton. Suddenly, with the stroke of a pen, cycling edged closer – however marginally – to the extraordinary income levels offered in tennis, golf, soccer and Formula One racing. LeMond would do it again at the end of 1989 when he signed with Z in 1990 for a $5.7 million, three-year deal – although the worldwide recession soon after would see wages plummet just as suddenly by the end of 1991 and 1992.

LeMond's deal with Tapie provoked a critical response from the French press. In an interview with one English magazine in 1987, LeMond recalled the reaction: 'French journalists don't understand American mentality. I think a lot of it has to do with friendships within French cycling . . . before I left Renault to join La Vie Claire I always had good press relations, but there are quite a few journalists who are friends with Guimard. And when I left Renault . . . boom, I started getting bad press.'

LeMond was also aware that other cyclists were benefiting and was happy about it. 'The average rider is making a lot more now,' he said in 1987: 'At Renault, Guimard would pay at least 70% of his riders under 10,000 French francs (then $1,000) a month. Incredibly low salaries. Now in La Vie Claire almost all the riders are well paid. A neo-pro might start with 7,000 or 8,000 francs a month but as soon as he performs well he's paid at least 15,000 francs (then $25,000 +). And each rider on our team makes another $25,000 a year in prize-money when we divide everything up. So the average rider is making between $40,000 and $50,000 a year.'

Tapie, just like Z's 'patron' Roger Zannier later on, recouped a good return on his investments too. At La Vie Claire LeMond and Hinault had their notorious clashes in the 1985 and 1986 Tours, but between them they were a virtually unbeatable force for anyone else. LeMond back-pedalled under Tapie's orders to let Hinault win the 1985 Tour for a fifth time. LeMond finished second. Then in 1986 he came up against Hinault who, despite promises to help the American in return for support the year before, clearly had winning a record sixth Tour on his mind. LeMond's resolve, strength and ability held out. And on July 27, 1986 the Tour de France had its first ever American on the winner's podium, wearing the yellow jersey.

In 1987 LeMond returned to the US in early March to recover from a broken wrist sustained in Italy's Tirreno–Adriatico. Had he stayed on the Continent he would not have been shot. But then something would be missing were there no 'ifs' to speculate about. And that alone makes him one of the most intriguing Tour de France champions ever seen.

Sometimes the publicity around LeMond pretty much clouded the achievements of all other Anglophile mavericks and legionnaires too. But while

LeMond did as he felt was right – and made more fans than arguably any cyclist in the peloton today – there was still a tidal wave of adoration and respect for Kelly.

In Kelly and his more conservative and stoic Irish approach, the European cycling world was given a perfect counter balance to LeMond. In Kelly, we have a living reminder of the old school of cycling. Kelly and LeMond may be two mavericks of different kinds, however their motivation is the same. And their formidable careers have left many other Anglophile mavericks in their wakes. But for Kelly and LeMond, we would still be wondering what really is possible for the English-speaking rider to achieve. Competitively, financially and personally both riders have emerged victorious. Yet both have proved that success does not come without sacrifice. They proved to all that the ACBB and Peugeot route was not the only one. What counted was that good old fashioned and very basic will to win.

9 AN AMERICAN DREAM AND BRITISH NIGHTMARE

With the establishment of English-speaking individuals on the Continent came plans for complete English-speaking teams. By the 1980s battle plans were drawn up, first by the United States and then by Great Britain. However their implementation was starkly different. The US front was led by the 7-Eleven team, which since 1991 has been known as Motorola. Britain's first bid since the 1960s to field a team in the Tour de France came in 1987 with the creation of ANC-Halfords.

The destinies of both may have taken different paths, but they nonetheless excited interest in a world which had never seen anything like it. The American dream of 7-Eleven and Motorola is laden with success, and its trail full of glory, whereas the fate of ANC-Halfords stands as a sorry reminder of what is at stake for the ill-prepared.

Both teams came close to a premature end at one time or an other, but the saving element for 7-Eleven was better planning, longer term objectives and a greater sense of purpose. The apparent objective of ANC-Halfords went no further than getting to the start line of the Tour, let alone finishing or even winning it!

7-Eleven – an American dream

The creation of an all-American professional team to race in Europe and be sponsored by 7-Eleven was seen as a natural evolution to the American foodstore chain's Olympic sponsorship programme between 1981 and 1984.

Up until then 7-Eleven's parent company, the Southland Corporation, had focused its attention on a $40 million investment in the contruction of an Olympic outdoor velodrome at Carson, Los Angeles. Then in 1981 it was attracted by a proposal from Dutch-born sports marketing consultant, George Taylor to invest another $350,000 and sponsor a men's amateur team which would gear itself towards the 1984 Olympics in Los Angeles.

'The focus of the 7-Eleven team in the beginning was to give its Olympic sponsorship involvement an umbrella. This meant finding a way to get the most mileage possible out of Southland's $40 million velodrome investment.' Taylor once told the American magazine, *VeloNews*, of 7-Eleven's desire to get as much from the sport as possible for its investment.

The team quickly grew in size, ability and reputation in the US; a feature boosted by the fame of former five-time Olympic ice-skating gold medallist Eric Heiden as team captain. Heiden, like so many ice skaters, had taken to cycling as a form of training. He progressed to cycle racing and even contested the 1986 Tour de France.

The 7-Eleven programme expanded in 1983 to include a women's team as well. The US won the 1984 Games, and when the euphoria had settled, the future of the team's continued support fell into immediate doubt. What more could the Southland Corporation and 7-Eleven get out of their investment? Taylor could understand why there were doubts, as too could the team's director, Jim Ochowicz. Although Ochowicz felt he had the answer: 'Och's idea was make the team professional, take it to race in Europe and one day take on the best European professionals'. Taylor disagreed and their conflicting opinions led to a rift which is still debated in American cycling circles today. But the facts prove that Ochowicz's convictions were sound, he is still at the helm of America's greatest cycling coup today.

The 7-Eleven team, made up mostly of former US Olympians, ventured to Europe for their first taste of cut-throat European racing in 1985. Despite the steep learning curve, the team still returned home with some formidable success in their wake. Ron Kiefel, the US team captain at the Olympics, won the one day Trophy Laigueglia in Italy in February, and then stage 15 of the three-week Tour of Italy. Davis Phinney made a name for himself as a sprinter to watch out for with two third places in the Tour of Italy and fifth in Milan–Turin. Still, as 1986 would confirm much tougher struggles lay ahead.

The 7-Eleven team's first full season in Europe was in 1986. It still had to try and fulfil obvious racing obligations in the US with events like the Coors Classic and the US titles. In the US, they were virtually unbeatable, but as much as Europe was known to Americans as 'the old Continent', for 'Och', Kiefel, Phinney and others, it was a new frontier. They were very much little fish in a very big pond.

The press welcomed the arrival of an American team as a development in cycling's 'mondialisation'; European riders didn't hide their initial resentment. Kiefel's recollection of an in-race fight with Italian Silvano Contini in the Tour of Italy the year before made that clear to him. 'He grabbed my brake levers while we were racing one day. He looked at me to say he had control over me, like a threat. I felt so scared when he did that.' he says.

The season objective for 7-Eleven was that year's Tour de France. And the team, while struggling through classics like Paris–Roubaix, had bolstered its line-up with that race in mind. But experience was something they still lacked, although in hindsight the 'program' as Ochowicz always called it was far better organised and realistic than ANC-Halfords'. Ochowicz was not a 'hands-on' director, as he travelled from the US to Europe supervising the operation of the South Club which he set up to run the team, the day-to-day direction in Europe was left to Mike Neel. His experience of racing in Europe in the 1970s was invaluable, as was rider Doug Shapiro's who had ridden the Tour the year before with the Dutch Kwantum team.

The team had no choice but to persevere as it battled through the pre-Tour races at the same time being subject to frequent cutting remarks and scathing criticisms. Other teams were told at race meetings to stay away from any 7-Eleven rider. They were labelled as dangerously inexperienced and even blamed for causing crashes they never witnessed. 'I remember we were always told to watch out for 7-Eleven riders, keep as far away as possible from them,' recalls Phil Anderson who was then on Panasonic.

The 7-Eleven team in many ways attracted a large share of animosity. 'I guess we came to Europe and we always thought we knew better. We tried to keep up our American image. We were proud of it, although it became less of a thing as the team adapted, became better and finally respected in later years,' concludes Kiefel, who also said that one of the most provocative incidents involved 1984 Olympic champion Alexi Grewal in the 1986 Three Days De Panne.

Grewal, a long-time *provoqueur* in US cycling, didn't last the season in 7-Eleven. He hit the headlines when he was quoted as saying something to the effect of 'I piss on Belgium' while he stopped to relieve himself. Understandably, Grewal never adapted to

Tony Capper 'with the lads', minutes before the 1987 Tour first stage start in Berlin

Shane Sutton, 'first-off' in the 1987 Tour prologue, and thinking of better places to be on a hot July summer day

European racing life, nor was he adopted by the Europeans.

The team went into the 1986 Tour blind. They didn't know what to expect, neither did anyone else. Hence the surprise when Canadian member Alex Stieda took the yellow jersey after the first stage when he was fifth but benefited from a tally of time bonuses which gave him overall leadership. He became the first North American to ever do so. But reality quickly came bounding back when later that day on stage two he not only lost the jersey, but was dropped in the team time trial and barely made the time limit! Still, 7-Eleven's shortlived glory was rekindled on stage three when Phinney got into the winning break and won the stage. Suddenly, these much maligned 'yankees' were turning heads for the right reasons.

From there, the Tour became an education for every member. The morning head count in the team's hotel grew smaller each day as fatigue set in. Team personnel tried everything to prop up their spirits. Team *soigneuse*, Shelley Verses – the first female to work in European cycling – even cut out photos from a *Playboy* magazine and snuck them into their feed bags in hope it would boost morale. For the record, it worked!

By the time Paris rolled under the peloton's wheels and Greg LeMond had taken Stieda's stage one achievement further by winning the Tour altogether, five 7-Eleven riders were in it – Raul Alcalá who was the first Mexican to race the Tour, Stieda, Kiefel and fellow Americans, Jeff Pierce and Bob Roll. Phinney, Heiden, Grewal and Chris Carmichael were the absentees. Considering the circumstances, it was a veritable success. It was painful, exhausting and sometimes – due to persistent ill-feeling from some Europen teams – humiliating. But with LeMond in yellow, his team-mate Hampsten in white and fourth overall and five 7-Eleven riders with finishers' medals to their credit, Europe had no choice but to stand up and accept that American cyclists had earned their right to be there.

Since 7-Eleven's eye-opening baptism to European cycling, their performance has gone from strength to strength. The 1987 season saw Hampsten join up to be a true leader for the Tour, and several new names like Denmark's Jens Veggerby, Norway's Dag-Otto Lauritzen who had ridden at ACBB and then Peugeot and American Jonathan Boyer.

Unlike ANC-Halfords, 7-Eleven embarked on further recruitment programmes as the years went on. Riders came and went and gradually the team took on a greater international image. No longer did we see the team turning up to races with baseball bats, gloves and balls and practising pitches at the team hotel. European racing they learned, was serious and tough. But they proved they could be as good or sometimes better than the best that Europe had to offer. That was proved by Hampsten and the team when they won the 1988 Tour of Italy. Other highlights include Bauer's nine-day yellow jersey exploit in the 1990 Tour, his second place, by a centimetre, in the 1990 Paris–Roubaix, Pierce's victory in the prestigious final 1987 Tour stage on the Champs Elysees in Paris, and Phinney's success over Dutchman Jean-Paul Van Poppel and England's Malcolm Elliott in the 1987 Tour at Bordeaux.

7-Eleven may no longer be a part of European cycling, but the team carried on as Motorola, named after the American multi-national electronic equipment manufacturer who took over in 1991. The ten-year association between 7-Eleven and cycling was itself a glorious one. There were hardships, sorrows, a few scandals and a measure of drama. But there were great moments of success and celebration too.

As Motorola, the team diversified further. And while Motorola too announced that 1993 would be its finale to its sponsorship commitment, the team is fully international now, having had Australian, English, Canadian, Norwegian, German, Italian and French riders pass through its once all-American ranks. However, Tour and major classic victory had still to be won when the 1993 season began. But they may not be far away.

Phil Anderson proved so in 1991 when he joined Motorola and won 12 races, including a stage to Quimper in the Tour, as did Hampsten in 1992 when he was fourth overall in the Tour after becoming the first American to win the much sought after stage to L'Alpe d'Huez. And then the arrival of American 1992 Olympian Lance Armstrong opened the door even wider to such prospects when he struck a winning chord in late 1992 and then again in early 1993 with his victory in the Trophy Laigueglia and aggressive performances in Paris–Nice and Milan–San Remo.

The elusive great victory may never come. But one thing is certain – many thought the 'American Dream' would have ended long, long ago, and its enduring success was entirely due to the quality riders it nurtured. Although a 1994 season was under threat without a new sponsor being found by late June, any possible demise would only be due to commercial reasons.

ANC-Halfords – a British nightmare

On the day that the ANC-Halfords cycling team for the 1987 Tour de France was presented to the British press, there was an air of eager anticipation amongst those running the team and the attending media. Here was the first British trade team to tackle the Tour since the mid-1960s.

Elliott,leading ANC-Halfords in the Tour team trial in Berlin, was the sole member to further his career in Europe

Kiefel,a founder member of the 7-Eleven team, saw vast opportunity in Ochowicz's offer to race in Europe

Yate's recruitment to 7-Eleven in 1989 paid handsome dividends. Here he shares the workload with eventual winner Dutchman Gerrit Solleveld in Ghent–Wevelgem in a day-long two man break. The pair stay away, but Yates is second

In 1991, Motorola look over 7-Eleven's sponsorship of the all-American team. In early 1993 Motorola announced it would be ending its sponsorship after the season

ANC-Halfords did not have a rider who could win the Tour. Many people even thought they didn't have a rider who could finish. But Tony Capper, owner of ANC couriers and team sponsor, didn't want to dampen the fire of publicity, no matter what the **reality** was. Hard-core observers could only shake their heads in pity for the lambs he was sending to slaughter, when he said: 'I think we can reasonably expect to win a stage, possibly two, and I think as a real bonus we could find ourselves in the yellow jersey.'

Certainly it was great to see a British team join the Tour. After all the presence of two English-speaking teams seemed to confirm that professional cycling really was no longer just for Europeans. However all did not seem quite right. Amidst the clink of champagne glasses and offerings of *hors d'oeuvres* around the invited guests and dignitaries following the official presentation in London, the looks of those who were about to go into battle in the greatest battleground of cycling told a different story.

Doubts that the impending attack was a mistake were confirmed by Australian member Shane Sutton's appearance. His face was haggard, his eyes drained and he seemingly lacked the 'punch' of any rider about to start his first Tour. So too did his team-mates. 'Mate . . .' looking over his shoulder at the same time to make sure no one could overhear. 'I'm knackered, I'm crook and we haven't even got to the start yet. We shouldn't be doing this, we're all half sick.'

Before that exchange with Sutton I was one of the early supporters of ANC-Halfords. Barry Hoban's sceptical outlook on their entry seemed much clearer. Hoban thought they were ill-prepared, lacked experience and basically were heading for disaster. Sutton, without having even pedalled one kilometre of the awaiting prologue in Berlin, obviously thought so too.

What could you say to him? What could anyone say to any of the riders? The team had officially entered the Tour, its £25,000 entry fee had been paid, Capper and the team's *directeur-sportif* Phil Griffiths, had spent most of the recent weeks promoting this epic British-sponsored Tour effort. Everyone wanted it to happen, except for the majority of the riders who were mostly British but also an Australian, a Czech, a New Zealander and a couple of Frenchmen for good measure. Capper's 'dream-come-true' would end up being the worst nightmare for most of the riders contracted to him. Furthermore, it was proof for those who needed it that British cyclists were still not up to competing on equal terms in Europe.

Only four of the nine ANC-Halfords riders made it through the Tour – England's Malcolm Elliott and Adrian Timmis, Czechoslovakia's Omar Palov, and France's Guy Gallopin. The first to abandoned the Tour was Frenchman Bernard Chesnau. Then came Sutton at the foot of the very first Vosges mountain. Next was former Peugeot veteran Graham Jones who was a shadow of his former self but tried vainly to stay the course; and Paul Watson who simply stopped after being dropped for reasons that people still try to pinpoint today. The last to fall was New Zealander Steve Swart, a strong rider who now races in the US. Ironically, he was finding his legs as the Tour went on but his hopes of finishing were dashed by a crash which badly bruised his right foot and forced his retirement.

In fact, the closest the team got to cracking open a celebratory bottle of champagne was on stage 12 from Brive La Gaillarde to Bordeaux. There, Elliott was third in the bunch sprint behind American stage winner Davis Phinney of 7-Eleven, and Dutchman Jean-Paul Van Poppel. However, one can imagine that Elliott, Palov, Gallopin and Timmis savoured a well-earned beer when it was all over!

To say the Tour was a struggle for them is an understatement. After Elliott finished he gave a weary smile, thankful that the physical agony of the Tour was over. How could he know that the toughest battle in the courts for unpaid wages was yet to begin – a dispute which brewed throughout the Tour itself and made the ordeal even harder to bear.

Where did the team go wrong? Should it have started the Tour at all? These were some of the questions being asked by every cycling observer before, during, and after the Tour. The argument always came back to one man – Tony Capper. The antics of Capper and the consequences of his decisions which led to only four riders making it to Paris were summed up well in the title to Jeff Connor's book *Wide Eyed and Legless*. For that is exactly how they looked.

Beginning with one rider in Mick Morrisson who retired soon after, the team grew quickly. The team was blooded on some Continental racing in 1986, a year highlighted with Liverpudlian Joey McLoughlin's fourth place in the Amstel Gold. Then in 1987 they raced more on the Continent as Capper and his fellow directors pitched their case for Tour selection around the negotiating table. Wanting results to back up their argument, the best provider for the team was Elliott. After the team rode Paris–Nice, Ghent–Wevelgem, then Flèche Wallonne where Watson took sixth, Elliott got into a five-man winning break in the Amstel Gold and finished third.

The team returned to England where Elliott won the Milk Race, then headed back to the Continent for the Midi Libre. And there Timmis revealed his climbing potential by finishing eighth in the mountainous Midi Libre stage race where he also won a stage. As far as Capper could see his detractors back home had got it all wrong, ANC-Halfords was Tour de France bound and nothing would stop them.

Once on the Tour, the walls came tumbling down around Capper and anyone who had anything to do with the team. There were personality clashes between riders, *soigneurs* and mechanics. Capper offended everyone by bringing his family on the race. It seemed to the riders and personnel that the Tour was one big holiday trip, and he had often talked of his ambition to one day 'lead' a team in the Tour.

It was plainly clear to all following the team that there was little communication. What else could explain what happened to Elliott when he reached the summit of La Plagne, well after the stage finish and saw the ANC-Halfords team car drive off into the horizon without him? Would any other team neglect its star rider this way?

The stickiest problem of the lot was that of unpaid wages. It's a common problem in any hastily fielded team, but the responsibility for it could clearly be traced to one man, Capper. He lived in tax exile on the Isle of Man, and had basically spent everything he had in getting to the Tour. The team was living his dream for free and worse, they didn't know until it was too late.

After the Tour, Capper ran for cover as riders tried every personal and legal avenue to retrieve what was owed to them. Even though he couldn't be found, the controversy went to the courts and most of the cases were not settled until several years later.

Capper was man who did a lot for cycling. However, his good intentions created ill feeling amongst many by pushing his own ambitions too far that year. And he tipped the scales as heavily against him as his 20 stone bodyweight would. He was a larger than life figure to British cycling. No one denied that. And it was typical of the man's irrepressible belief in himself that he later confided to some that he wanted to return to the sport. It was typical that some who remember him still break into a smile – however wary – shake their heads and hesitatingly admit that he wasn't all bad.

10 THE FUTURE

One of the most common reactions from those whose help I sought in writing *The Foreign Legion* was why it hadn't already been written. Upon reflection, it seems odd that it hasn't, but then as in many elements of life, people, their achievements and events often don't get the recognition they deserve until after retirement or worse, death. And it is a sad fact that the fruition of this book is largely due to the apparent end of the legion itself. What will happen after the doors close on the racing careers of Robert Millar, Phil Anderson, Sean Yates, Allan Peiper, Stephen Roche, Sean Kelly and Greg LeMond? Who will fill their shoes, if anyone?

Will the wildly mooted philosophy of *mondialisation* continue or fade away? What attraction will there be for English-speaking media to continue following the sport? And if that all ends, how much interest will multi-national corporations like Gatorade and Motorola have in continuing their sponsorships? Will cycling return behind the closed doors of European parochialism where it was once before? These are the questions which have since arisen. And most probably they won't be properly addressed until it's too late – if it is not already.

Were it not for a handful of thought provoking events in 1991 and 1992 which involved many of our legionnaires, this book may not have been written, let alone the aftermath of their farewell from the peloton be assessed. For good and bad, those seasons were the inspiration to many. Retirement is a topic of conversation amongst some and the odd victory race is still being ridden by others.

Admittedly every country one day faces the problem of having no champion to follow. But for countries like France, Belgium, the Netherlands, Italy and Spain supporting the systematic replacement of its stars is the heritage of cycling. Without an Eddy Merckx, Bernard Hinault, and Francesco Moser the Tours of France, Italy and Spain have no trouble surviving as the grand monuments they are. The same can be said of the Tour of Flanders, Milan–San Remo or Paris–Roubaix, they will continue long after Claudio Chiappucci, Miguel Indurain or Laurent Fignon.

Without Kelly, Roche, LeMond and Anderson *et al*, the English-speaking world has nothing to inspire interest from its youth. It is because of their success that races like the DuPont Tour, the Kellogg's Tour of Britain and Nissan Classic of Ireland became popular. Even though their international credibility and long term future have always been in doubt. Just as such races have enjoyed local popularity, so has their presence assured sponsor and television interest, making the sport of cycling accessible to all.

Sherwen and Jones are already long retired. Sherwen stopped racing in 1988, while Jones came to a halt in 1987. And Peiper, despite agonising over the decision during 1992, hung up his bike at the age of 32. Meanwhile his long time associate Yates, just 22 days older than Peiper, was also pondering whether to continue after 1993 for another year, depending his team's sponsorship odds.

In early 1993 Kelly, 36, and Roche, 34, had both considered their retirement – Roche definitely for 1993 while Kelly was considering that infamous 'one more year'. For both, such decisions could have been tempting to avoid because of their apparent late successes. But both also proved that there was no reason for doubting they could end their careers on a winning note. And that is the most fitting way any champion should bid adieu.

After all, Kelly's appetite for victory had been tantalised when at the age of 35 he won the Tour of Lombardy in October 1991 and then came back in March 1992 to win Milan – San Remo. Winning the last classic of one season and the first of the next is a rare feat. It had only been accomplished ten times before. And by recording his 11th strike for a classic victory Kelly, having already won the 'double' in 1985 and 1986, joined Italian Fausto Coppi in being the only riders to have ever done it twice.

As for Roche, he shed his years of sponsorship and injury woes to finish 15th in the Tour of Spain and ninth in the Tour de France in 1992, including a stage win to La Bourboule. The problems of a slipped disc during that season may have reminded us him of his age and limited future in the peloton. However, he battled on for most of the year, and proved his courage was still as fiery as in his heyday. It was also a far better path to retirement than the one he was following in 1991 where several years of sponsor disputes, knee injuries, and the humiliation of his Tour elimination after missing the team time trial start, came so close to pushing him out before he was ready.

By contrast LeMond's 'failure' in the 1991 Tour de France where he was a personal worst-ever seventh, raised doubts about his future in the saddle. Finally, it was proved that the American is vulnerable to defeat after all. It was the first dent in his steely reputation. Now at the age of 31, there is much speculation that the end is in sight. The 1993 season would decide that.

As for Anderson and Millar, their exit from the peloton seems to hinge on how long they will continue to get contracts. By the end of 1992, Anderson was on song 'for another two years' after salvaging his season with an Autumn run of success which included an overall victory and a stage win in the Nissan Classic of Ireland, victory in the Grand Prix of Isbergues in France, third in Paris – Brussels and sixth in Paris – Tours.

Millar's destiny is typically as hard to define as his personality. The Scot moved from LeMond's Z team to the Dutch TVM camp – alleged by some as more of a safe house for ageing individualistic high-paid pros rather than a haven for blossoming talent. It proved fruitless. His biggest headliner for the 1992 season was a positive dope test in the Tour of Spain against which he appealed, asserting that the test result was incorrect. As 1993 began Millar, at the age of 33, needed a major win if his career was to end on the same note of glory on which it began.

As the ranks dwindle, there will be a need for replacements. The question as to who will succeed is still wide open. There have been suggested candidates, but in reality the predicament is akin to that facing Belgian cycling which so longs for another Eddy Merckx. The instant a young Belgian hopeful distinguishes himself, the pressure of public and media expectation will come raining down and ruin what chances he may have.

Anglophiles have invested hopes in many: Joey McCloughlin and Adrian Timmis held strong promise while riding for ANC. But in 1988, once they crossed the Channel bound for the enclosures of the French Z team – formerly Peugeot and now Gan – their publicised promise counted for nothing. They were back home within a season.

Another ANC member, Malcolm Elliott went further. His sprinting prowess saw him become an asset for the long-disbanded Fagor team in 1988 – then led by Roche. And despite the huge domestic strife over wages and rider conflicts he even managed to win the Tour of Spain's blue points jersey in 1988. But a move to another

Spanish team, Seur, which concentrated mainly on home races, the year after took him down the path of virtual anonymity, little success, growing despair and eventually, by 1992, to the moment every professional rider confronts one day – virtual obscurity. European purists would harshly interpret his move in 1993 to the US scene where he signed up with the Chevrolet-LA Sheriff team as just that.

In that time none have looked set to follow in the path of the foreign legion. From the American fold after Mike Neel, George Mount and Jonathan Boyer, there have been Andy Hampsten, Davis Phinney, Ron Kiefel, Jeff Pierce, Chris Carmichael, Alexi Grewal and Bob Roll. Lesser known identities include Joe Parkin who lasted a year with Tulip in 1991, Paul Willerton who rode for Z before heading home in 1992 for Subaru – Montgomery.

From the American roadmen in Europe Hampsten nurtured the most success after LeMond by winning the Tours of Italy, Switzerland, Romandy and of course, the prestigious L'Alpe d'Huez stage of the 1992 Tour at the age of 30. But even he admitted, when asked about retirement that year, to having to 'start thinking about that'.

The same must be said of Canadian Steve Bauer, Hampsten's long time team-mate at La Vie Claire and finally Motorola. Bauer, a Tour de France yellow jersey wearer in 1988 and 1990 and so often on the verge of success in major classics and world championships, was heading down a sorry path by the end of 1992. Aged 33 and on a reported salary of $500,000 (US), he had won only two races in three seasons – a stage of the 1991 DuPont Tour and 1992 Tour of Galicia in Spain. Unsurprisingly Motorola did not renew their deal – a move that must have thrown a spotlight on his retirement prospects. Although it must be said that he never gave up, as his persistence to train alone and race as an 'invited' rider on Motorola in the 1993 Paris – Roubaix proved. A victory there would have resurrected his career as quickly as the yellow jersey did, but his 21st placing out of 66 finishers was hardly that of a failure in a race where most simply don't finish.

Bauer is not the first Canadian to race in Europe: there was Ron Hayman and Alex Stieda, a surprise yellow jersey wearer for half a day in 1986, who retired in 1988. Despite his time trialling qualities, Canadian Brian Walton's future in Europe was also brought to a halt after 1992 and he signed up with Saturn.

Australian's Stephen Hodge and Neil Stephens are worthy names to fill Yates' and Peiper's places. But as their value as 'super domestiques' only began to really shine in 1992 at the respective ages of 31 and 29 long-term expectation would be a little late in the day.

Englishman Harry Lodge rode with Tulip until the Dutch computer firm pulled out after 1992, compatriots Deno Davie lasted a year with Carrera in 1988, and Dave Rayner was with Buckler for the 1991 and 1992 seasons. Then Irishmen Paul Kimmage, retired in 1988 after four years riding for RMO and Fagor and Laurence Roche lasted two seasons in Europe after a season with Carrera in 1990 and then with another his brother, Stephen at the financially stricken Belgian team, Tonton Tapis.

To whom can we look to fill the void? Irish hopes were modestly placed in 1992 Milk Race winner, Conor Henry who was shortlisted for a pro contract with TVM for the 1993 season, but eventually made to wait another year. Australian chances lay in a 25-year old third-year professional named Scott Sunderland, while English hopes seem non-existant. The only safe investment appears to exist in a 21-year-old Texan named Lance Armstrong, and Americans like Bart Bowen, Nate Reiss and Mike Carter with the American Subaru-Montogomery team which made its first full-season European campaign in 1993.

Armstrong, a former national classed triathlete, saw his reputation precede his arrival to the professional ranks after the 1992 Olympic Games. In the US he had already won two pro-am races before embarking on a career. And while his professional debut at the San Sebastian classic in Spain, a week after finishing 14th at the Games was humbling to say the least, it carried some reward.

Armstrong was quickly off the back of the field, struggling with fatigue and probably wondering what ever made him feel he could be a professional. Were it not for his Motorola *directeur-sportif*, Hennie Kuiper's encouraging words the normally ever-confident Texan would have abandoned. 'Ride to the finish Lance. What you do now will benefit you later,' said Kuiper, former world and Olympic champion, winner of Milan–San Remo and a top ten Tour de France rider, including second in 1977 and 1980.

Armstrong heeded the advice. And while finishing last, alone and 25:00 behind the winner Mexican Raul Alcalá the Texan soon discovered what Kuiper meant. At the Championship of Zurich seven days later he was second and in the winning break. And then came two wins in Italian lead-ups to the world championships at Benidorm, Spain and victory in the King of the Mountains in the Tour de L'Avenir. In the space of a month, Armstrong had aroused English speaking expectation once more. He kept their hopes alive when he returned to Europe in 1993 to win the Trophy Laigueglia in February, feature in several prominant breaks in Paris–Nice and play a key role in Milan–San Remo. He also won the $1,000,000 'Triple Crown' and national title in the US in June.

The dilemma facing us is why many others haven't followed Armstrong, or the programmes adopted by American teams like Subaru-Montgomery and even Saturn. Subaru-Montgomery spent 1992 racing in Europe sporadically, then after a hefty winter recruitment of fresh European talent came into 1993 for a full season, which included a World Cup campaign and hopes of starting the Tour. So, besides Armstrong, riders like Bowen, Reiss and Carter were names that held American hopes for success. A similar plan was envisaged for Saturn, having progressed from amateur to professional status in 1993.

The interest in criterium racing in Great Britain and in the US during the mid-80s has had an effect. Series like the City-Centre Series in England in the 1980s unintentionally played a role in deterring riders from trying to make a living abroad. The same could be said of the US, especially with concepts like the National Cycling League which is as far removed from traditional Européan cycle racing as mountain biking.

English and Australian professionals in Britain and the US suddenly found a source of income which didn't require them to live and race on the Continent. Nor did they have to race day-in, day-out for seven hours to earn their money. As television supported the series, and hence British sponsors backed British based teams, they could live quite happily on a racing itinerary of two or three one-hour criteriums a week and several short tours per season. Why become 'cannon fodder' as British pro Steve Joughin once called it, and kill yourself racing on the Continent?

Others lay blame on the increased funding and support of national amateur teams – especially in the US and Australia – stopping the trend set by Sherwen, Jones, Millar, Anderson, etc. After all, in their epoch, they had little if any support. Yet without federation support, as Jones and Herety found out, those national bodies opposed certain individual measures they were taking to try and become professional.

The common denominator was over appearances 'back home' in races like the Milk Race and Sealink International. If they didn't give up their European plans and come home, they were officially shunned.

Italy, France and Spain may do the same thing, but then the sport thrives in Europe. American, Australian and even English monopolising of Olympic talent by national federations also enforced a distance from the hub of professional racing. Scare tactics often work. Invariably Anglophile national teams venture to Europe having heard second- or third-hand tales of a frightening and rampant use of drugs, blatant pay-offs and a ruthless manipulation of human resource by professional team directors, sponsors and race organisers. If this doesn't work, then poaching can be simply fended off in other ways. For instance, protective national coaches can tell professional managers interested in one of their amateurs that he is not available because he is still under contract to that federation – even if he isn't.

What is certain, is that there seems to be fewer hardened tough-nuts in the English-speaking cycling world than before. All those who previously succeeded had a strong personality. They stood out from the rest on personality alone. They may not have been the most popular. They may bear the scars of controversy from their amateur days. They may not have even won the most races. But what they do have is an inner psychological strength essential for professional racing. And Armstrong is the first Anglophile rider to be detected with it since the mid-1980s.

Anderson and Yates, both Armstrong's team-mates, agree. 'When you talk to him, you'd think he has been a professional for ten years. But he has only just begun,' Yates said in early 1993. And Anderson was just as quick to support the Texan for his manner. 'A lot of people misunderstand his self-confidence for cockiness. But he is not cocky. He is just professional. It's remarkable that he is like that so early. But it's great,' remarked the Australian.

And who knows, Armstrong's presence may just spark another flood of English-speaking stars. Bowen, Reiss and Carter are already there, after all. And we can't forget that when Sherwen arrived in France, he came as Barry Hoban was on the verge of retirement. There were very few others in Europe, except for Kelly, and Englishmen Bill Nickson and Phil Edwards.

Perhaps the answer is not to look for a new LeMond, Kelly, Anderson, Roche or Millar, but to nurture new talent as it comes and encourage the rider to be as individual as his racing ancestors, in this way echoes of the legion may continue.

TEAM HISTORIES AND CAREER HIGHLIGHTS

THE ACBB

1955	Shay Elliott (Ireland)
1974	Jonathan Boyer (USA)
1977	Alan Van Heerden (SA)
	Paul Sherwen (England)
	David Mayer-Oakes (USA)
1978	Graham Jones (England)
	Van Heerden
	Neil Martin (England)
1979	Robert Millar (Scotland)
	Phil Anderson (Australia)
	Russell Williams (England)
	John Parker (England)
	Martin
1980	Stephen Roche (Ireland)
	Parker
1981	Sean Yates (England)
	Jeff Williams (England)
	Kevin Riley (England)
	John Herety (England)
	McIlroy (Ireland)
	R Parker Williams

1982	Allan Peiper (Australia)
	Pete Longbottom (England)
	Neil Hunter (England)
1983	David Akam (England)
	Alan Gornall (England)
	Rick Flood (Australia)
	Pete Saunders (England)
	Tony Mayer (England)
	Raphael Kimmage (Ireland)
1984	Paul Kimmage (Ireland)
	Christian Yates (England)
1987	Brian Smith (Scotland)
1988	Deno Davie (England)
	Smith
1989	Laurence Roche (Ireland)
1990	Matthew Stephens (Scotland)
	Dave Cook (England)
	Clayton Stevenson (Australia)
1991	Stephens
	Cook
1992	Stephens
	Cook

THE LEGION

Sherwen
FIAT (France) 1978-1979
La Redoute (France) 1980-1985
Raleigh (England) 1986-1987

Jones
Peugeot (France) 1979-1982
Wolber (France) 1983

Systeme U (France) 1984
EverReady (England) 1985
ANC-Halfords (England) 1986-1987

Millar
Peugeot (France) 1980-1985
Panasonic (Neth) 1986-1987
Fagor (Spain) 1988

Z (France) 1989-1991
TVM (Neth) 1992-1993

Anderson
Peugeot (France) 1980-1983
Panasonic (Neth) 1984-1987
TVM (Neth) 1988-1990
Motorola (USA) 1991-1993

Roche
Peugeot (France) 1981-1983
La Redoute (France) 1984-1985
Carrera (Italy) 1986-1987
Fagor (France) 1988-1989
Histor (Belgium) 1990
Tonton Tapis (Belgium) 1991
Carrera (Italy) 1992-1993

Yates
Peugeot (France) 1982-1986
Fagor (Spain) 1987
Fagor (France) 1988
7-Eleven (USA) 1989-1990
Motorola (USA) 1991-1993

Peiper
Peugeot (France) 1983-1985
Panasonic (Neth) 1986-1990
Tulip (Belgium) 1991-1992*

THE MAVERICKS

Sean Kelly
Flandria (Belgium) 1977-1978
Splendor (Belgium) 1979-1981
Sem (Belgium) 1982-1983
Skil/Sem (Belgium) 1984-1985
Kas (Spain) 1986-1988
PDM (Neth) 1989-1991
Lotus/Festina (Spain) 1992-1993
Lotus/Festina (Spain) 1993

Greg LeMond
Renault (France) 1981-1984
La Vie Claire (France) 1985-1986
Toshiba (France) 1987
PDM (Neth) 1988
ADR (Belgium) 1989
Z (France) 1990-1992
Gan (France) 1993

ENGLISH SPEAKING RIDERS IN EUROPE 1976–1992

| 1976 | Barry Hoban – Mercier-Gan |
| | Phil Edwards – Sanson |

1977	Sean Kelly – Flandria
	Bill Nickson – TI Raleigh
	Hoban – Mercier-Gan
	Edwards – Sanson

1978	Paul Sherwen – FIAT
	Hoban – Mercier-Gan
	Kelly – Flandria
	Nickson – TI Raleigh
	Edwards – Sanson

1979	Graham Jones – Peugeot
	Hoban – Mercier-Gan
	Kelly – Splendor
	Sherwen – FIAT
	Edwards – Sanson
1980	Robert Millar – Peugeot
	Phil Anderson – Peugeot
	Jones – Peugeot
	Hoban – Mercier-Gan
	Kelly – Splendor
	Sherwen – La Redoute
	Edwards – Sanson
1981	Greg LeMond – Renault
	Stephen Roche – Peugeot
	Millar – Peugeot
	Anderson – Peugeot
	Jones – Peugeot
	Kelly – Splendor
	Sherwen – La Redoute
	Boyer – Renault
1982	Sean Yates – Peugeot
	John Herety – CO-OP-Mercier
	Eric McKenzie – Capri-Sonne
	Steve Jones – Splendor
	LeMond – Renault
	Kelly – Sem
	S Roche – Peugeot
	Millar – Peugeot
	Anderson – Peugeot
	Jones – Peugeot
	Sherwen – La Redoute
	Boyer – Sem
1983	Peiper – Peugeot
	LeMond – Renault
	Kelly – Sem
	S Roche – Peugeot
	Millar – Peugeot
	Anderson – Peugeot
	Yates – Peugeot

	G Jones – Wolber
	S Jones – Ayel-Gipimme
	Sherwen – La Redoute
	Herety – CO-OP-Mercier
	McKenzie – Capri-Sonne
	Boyer – Sem
1984	Michael Wilson – Alfa Lum
	David Akam – GIS
	Chris Wreghitt – Bianchi
	Gary Dowdell – Systeme U
	Herety – CO-OP-Mercier
	Kelly – Skil/Sem
	LeMond – Renault
	S Roche – La Redoute
	Millar – Peugeot
	Anderson – Panasonic
	Jones – Systeme U
	Yates – Peugeot
	Peiper – Peugeot
	Sherwen – La Redoute
	Boyer – Skil/Sem
	McKenzie – Capri-Sonne
1985	Ron Kiefel – 7-Eleven
	Bob Roll (USA) – 7-Eleven
	Chris Carmichael (USA) – 7-Eleven
	Jeff Pierce – 7-Eleven
	Eric Heiden (USA) – 7-Eleven
	Davis Phinney (USA) – 7-Eleven
	Alex Stieda (Canada) – 7-Eleven
	Alexi Grewal (USA) – Panasonic
	Steve Bauer (Canada) – La Vie Claire
	Paul Kimmage (Ireland) – RMO
	Neil Stephens (Australia) – Santini
	Doug Shapiro (USA) – Kwantum
	LeMond – La Vie Claire
	Kelly – Skil/Sem
	S Roche – La Redoute
	Millar – Peugeot
	Anderson – Panasonic
	Yates – Peugeot
	Peiper – Peugeot

Sherwen – La Redoute
Wilson – Alfa-Lum
Boyer – Skil/Sem

1986 Andy Hampsten (USA) – La Vie Claire
LeMond – La Vie Claire
Kelly – Kas
S Roche – Carrera
Millar – Panasonic
Anderson – Panasonic
Yates – Peugeot
Peiper – Panasonic
Kimmage – RMO
Bauer – La VieClaire
Wilson – Ecoflam
Martin Earley (Ire) – Fagor
Kiefel – 7-Eleven
Roll – 7-Eleven
Carmichael – 7-Eleven
Pierce – 7-Eleven
Phinney 7-Eleven
Heiden – 7-Eleven
Shapiro – 7-Eleven
Stieda – 7-Eleven
Grewal – 7-Eleven
Boyer – 7-Eleven

1987 Steve Swart (NZ) – ANC-Halfords *
Adrian Timmis (Eng) – ANC-Halfords
Joey McLoughlin – ANC-Halfords
Malcolm Elliott – ANC-Halfords
(Eng)
Paul Watson (Eng) – ANC-Halfords
Shane Sutton (Aust) – ANC-Halfords
David Akam (Eng) – ANC-Halfords
G Jones – ANC-Halfords
Jeff Bradley (USA) – 7-Eleven
Stephen (Australia) – Hodg – Kas
LeMond – Toshiba,
Kelly – Kas
S Roche – Carrera
Millar – Panasonic
Anderson – Panasonic

Yates – Fagor
Peiper – Panasonic
Earley – Fagor
Bauer – Toshiba
Hampsten – 7-Eleven
Kimmage – RMO
Kiefel – 7-Eleven
Pierce – 7-Eleven
Boyer – 7-Eleven
Roll -7-Eleven
Phinney – 7-Eleven
Heiden – 7-Eleven
Grewal – RMO
Stephens – Zero Boys

1988 Deno Davie (Eng) – Carrera
Peter Stephenson (Eng) – 7-Eleven
Nathan Dahlberg (NZ) – 7-Eleven
Elliott – Fagor
Timmis – Z
McLoughlin – Z
Watson – Hitachi
LeMond – PDM
Kelly – Kas
S Roche – Fagor
Millar – Fagor
Anderson – TVM
Kimmage – RMO
Yates – Fagor
Earley – Kas
Peiper – Panasonic
Hampsten – 7-Eleven
Bauer – Weinmann-La Suisse
Wilson – Weinmann-La Suisse
Hodge – Kas
Boyer – 7-Eleven
Kiefel – 7-Eleven
Phinney – 7-Eleven
Pierce – 7-Eleven
Roll – 7-Eleven
Knickman – 7-Eleven
Stephens – Artiach

1989	Norm Alvis (USA) – 7-Eleven	Millar – Z
	Andy Bishop (USA) – PDM	Anderson – TVM
	Scott McKinley (USA) – 7-Eleven	Yates – 7-Eleven
	Brian Walton (Canada) – 7-Eleven	Hampsten – 7-Eleven
	Wayne Bennington (Eng) – Systeme U	Bauer – 7-Eleven
	Scott Sunderland (Australia) – TVM	Peiper – Panasonic
	Davie – Carrera	Earley – PDM
	Daryl Webster (Eng) – Teka	Elliott – Teka
	Eddy Salas (Australia) – Amore & Vita	Wilson – Helvetia-La Suisse
	McLoughlin – Z	Sunderland – TVM
	LeMond – ADR	Hodge – ONCE
		Alvis – 7-Eleven
	Kelly – PDM	Bishop – 7-Eleven
	Stephens – Caja Rural	Kiefel – 7-Eleven
	Elliott – Teka	Phinney – 7-Eleven
	S Roche – Fagor	Roll – 7-Eleven
	Kimmage – Fagor	McKinley – 7-Eleven
	Millar – Z	Walton – 7-Eleven
	Anderson – TVM	Dahlberg – 7-Eleven
	Yates – 7-Eleven	Bennington – Z
	Hampsten – 7-Eleven	Salas – Amore & Vita
	Bauer – Helvetia-La Suisse	Stephens – Artiach
	Earley – PDM	
	Peiper – Panasonic	**1991** Frankie Andreu (USA) – 7-Eleven
	Wilson – Helvetia-La Suisse	Steve Larsen (USA) – Motorola
	Hodge – Caja Rural	Mike Carter (USA) – Motorola
	Dahlberg – 7-Eleven	Paul Willerton (USA) – Z
	Kiefel – 7-Eleven	Colin Sturgess (Eng) – Tulip
	Knickman – 7-Eleven	Harry Lodge (Eng) – Tulip
	Stieda – 7-Eleven	Dave Rayner (Eng) – Buckler
	Roll – 7-Eleven	LeMond – Z
	Phinney – 7-Eleven	Kelly – PDM
	Pierce – 7-Eleven	S Roche – Tonton Tapis
		Millar – Z
1990	Laurence Roche (Ire) – Carrera	Anderson – Motorola
	Joe Parkin (USA) – Tulip	Yates – Motorola
	LeMond – Z	Bauer – Motorola
	Kelly – PDM	Hampsten – Motorola
	Davie – Carrera	Earley – PDM
	Stevenson – RMO	Peiper – Tulip
	Nick Barnes (England) – Teka	Elliott – Seur
	Dean Woods (Australia) – Stuttgart	L Roche – Tonton Tapis
	S Roche – Histor	Hodge – ONCE

Woods – Stuttgart
Wilson – Helvetia-La Suisse
Sunderland – TVM
Parkin – Tulip
Bishop – Motorola
Dahlberg – Motorola
Kiefel – Motorola
Carter – Motorola
Roll – Motorola
Bennington – Z
Salas – Amore & Vita
Stephens – Artiach
Stevenson – RMO

1992   L Armstrong (USA) – Motorola
Rayner – Buckler
Lodge – Tulip
LeMond – Z
Kelly – Festina
S Roche – Carrera
Millar – TVM
Anderson – Motorola
Yates – Motorola
Hampsten – Motorola
Bauer – Motorola
Earley – PDM
Peiper – Tulip
Elliott – Seur
Stephens – ONCE
Hodge – ONCE
Sunderland – TVM
Andreu – Motorola
Bishop – Motorola
Kiefel – Motorola

Walton – Motorola
Larsen – Motorola
Alvis – Motorola

1993   Bart Bowen-Subaru-Montgomery
Nate Reiss-Subaru-Montgomery
Mike McCarthy – Subaru-Montgomery
S Roche – Carrera
Millar – TVM
Anderson – Motorola
Yates – Motorola
Hampsten – Motorola
Bauer – Independent-Motorola
LeMond – Gan
Kelly – Festina
Earley – Festina
Stephens – ONCE
Hodge – ONCE
Sunderland – TVM
Andreu – Motorola
Alvis – Motorola
Armstrong – Motorola
Bishop – Motorola
Larsen – Motorola
Carter – Subaru-Montgomery
Willerton – Subaru-Montgomery

** ANC-Halfords did race in Europe in 1986, but 1987 was officially recognised as their first full assault on Europe, culminating with the Tour de France.

* Subaru-Montgomery did race in Europe in 1992, but 1993 was officially recognised as the team's first full season.

BIBLIOGRAPHY

Kings of the Road, Robin Magowan and Graham Watson, Springfield Books 1988

1988 Tour du France, Phil Liggett, Harrap

The Agony and the Ecstasy, Stephen Roche and David Walsh, Stanley Paul 1988

Greg LeMond: The Incredible Comeback, Samuel Abt, Stanley Paul 1990

Kelly, David Walsh, Harrap 1986

Velo, Harry Van den Bremt and Rene Jacobs, Editions Velo 1987 – 1993

Wide Eyed and Legless: Inside the Tour de France, Jeff Connor, Sports Pages-Simon and Schuster 1988

The Fabulous World of Cycling, Winning, all volumes 1983 – 1992

Hearts of Lions, Peter Nye, Norton 1987

Archive material from:
L'Equipe newspaper (Fra), *Cycling Weekly* (UK), *VeloNews* (US), *Winning* (UK), *Velo* (FRA), *Pedal* (Canada), *Cycling World* (Australia), *Bicycling Australia* (Australia), *Mirroir du Cyclisme* (Fra).